RULING THE ELITE

Moving Power from the Parties to the People

TIM HORN

"Joe American"
viewed by millions on YouTube

Ruling The Elite: Transferring Power from the Parties to The People

For information about this title or to order other books and/or electronic media, contact the publisher:
NonPartisan Americans, LLC
NonPartisan Americans.com

ISBN: 978-0-9836182-0-1

Printed in the United States of America

Cover and Interior design by 1106 Design

DEDICATION

To ordinary People everywhere who have preceded us and will follow us in the eternal pursuit of Freedom.

CONTENTS

INTRODUCTORY REMARKS

The "spirit of party," which George Washington referred to in his Farewell Address as "part of human nature" and government's "worst enemy," is a manifestation of the innate drive within some people to control others. That powerful need to dominate has caused the organization and rise of the political Parties in response to democracy, just as it caused the rise of the controlling royalty, emperors and dictators of history; Parties are the current expression of the desire of the few to control the many.

Political Parties were not part of the self-governance plan prepared by the authors of democracy. George Washington detested them and warned against their negative influence on our liberty and welfare. We can see the disunity that they cause, and we are experiencing how far away from the traditions and intent of democracy a dominating Party can take us. Parties are highly controlling *consumers* of Liberty and have wedged themselves between us and our government. It is our need, and it is our duty, to correct that.

— *Tim Horn*
America, 2011

The Ordinary Author and the Book

Some years ago, I enjoyed constant interaction with a friend who represented the idea of character better than any man I have known to date. He expressed well all the values he was committed to, and one of them was humility. As if to underscore his personal acknowledgment that he was no better than anyone else, he would often sign off on a message as "only Don." As his neighbor, I would go by his house nearly once a day. You would recognize him, and he would recognize himself, as an ordinary person living on an ordinary road near an ordinary Midwestern town. There are millions and millions of ordinary People in our country and worldwide—millions who just seek to independently improve their lives and are willing to work hard and honestly to secure a good and happy life. They don't want to be controlled in their lives nor to control others in theirs. Like Don, I am one of those millions.

But we must understand that there are those who see themselves differently, as part of a ruling class. This group exists naturally everywhere and has found a ready nest in the political Parties of the world's democracies. In America, the mother of modern democracy, they are tightening their grip, and we ordinary Americans are their targets. To them, we are in the "Fly-Over States," we are "Outside the Beltway," and we are the "Sheeple." We are people (as sheep) to be herded and shorn, mocked and ignored. Usually hidden, sometimes the scorn of those who seek control becomes evident. We must realize that any democracy, while not yet reaching either its broadest reach or its highest level, has internal enemies. They are at work. And we, the beneficiaries of democracy and the capitalist system that fuels it, need to know who these enemies are in order to protect ourselves and ours. We, fellow ordinary, hard working believers, are *the source*. We accept personal responsibility, commit to a lifetime of work, support our families, communities and faiths with our time and money, follow the rules, create new ideas and businesses, and pay most of the taxes. We are the producers. Without us, there is no nation. You know it. I know it. There is no one who will stand up for us because all of them use us. *We* must stand up for ourselves. As a reader of this book, you are, most likely, an ordinary American like me, and it is for us, and for our international ordinary brethren that I have written this book.

Like you, I was not born with a "silver spoon in my mouth." I got the "live above a garage and have a divorced mother who was a waitress in a donut shop" spoon. For years I was raised by my grandparents in an apartment in the Midwest. I learned early that the outcome of your life was in your own hands. I started working a job at age 14. In high school, I was a successful student athlete and I believed my American Government class. With one brief exception, I have lived my life working in non-government jobs. I have been previously active in both political Parties but have not been in any Party for a long time. I have been a ditch digger, a construction laborer and was the first in my family to go to college, a state college. I worked

my way through college as a janitor, a dishwasher, a handy-
man, a salesman and a truck driver. Sometimes I had to make
tomato soup from free ketchup packs and hot water in order
to eat. I have been in three unions. As an employee of both
large organizations and small companies, I have felt the pain
of economic downturn and backstabbing internal warfare. I
usually have had more than one job. I started a business from
scratch while I continued working my 60 hour weeks. Then I
risked everything, and worked 80 hours a week or more for
my own company. After three years of that, I took my first
paycheck. Eventually, I sold it and did well. I have spent a
lifetime volunteering for charities and helping my neighbors;
I did all the 'kid things' with my stepson and have served my
church and my community.

If you are in that ruling class of Elites, you probably think
my life is funny, pathetic, and maybe even meaningless. It is
no wonder you fly over without even noticing. But, if you are
an ordinary American, then you can probably connect with
some—or maybe even most—of my experiences. You and I
can identify with each other because we ordinary Americans
have much more important commonalities than we do differences. When we set aside our skin color and family origins,
our gender and religion, as all Americans know we must do,
we ordinary People find unity in our values, commonality in
our spirit, and commitment to our country that is unstoppable.
We have seen it in our steady national improvement, exhibited
it on hundreds of battlefields, and experienced it in countless
human relationships.

The thing is, most of us ordinary People in America and
other democracies have been asleep politically. We have assumed
that everything is already set. We have believed that all is
either just the way it is, or the way it should be. It is not. We
did not see the Parties, using our government, acting to cause

disunity and to reduce our Liberty. We have been called the "Silent Majority." This book is intended to help strengthen the wake up call. We see now that we cannot silently go about our work and lives any longer. It is past time for us to be loud, very loud, and time to act; but act we will.

As an ordinary person, I have worked hard all my life. I live on a nice street, count my blessings, and just want my family and friends to be safe and happy. That is what we ordinary People do. We expect that reward should go to those that earn it, that people behaving badly should be punished, and that the government should make sure that both happen. I have spent years listening, reading, and thinking about these current times. The following pages are personal thoughts about the alarming state of ordinary People in the American democratic republic and others we spawned, how we arrived here, and what we can do about it. I don't know all of the answers. But here are some things to consider and perhaps stimulate all of us to more thinking. Together we can get to the solution. We can allow ourselves some confidence because, and perhaps only because, of the gift our Founding Fathers left for us. If we act in unison, we ordinary Americans are the force that can cause *true* change that will fluff the covers of America, and perhaps the whole world.

We actually can do this, and together, no one can stand against us.

* * *

POST PREFACE

Well, if you are thinking that this author loves America, you would be right. And despite what you may have heard, a *huge* majority of ordinary Americans, like me, feel the same way. If you too love America, the idea of democracy, or if you just like America, or are "on the fence," this book is for you. If you don't like America and would like to see the demise of the Values it represents for ordinary People, this book may not be for you. But then again, if you have the slightest opening in your mind, perhaps even you should read it; this book is about what may become the next "Evolutionary Point of Change" in the human community, and of that we all are a part.

ONE

The Legacy of the Ruling Elite

Every nation has its own, unique set of problems. Common issues that trouble the people of most nations often come neither from nature nor from enemies outside their borders. Problems of the majority in a nation emanate from the wrangling of relatively few people from within who seek control of their countrymen and access to their money. American-style democracy, exceptional in so many ways, does not escape this axiom.

Looking back to the earliest human history, it is likely that there were always at least a few who held the notion that *they* should control everyone else, usually for the majority's "own good." Of course, that same few believed that they should be well compensated by the majority for their leadership and control. Perhaps such behavior was innate to primitive mankind, or maybe it was a reflection of the natural existing world that human communities developed into. Science says that by the time humans appeared, there existed a hostile environment of danger and death, inhabited by all sorts of life forms that already had well defined hierarchies and behavior patterns.

The primary pattern was that the biggest, the fiercest, and the most swift and savvy would prey upon others and brutalize even their own species for the benefit of themselves. Whether T-Rex or velociraptors among dinosaurs, or the largest gorilla in a pack, this was the pattern of life that was evident. To the humans, perhaps it seemed incontrovertible; it just "was the way it was."

It is conceivable that our human predecessors simply mirrored this animal world pattern in the beginning of their community development and then, over the eons, embellished it with trappings of all sorts, like rules, buildings, and class divisions. The few who controlled the many eventually elevated themselves to the status of royalty. Some claimed to have been sent by gods to rule or were even said to be gods themselves, worthy of praise, power and even prayers. For various reasons, the daily lives and the wealth of the many came to be controlled by the few. While the small number in control lived long and well, those being controlled lived as assets of the few, to be used and eventually discarded—all by incident of their birth. Those in opposition to such control would be punished or eliminated because it was said to be "necessary" for the "benefit of the people/culture/crown/state." Those who supported the ruling class were offered protection and perhaps even some share of the wealth. Most of those who produced wealth lost it to the rulers, much like lesser animals lost their dinner to the T-Rex, who found it easier to take than to work for their own. After all, it "was the way it was."

A truly amazing thing occurred around 1750 BC, an event that would begin to change the way the masses would think about themselves. Hammurabi, a Babylonian king, provided a body of rules for his people that they, and he, would follow. They were chiseled into stone columns and erected in public places. For perhaps the very first time, the people who were being ruled could know the limits of their ruler's power through this means of mass communication. Instead of royal whim, the people had guarantees or "rights" to certain behaviors and they were literally "cast in stone" before them. One of these pillars is in the Near Eastern Antiquities Collection of the Louvre in Paris. Because it was an event of such great consequence, I term it an "Evolutionary Point of Change" within the human community. A slow but steady expansion of these ideas began. Many times over the subsequent centuries, the ideals of what came to be known as democracy, where ordinary People would seek to gain more control of their lives and destinies, would cause change and unrest and even revolution. Another important Point of Evolution of the human community came 3,526 years after Hammurabi's Stele was offered to the ordinary People, who have been sometimes referred to as "the unwashed masses" by the elite few. This occurred long after an entire "New World," as it was termed then, had been settled by the Colonies of Great Britain and others. In 1776, the Declaration of Independence by the American Colonies would, while outlining its case for freedom from Great Britain, make the case for a new origin for "rights" for all humankind. The rights of the people, the Declaration stated, were not only equal, but also did not emanate from any earthly ruler; they came from the Creator of the earth. It declared that people were born with rights, rather than granted rights by some changeable ruling class of elite humans. Even if one did not believe in a Creator, as the American Founders did, the understanding that every human has basic rights because they simply exist was an exciting new premise. This was a Evolutionary Point of Change in the thinking of how humans related to being ruled, and it would come to influence greatly how our twenty-first century world is arranged.

From our vantage point today, about 235 years later, it is difficult to understand how great a change in thinking the Declaration represented. The American Colonies, after all, had been established as a reflection of England, where there was some democracy, but the ultimate authority at that time was reserved for the English royal family. Imagine how shocking the words of the Declaration were to the entire world of ruling families, wealthy land owners, slave owners, indeed, the sheiks, the dictators, and all their families and business people whose life was based upon control by their elite ruling class. Certainly those that benefitted from the existing structure wanted it to remain as it was, and surely they found such words of Thomas Jefferson and his American co-signers unacceptable. They likely viewed our Founders as traitors to their elite group, and hoped that a nation based on such thinking would fail and fail quickly.

Many of the Founding Fathers of the United States of America were of the ruling class of the Colonies, and others could make themselves part of it in the process of creating a nation. This fact makes their story truly amazing. They chose to found a nation and prepare a Constitution that would establish a nation that would *not* be under their control. Instead, they ceded much of the control to its more ordinary "common" citizens. They all could have become royalty themselves, assuring incredible status and vast power and riches for many generations to come, but they chose not to. These families put their prominence and wealth behind ideas which would not be to their own maximum benefit. The Founders set up our great Founding Documents because they believed the idea of liberty and self rule were right for America, right for all people, and right for all time.

Before the America they envisioned would be established, almost all of its once wealthy and prominent Founders lost everything they had begun with. Of the 56 who signed the Declaration, five were tortured to death, 12 had their homes destroyed, nine died by hardship or by gunshot wounds. Many who signed the Declaration had their families destroyed, and most of them died in poverty.

We owe so much to the Founding Families. Because of their ideas and their will to act and to sacrifice, the most free, as well as the most economically and militarily powerful nation the world has ever known, was birthed. The values that they helped to establish were responsible for this feat. They understood that the nature of men and women is to improve their lives and, in response, the Founders established that the right to control one's own person and property were part of every person's human existence. Coupling this Liberty with a capitalist economy, which would reward ordinary citizens who would work the hardest and risk the most, they established an incredible engine of prosperity that has changed the world of ordinary People. The earlier opportunities to construct such an economic engine, and improve the lot of ordinary People, had been squandered for all previous history by the ignorant and selfish desire for control by generations of the world's Ruling Elites.

Through the Founding Families came the values of the American people and it is these Values that drew millions. American Values struck a chord with people throughout the world, and that chord has been vibrating for more than two centuries: the opportunity to keep almost all of what you earn instead of being forced to give it to a government; the ability to select one's own future without the government disfavoring you and favoring others; the independence in pursuing your religion and all happiness without government influence or direction. These Values have drawn people from every corner of this planet and have encouraged many in other nations to emulate America. It quickly became the beacon for the world because its Values incorporated freedom and fiscal opportunity for all. The millions who sought freedom from unequal treatment or from some forced belief by their government, came to America. Those who wanted the opportunity to gain from their own enterprise came to America. And later still, others came to escape from socialist countries where they saw the fruits of their work given to others who did not work and also to the Ruling Elite and their supporters. Those millions of poor immigrants thrived in the American Values that they adopted as their own. My own family did that, and it is likely that your family did too.

It can be argued that America, in support of economic freedom and democracy in the World Wars, has twice conquered the world militarily. Incredible enough, that, but even more incredible, and totally unmatched in world history, America gave it back, and helped former enemies become peaceful democratic nations of the world. Certainly, trade benefits to America accrued from those actions, but it was an opposite step from the subjugation, domination, and even enslavement that had been the spoils for the conquerors over thousands of years of human existence. Was that done by the Egyptians, the Mongols, the Greeks, the Romans, the Muslims, the Byzantines, the Aztecs, the Incas, the American Indians, the Spanish, the British, or by any military power in history? No. America's acts are inconceivable from the view of history. America's actions then, and then again, have been driven by its special Values. It is the true melting pot of all nations; it is a "united nations" that works.

But even with America's success and emulation, the struggle of ordinary People versus their rulers continues today in democracy-based nations throughout the world, including the United States. Since 1776, there has been a rise in democracy and a reduction in all forms of autocratic rule by kings, families, dictators and all forms of the "exalted." Because of American style democracy coupled with capitalist economic systems, previously unimaginable numbers of ordinary People have been living longer, better lives where they can follow dreams, participate in their own success, and if they desire to do so, they can praise a deity instead of the people who control their earthy life. But we must all understand that the struggle to maintain our Values and our Liberty is *not over.*

There is no steady state, especially when it comes to human behavior. As long as humanity exists, there will be people who seek to increase their power and rule over others. To do that, they have need of those ordinary People. Of course they need our power. Of course they need our money. Of course it is all about their concept of what is right and what is wrong for us. Of course they will influence the direction of our lives. Of course the power seekers and their special interest groups will want to use the tools of government to get their way. And, of course, it will all be "for our own good." Of course it will be.

TWO

The Citizens' Rights Movement

The political Parties are the current embodiment of the Ruling Elite that has always sought control over the ordinary People. Over the years since the Founding they have emerged and then matured into the most potent force in contemporary America. As the originator of modern democracies, America is a perfect case study in how political Parties have circumvented the structure of democracy and diminished freedom. The American Parties have essentially taken control of government in order to expand their power and wealth and in that process have become the agents for the denial of Rights.

There are five fundamental Rights that American citizen's feel are guaranteed in the Founding Documents: Life, Liberty, the pursuit of Happiness, Equality and the Right to Vote. Like the Ten Commandments, there is a lot of detail underneath each topic, like free speech, the bearing of arms and much more, but overall these are the "big five" of the Rights of American citizens. The view of perhaps most of the citizenry in 2011 is that these Rights have been slowly eroded for a long time, certainly since the time of President Franklin Roosevelt in the 1930s.

Many believe that this erosion quickly and forcefully expanded when the Obama Administration came into control; as erosion in nature would be rapidly increased by a raging storm. Most ordinary Americans attribute the 2010 historically heavy losses by the Democratic Party in the midterm elections to the Obama Administration's broad attack on our democracy and its seeming disdain for our Rights. Let's review the status of these Rights as perceived by ordinary citizens in the early twenty-first century.

The Right to **Life** relates first to the capability of the state to take your life from you, causing your death. That was a major concern to the Founders as they wrote our Declaration of Independence because the norm in the 1700s was a world of royalty in which an ordinary person could be put to death for simply being disrespectful to a royal family. Today, our Rights seem fully intact at this base level, having a full complement of due process hurdles protecting us from inappropriate extermination at the hands of the state. We all understand that one forfeits their individual Right to Life to the state for specific unacceptable behaviors. But there is more to this Right than just having it revoked by our government. Many of us ordinary People view any Right as *diminished* by the failure of our government in *protecting* that Right. Regular People have their life threatened each day by sources other than the state. Violent crime is perpetrated upon them in every corner of the nation and murder is a frequent result. People are beaten to death at home in the night, innocent kids are gunned down in the street, our daughters are raped and discarded like trash and our sons are often molested by male religious figures and by female teachers. Fully realizing that perfection is impossible, none-the-less the government consistently fails to protect our Right to a Life well lived from ever present threats.

The government, run by one Party or the other, affects our Rights by what it does *and* by what it does not do. Government *reduces* our Rights by its failure to do its job of *protecting* our Rights. Within the confines of the Constitution, it is the primary job of our Federal government to *protect* our Rights. This includes protection from any internal source such as from one citizen or group against another citizen or group. It also includes any external source, such as a foreign citizen, group or government. It is this latter point that is a special source of rancor for ordinary People regarding border control. By not controlling the border and allowing noncitizens to enter and commit crimes including violent attack and murder of our citizens, government becomes complicit in reducing or denying our Right to Life.

We reason that the southern border can absolutely be physically controlled. Those that argue that it cannot be physically controlled are doing so out of untruth, marked ignorance or, most likely, blinding acceptance of ideology. There is little new that can be said about liars, they will consecutively create new and even less conceivable lies to defend the earlier ones, and, if left no avenue but the truth, will name call and run away; this remains the same as children have always done. As for the ignorant, if one has the will, it is easy to know of history with its Roman distant barrier against the Anglo Saxons, the Great Wall of China, the lagoon in which Venice is positioned and the twentieth century division of East and West Germany. The Israeli control of its borders to keep the crossing of unauthorized individuals and the knowledge of U.S. observation satellites that can read a license plate day or night are on twenty four hours a day make it clear that we can detect and control most trespassing, if there is only a will to do so. This is where it becomes hurtful for us ordinary People. There is a choice being made by the Parties controlling our government that favors those that support them. This is a choice that favors access to our nation's jobs, benefits and even voting booths by noncitizens over The

People. The Parties choose to benefit themselves rather that to protect American citizens. Both Parties favor those entering illegally even over the *Right to Life* of American citizens. The Republican Party seems to desire cheap labor for its business supporters. The Democratic Party knows that most illegals will vote for Democrats and they want them here and voting to counteract the opposition voting of legitimate citizens. And they add the additional insult against the Right of Equality by promising special programs and benefits based on the ethnicity of these quiet invaders. Governments can fall under the weight of such egregious wounding of the citizenry alone, but there is an even greater diminishment of the Right to Life looming: the issue of government management in healthcare.

Every citizen's life is emergently or eventually in the hands of the healthcare system. The increasing intention of the government is to move from regulation into *management* of the healthcare system. That very idea seems by its nature a threat to our Right to Life. Forget the issue of potential "Death Panels" deciding who will get services and who will not, and set aside the issue of morally opposed providers mandated to perform abortions against their beliefs. Just the fact that the government cannot manage *anything* well seems to present clear evidence that they will be further reducing our Right to Life by attempting to manage the healthcare system. We must expect, based on track record, that government/Party management will increase cost, lower productivity, cause delays, put people who are unqualified in positions of decision making and put those that are incapable directly into frontline service. We can expect special favor and programs for those that are part of or support the government "family" and unfavorable treatment of those that are not or do not. The result will be confusion and dismay by patients and their families and delay which will cause anguish, suffering, loss and needless death, all with no recourse. Rather than protecting our Right to Life, it will once again be reduced.

Liberty is the Right defined as the individual's control of person and property. Each American citizen is guaranteed the ability to control their own life and to have similar control over their property. We take this as fact today, but property rights were at one time a major issue for ordinary People. Property was generally owned by the rich and powerful families of the rulers and ordinary People were usually renters of most property like homes, businesses and farm land. Because of this it was difficult both to be certain of the future, because one could be removed by the landlord, and to create wealth. The ability to own and control property, added to the capitalist economic model (detailed in pages ahead) has enabled the creation of vast collective wealth for the ordinary Americans. This Right too seems currently under assault. Constantly rising property tax rates, the establishment of tax on income and constant expansion of taxable transactions seem to diminish the Right. The first federal income tax was a flat income tax passed in 1894 but found to be unconstitutional and stopped. In 1913 Amendment XVI established the national income tax that today's much higher income taxes are based on. Even further, the current Democratic Administration has openly followed a "wealth transfer" policy intending to *take* property from some citizens and *give* it to others. To most of us ordinary Americans, this denies the Right of Liberty upon which the nation was founded. It is this Right that has been a primary motivator of citizens to be personally responsible, to become educated, and to work hard so as to be successful in the marketplace. Ordinary Americans have long proven themselves to be the most giving and charitable people in the world when it comes to helping the truly helpless and the victims of disaster. However, we almost uniformly bristle at helping those who can help themselves but choose not to. These people must become personally responsible like most of us. To us it seems that if poor, unlawful, or slovenly behavior is rewarded, it will only encourage more of it. The "Greatest Generation" had it right; "a few rotten apples will ruin the whole basket." If a substantial majority of a country's citizens do *not* take personal responsibility, it cannot survive. It seems that the Parties use taking our money and giving it to those that did not earn it as a means of securing their vote from them. It is similar to rewarding a thief for stealing on their behalf and then asking for more. "Wealth Transfer" is *theft of property* that we have a Right to control. Any theft is a violation of one of our basic Rights, whether committed by a burglar or a politician. It is being committed by political Parties using our government as a tool and plundering The People for their own purposes. Instead of disregarding our Rights, they should be controlling spending and stopping favors to their supporters. The opposition to these actions is now beyond concern or mere disappointment by most of us ordinary People; we are *angry*. And anger is a damper on the Right to pursue Happiness.

The pursuit of **Happiness** is not some mystical or abstract vision. This is the Right to live life the way we individually believe will most please us. Certainly there are expectations about personal responsibility inherent in this. Implicit in this Right is the duty to take care of your own needs and to contribute to the society in which you live. *Freedom* cannot allow *freeloading*.

There are rules and responsibilities in all collections of humans and the collection called the United States of America has them too. Within these rules, we citizens were granted the Right to pursue our dreams. But today, the ordinary People are unsettled. We view the country as unstable. We are concerned about its continuance as we know it. These concerns are keeping us hunkered down, not spending, not increasing investments or beginning new businesses. We saw nearly a trillion dollar "Stimulus Package" that was hurriedly passed by a single Party and did not meet the promised goal of capping and lowering unemployment rates. Most of the money seemed to not be spent on shovel ready projects but rather on Party payback projects and much was wasted. Our Administration seems all about expanding government size and its control. It is pursuing wars that it plans on losing at great expense in money and lives. All this impinges on our pursuit of Happiness, and layered upon that are additional actions that enhance our anger.

We have Congressional representatives from both Parties that do not read their bills, whose policies send our jobs overseas and spend beyond our means. We had a leader of the House who said, we must "pass it to see what is in it" regarding a huge bill giving management of healthcare to the government, and indicated that opposition demonstrators seemed like Nazis. We have an Administration with a President that has verbally disparaged us and our specifically written Rights to bear arms and to practice our religion, saying with derision that we ordinary Americans "cling to our guns and religion." These same Party leaders are funding groups like Acorn and its successors with our money, which have an objective of corrupting our voting process. Meanwhile the leaders of the Parties do not stop it, and then they refuse to secure the border. Now the Democrats have set multiple ultra high records of spending and, post midterm election, claiming not to see why there is this anger directed at them by many ordinary People. Let us be clear: we are angry at your attacks on our Rights and values, at your arrogance and ineptitude, and at the manner in which you adhere to a socialist agenda of big spending and big government control. These things stand against The People. Understand that *any* Party behaving in such a manner would raise our anger and understand that our anger has not abated. By impinging upon our Rights you have created anger and impeded our Right to pursue Happiness.

Equality is a Right that has always run counter to the efforts of the Ruling Elite, and so it is today. History is evidence that a primary tool of those in control is to show favor to those that support them but no favor and perhaps disfavor to those that do not support them. Following the American Right to equal treatment before the government is something that the Parties of the Ruling Elite do not want to do; it would stop them from using public money to buy supporters and votes. The Parties always cover their unequal treatment with appealing program titles, but just as Shakespeare said, "A rose is a rose by any other name"; and so does unequal treatment of some in favor of others by any name remain unequal treatment. It is the citizens that suffer the diminishment of their Right to Equality while their government is used to gather more Party power through the distribution of favor.

The Right to **Vote** is the special ability of us ordinary citizens to have meaningful participation in controlling our lives and our government. The Parties seem hard at work to diminish this Right too. It is well known that Arizona's southern border with Mexico is the crossing site of millions of illegals entrants into the United States and that such a large presence creates opportunity for voter fraud. As this is being written, the United States Court of Appeals Ninth Circuit in San Francisco has recently denied the State of Arizona's referendum law that requires those registering to vote to show specific documents proving their American citizenship. Consider also the comments of the Sheriff of Arizona's Cochise County who is head of the Border Sheriff's Association. In a television interview in early November 2010, he stated that he has towns in his county that have three or four hundred residents but routinely generate three to four thousand election ballots. Any such allegations *should* be thoroughly researched and if true, cleaned up by the government. It is logical that illegals would seek to vote in our elections in order to sway issues and elect politicians favorable to them. This cannot be allowed. If noncitizens are voting in any country's elections, it clearly is undermining their ability to be a democracy that its true citizens control. The legitimate voters are displaced by illegitimate voters, and the Right for every citizen's vote to count is directly violated. It is the Federal government that is legally responsible to protect the Right to Vote and to protect the border, but neither is being done. The current Party in power is not controlling the border, although it could, nor is it investigating even blatant potential voter fraud. This group then must be considered complicit in the fraud, yet the law enforcement system seems to protect them from prosecution. Meanwhile, the Administration is suing Arizona to block them from enforcing the Federal immigration law, demeaning the state internationally, and encouraging national disunity by stating that Latinos should "punish" those who oppose them. And the liberal Ninth Circuit court is allowing the Administration's suit, but not allowing the legitimate citizens to have their state verify citizenship to vote. You cannot even make this stuff up! Truly, is there *any* wonder that legitimate ordinary citizens are *angry?*

Anger results when humans are forcefully denied what they know is theirs. It was anger that drove the Founders of America to stand against England. It was anger over the attack at Pearl Harbor that ignited victory in WWII. It was anger that stopped slavery and then racial abuse. I contend that anger will help us now make an Evolutionary Point of Change that will correct the current abuse at the hands of a government that has become little more than a tool for the political Parties to squander the wealth and opportunity of America for their own benefit. This book will detail the roots and nature of the actual mess we are in; it will say things that must be said on behalf of the ordinary People.

Our situation was brought about by the Parties themselves, although they constantly blame the ordinary People. They say that our deficits are rising because of "The People's desire for more government spending," not their Party efforts to buy more votes and control with our money. It is a "deterioration of the moral fabric," not their push of faith from our institutions that they have expanded to control. "The schools are underfunded" they say, when they control what is taught, to whom and fail to teach citizenship and personal responsibility. "The family unit has deteriorated" is their speech, when they have encouraged dependency and illegitimacy by their welfare policies. "The People spend too much rather than save," when the tax policy and interest rates reward those who borrow and penalize those who accumulate money. We hear that "There are problems between economic strata and races," while the Parties vilify the top earners (but take from them 59% of all collected income taxes) and single out strata and races for favor. They say "The People need more government jobs" when they levy among the highest business taxes in the world and don't protect our private sector markets. It is time for major change. We must change *structure* in order to protect our rights, because changing personnel has shown to not be enough. It is time for a walk to the woodshed. It is time for a real "butt whippin'" to get some minds right, even if we have to pave D.C. and make it an alternative landing site for the space shuttle.

We know that in order to deal with a problem, one must first know what the problem is. We must ignore the Party blaming and other disunity tactics and realize that these accusers are a major problem. The Parties, *neither* of them, are our friends. By their origin and nature they are more an enemy than a friend of us ordinary People. This book will help you to consider that possibility and perhaps, as I have, come to that understanding. Part of that understanding comes from knowing that political Parties are not given *any* power nor even mentioned in the Constitution or any of the Founding Documents. George Washington, a Founder and the first President, disliked the very idea of political Parties and warned about them and about the spirit of domination that drives them. Today, we see the evidence of the special treatment and power that the Parties receive: the public pays the Party leaders inside Congress extra money for representing their Party; the parties have allowed government workers to become much better paid than those in private enterprise with much better benefits and paid retirement decades before the private sector; every ten years the Party in power redraws all the voting districts of the country which manipulates our votes to best benefit them; not only do these super interest groups decide who the candidates will be, but also the public pays for the "Primary" elections to assist them in *reducing* our choices! The 2010 primary campaign for Senator by Pennsylvania Congressman Joseph Sestak, showed that the Parties may even trade off other of our public jobs to manipulate elections to get the candidate that will best serve the Party; the *Party*, not The People. Sestak admitted he was offered an appointment by the Obama Administration if he dropped his primary run against their preferred Party candidate, Arlen Specter. He refused and then was later defeated by Republican Pat Toomey in the general election. At the time of the disclosure, there was talk of the investigation of three felony charges by Republicans. Post election, with Republican control of the House Oversight Committee and the certain capability to conduct such an investigation, it was dropped. A spokesman for Committee Chair, Darrell Issa, said, "If you are going down that road, you have to go back to every administration." This exemplifies how the two Parties routinely cooperate and control the enforcement of laws so that little happens to either Party's members who reduce our democracy and diminish our Rights. Consider also the consistent misconduct by Congressmen that we would be fined and incarcerated for; they go free with some negative words and get to keep a huge public pension that is completely out of reach for we ordinary People who pay for it.

And there are other ways that the Parties reduce our representation in government and our value in the process of government: having already noted that they deliberately do not protect our voting process, they also fail to meaningfully pursue vote fraud allegations: the Attorney General reportedly refuses to pursue any allegations against Blacks; the Parties disguise the intent of legislation from us by using misleading titles; they bury important laws inside of unrelated legislation; and they write bills in ways that are difficult to understand, including making them thousands of pages in length; they prepare bills in ways to reward supporters with millions in contracts or millions in reduced taxes. In the ObamaCare bill, after receiving millions in support from labor unions, the Democrats excused union members from having to pay a 40% excise tax on the best level of health benefits until five years after all others with such plans are required to pay it. These sorts of actions demonstrate that under the current structure *any* Party is able to openly abuse the values, the finances and the standards of government operation if they want to. By such actions, the idea of what a government is for ordinary People begins to *fade* and our noble experiment becomes a forced labor camp run by thugs, where the ordinary workers produce *everything* and support the thugs and their friends who run the camp and produce little.

We also know that rather than working to unify us, the Parties can intentionally cause disharmony among the citizenry for their own benefit. We know that we are suffering a huge economic downturn that may be mostly because of what they have done which will be detailed in these pages. We have witnessed the previously unimaginable consequences of the arrogance of a single Party's control over our government in the Democratic Party's open call for a "transfer of wealth" from one group of citizens to another. What we really need is a "transfer of power" from the Parties so that similar direct attacks on the Rights of the ordinary People can *never* happen again.

There was no grand conspiracy that brought us to the situation in which we find ourselves. Rather, it was rooted in the very nature of humankind that our Founders knew of and chose to defy; the natural human tendency of some few who will always seek to dominate over the many. These are the would be Ruling Elite and they will always seek control over the masses of ordinary People. By their nature they can neither help cure their malady nor want to. For all of history the world has seen them use many tools and guises to gain control: terror, slavery, dictatorships, war, royalty, religion, fear and others. For those of us in twenty-first century democracies, that tool is the powerful political Party. We ordinary People have been pushed aside by these groups who have used our trust and exploited the power loopholes they have found. It is from this marginalized state that we, and perhaps all democracies, must begin our journey to *shift* the power from the Parties to The People. The Party boldness has now shown us beyond question that they can have too much control and that government can become too large and powerful. Party-controlled big government seems uninterested in protecting our *Rights*; perhaps it is because it is too busy protecting *itself*.

> "Party-controlled big government seems uninterested in protecting our *Rights;* ...it is too busy protecting *itself.*"

The Citizens' Rights Movement is an attempt to provide a focal point for all citizens to escape the yoke that the Parties have placed upon us and to dislodge them from their position between us and our government. My background of faith and my review of history make me believe that the Founding Documents of our Country were divinely inspired, although not to the level of scripture; most of those who wrote them and then went to war for them believed that too. As this book will detail, we have been given a great and unique gift. If you are not of faith, consider our Founding Documents a gift from inspired men. If you are of faith, then consider them a gift from God, just like our Rights. Either way, all of us equally own this gift and we all must join in that commonality and in common sense to protect it.

The objective of the Citizens' Rights Movement is to reestablish the Rights we are guaranteed and to restructure government so that the control of those Rights transfers from the Parties and into the hands of The People who own them. Over many years, these political groups have taken control of our government and the control and protection of our Rights. The pages before you will detail that they are wholly unqualified to do so and demonstrate inadequacy daily. We will examine the nature of the Parties, review the Founding Documents that all who seek improvement need to be familiar with, detail the problems we suffer because of the powerful Parties, and propose a solution which we need to refine, agree to and embark upon very soon. There is an opening now for those who are not aligned with a Party to make a lasting impact on democracy for the benefit of all ordinary People. We have thousands of disparate groups and millions of The People who need to not just complain but to adopt a direction. By combining behind a set of ideas, The Tea Parties, Independents, American Solutions and Freedom-Works members, the stop government folks, the

Town Hall men and women, the disenchanted former Party members and numerous other similar groups can become "The New Middle." Together we will outnumber either of the Parties. By uniting behind a set of intentions and a plan, with goals to be achieved and steps to be taken, *we can win*; we can modify the path of our country so it can fulfill its centuries-old promise for the ordinary People of America and the world.

We can still remain discreet units and remain outside the Parties, but we must promote our commonalities and define our mutual goals. The Citizens' Rights Movement is offered for consideration as a starting point for our new and prosperous future. As our Founders were the *Revolutionaries* of their time, we are the *Evolutionaries* of ours. Together, our numbers are huge and by using our voting size in combination with today's communication technology, we can achieve what once took weapons. It will take many of us, but there *are* many of us.

THREE

We the People Versus the Political Parties

Most Americans have a pretty good "feel" for how all the democracy stuff works. If they were to explain it to someone from a non-democratic country, it would be something like this: "American citizens elect men and women from each district that are similar to themselves and whom they believe would generally represent the ideas and beliefs of those they represent in whatever government office to which they were elected. These people are accountable to the voters who put them in that office, as are their staff people and all hired employees that work under them. The voters trust the office holders to consider laws and policies on their behalf and according to the provisions of the Constitution. At the next election, they might run again on their record of representing the voters well."

The foreign visitor might surely expect that as far as personal conduct while they were representing whatever district it was, the elected person would be mindful of all laws and would behave in a manner consistent with their constituents' wishes. They might well assume that the representatives would be subject to the same laws and standards that govern their constituents and have similar pay, benefits, and job security that ordinary voters experience. Now, that sounds like a reasonable explanation and expectation, doesn't it?

Sadly, there is virtually no truth in the above paragraphs. Although most of us do not realize it, all of us see what we want to see or what we have been taught to see and that may have little to do with what is real. Everything above is almost exactly the opposite of the truth. Please understand that I am not here to spin some sort of "conspiracy theory." I have never thought a single such theory had any weight to it. No, what I am about to present is more like a "realization theory." It is a wakeup call to shake you into understanding the world in which we live. What I am about to describe is similar to someone telling you as a child that "there is no Santa Claus." When someone told you the truth about Santa, you probably did not want to believe it, even though you had perhaps seen some evidence already and maybe even questioned its reality earlier. It is natural to resist a mental move to an understanding based on truth.

Another analogy would be what happens when fans of "professional" wrestling realize that the whole thing is not real. After all, the fans had the hats, the tee shirts and had given financial support to their heroes. Their perception of the sport and those they held in esteem was based on what they had come to believe, not on what was real. When there is a shift to reality, we never look at the subject matter in quite the same way. To some extent, we all experienced this kind of unwanted reality shift in the way we look at things when we found that our parents are just people like us, sex and all. And right at this very moment, I am about to challenge you readers with a reality shift that few have been through yet.

The reality is, that American politics, for all of its colorful flag waving, memorable slogans, smiling people and perfect sound bites, is not at all what it seems to be. Instead, it is an attractive illusion, carefully crafted by the major political Parties. The purpose of this illusion today is the same purpose as in the decades past; to take more power and money from the citizens each year to put toward achieving the goals of the Parties. It is not about The People. I am not referring to any individual here. The goals of the political Parties are mostly to place and keep its candidates in positions of control at all levels of government, so that, as you may have guessed, the Party gains even more power and more money. Can you see how, with both Parties doing this decade after decade, the government just continues to grow? At the beginning of the 1900s government accounted for about 7% of America's Gross Domestic Product (GDP). That means the government was responsible for 7% of all items produced and every service performed in the nation in a year. Now it is 44%, and that is before taking over the healthcare that has always been in the free market.[1]

The government of our nation has become the mechanism by which the political Parties control The People for their purposes. Most people don't see this and for most of my life, neither did I. Like many, I was also a fish who did not know that I was in water. The reason for this blindness to the obvious was simple: the whole thing was "hiding in plain sight," and I did not *want* to believe it. I spent years following and supporting first the Democrats and then the Republicans. It was over a period of many years that I came to understand what the relationship truly is between these Parties and our government.

---

[1] USGovernmentSpending.com. (2010. September 28). U.S. Government Spending As A Percent of GDP from FY 1903 to FY 2010. http://www.usgovernmentspending.com/us_20th_century_chart.html

Getting Real About the Political Parties

It was a process of realization that began when I prepared for a debate in grade school covering the issues of the upcoming presidential election.

As an eager school boy, I worked diligently putting together facts and figures as to why my fellow student voters should select the Democratic Party candidate in the mock school election. In preparation, I went to my classmates to discern what key points to stress about the platform and qualities of my candidate. Surprisingly, most of those that seemed to like him did so because he spoke well and was handsome with a "neat" wife. The detractors seemed to not like that he was Catholic and thought that he would use the position of President of the United States of America to hurt Protestants. As the school votes were later counted, the pretend election was indicative of things to come. Although a big deal to me, John Fitzgerald Kennedy certainly did not feel the first flush of electoral success because of the results at our school. We were just ordinary People there on Havens Corner Road in Gahanna, Ohio, a growing farm town that had recently put in its second stoplight.

But "JFK" was the catalyst that began my lifelong interest in "politics." It was about that time that I came to believe that "politicians" referred to the people who lead the process by which ordinary People in a democracy select those who will represent their views to the government. Looking back, it seems that I might have been clued in to the error of my thinking by simply looking at the dictionary. The American Heritage Dictionary says a "Politician" is: "One who is actively involved in politics, esp. *party* politics" (emphasis mine)[2].

---

[2] American Heritage Dictionary (2nd College Ed.). (1985). Boston: Houghton Mifflin Company.

Even a standard dictionary seeks to tell us that the people we like to believe are about representing us are actually about representing their respective Parties. But that just isn't what we ordinary People believe. We just do not think it through, or perhaps we give them too much credit, especially when we are young students.

Most kids in college consider themselves to be left-leaning; there are several reasons for this. Most of the professors are left leaning and are strong influences on the student body. College students are exposed to social issues that are new to them. Such issues are combined with the passion of youth and its arrogance which drives the students to believe that they are different, that they are seeing things in a new way and that something can be done about it. As a college student, I thought precisely this way. Social change and engineering the nation to achieve it seems a reasonable approach in college. Such ideas are appealing because the student lives in a somewhat isolated environment which is, itself, socially engineered. Social engineering and free will are opposites, and more of one makes for less of the other. America has always been somewhere between the two. If these approaches were the colors black for social engineering and white for free will, America would be some shade of gray. Colleges would be a much darker gray.

American colleges have long been a collectivist interlude between the preparatory education and parental provision of the grade school years and the real post college working world. In college, students spend years experiencing an egalitarian environment in which thousands of inhabitants uniformly experience minimalist shared quarters and conversely vast and impressive public spaces. They wear similar clothing and live under their school identity package of colors, flags, logos and glories. They have their own president, and their own rules. Most students historically work little or not at all, or have loans which will defer their expenses to another time or to another person. Yet, shelter is convenient, food and comforts are plentiful, and all are provided for the student as if it is just supposed to be that way. A student's free time is used to pursue thinking about whatever one chooses, and about doing what seems fun at the moment. Having spent four years "on campus" to receive my undergraduate degree and another two years for my Masters degree, I can fully vouch for its influence in making the unreal seem very real. During my time at a Midwestern university, I could passionately feel the error of all "right" thinking. I just knew that Nixon and his ilk were part of the complex of injustice that was oppressing our nation and the world. Even though I was one of the minority who had to work my own way through, my state university was an idyllic place from which I emerged with a socialist point of view and a solid commitment to the Democratic Party. Many of us did.

The working world can be a big adjustment for many college graduates. Those who did the ideal routine of parental sacrifice may find it even more difficult, I think. First, they have to rework their entire life of waking and sleeping. While they struggle there, they actually must produce something for long periods of time, cut their play, and be responsible for providing for themselves. Food is no longer prepared and waiting, and it has to be paid for. Even for those of us who didn't have someone provide money for our college, the "real" world challenged our thinking about what we thought was reality in college. It is understandable that so many more recent college graduates seek to move back home.

The working world is competitive, mostly uncaring, and complicated, and can be shocking for new recruits, especially when that first post-graduation Spring break comes and they aren't there. For me, only working and not also going to school seemed more of a vacation compared to the work-and-go-to-school combination that I had endured, so I resolved to use the work habits I had acquired by necessity to help move my career forward. Instead of working a salaried forty hour work week, I put in 55 to 60 hours a week. Although I got paid no more, I got more done and gained more knowledge and experience in the process. This allowed me to move up in responsibility quickly. If you have recently graduated and followed a similar work/school track, consider this approach and the responsibility, experience, and opportunity that can come from it.

As my post-college career unfolded, I was traveling the country and going to exciting cities and meeting important people. I frequently worked with politicians to acquire and execute professional services agreements for large government construction projects across the country. My eyes were forced open to see another part of the real world that I truly did not want to see. The government construction arena was filled with lies and bribes. I learned that in order to get a part in these projects, your firm must show financial support for the political Party in power, for starters. Our firm was absolutely one of the very best at what we did. We had a large gallery of successful projects, a long-time staff of dedicated, knowledgeable professionals and in-house specialists who had actually spent entire careers in the detailed operation of our type of buildings. I was proud of the organization I worked with, and I still am. Without exception, they were top notch, hard working and well-intentioned professionals. You would think that our firm's pedigree would be enough to open the door for consideration on any project in our specialty. It wasn't. Too often, the real world of political Parties and their politicians stood between us and executing a project paid for by the public. Often that meant learning things that were not taught in the ideal world of the college campus.

Early on, I was involved in a project in Dallas County, Texas, that was a real "eye-opener" for a solid young Democrat. I was in the office of famed Democrat Henry Wade in the Dallas County building where he was the County Attorney. I recall that he had been there for about 25 years and was known as one of the most powerful men in Texas. Now, I was just an ordinary young guy from Ohio working on a project that was under his control and I had never even been near a man like this. (He would later become the "Wade" in "Roe v. Wade.") So there we are, standing alone, side-by-side, on a sunny Texas day. We were chatting and admiring the view from the many windows of his large office, which overlooked the JFK Memorial that was constructed across the street after President Kennedy's assassination. I mentioned how beautiful it was, perhaps with a tone of fondness that I had long carried for that man. Wade's reply was—and these are the words that burned into my memory, "Yeah, I am glad the son of a bitch got killed here."

In the next few moments, my mind must have raced over a hundred things, and gratefully my mouth said nothing. I thought, "He was referring to JFK! He was assassinated! What about his family? He was a Democrat! Was there that much hatred between the Democrats of the North and the South? Who *did* kill Kennedy?" I uttered none of these questions aloud, so there were no answers offered, but I will never forget that moment. It was as if more than my innocence was lost. It was a *reality shift* for me. In the days that followed, I began to see for the first time that the Party was just an organization of men and women—not inspired people of great character nor well-intentioned guides for citizens. No. Rather, these were coarse, heartless people with personal drives and intentions. In the years that have followed that incident, I have experienced, time and again, the teaching point of that memorable first encounter with the real world of Party politics.

I learned by personal experience that a high percentage of politicians wanted some sort of payoff to support their selection of—or perhaps even a consideration for—a public contract. This sort of tawdry practice might be about paid vacation, envelopes of cash, or worse. The "pay for play" activity seemed frequent at all levels of government. In the cities, the counties, the states, and even at the federal level. The odd thing is that it is just not spoken about. It is like the secrets of a fraternity where everyone knows about it, but never talks about it; not only because someone could overhear, but also because speaking about it is against some understood "code." And speaking about it could also get you into trouble.

It is for that last reason that I am pleased that I cannot remember the politicians and other government officials that I have had demands from. I cannot detail involvements such as the one with a U.S. Senator who had made an arrangement with local officials, using public money, that would net him hundreds of thousands of dollars delivered into his own pocket. His scheme would cost the taxpayers much more, as well as disrupt the lives and businesses of people of his state. When I hesitated at going along, they threatened that they would ruin my career forever if I stood in their way. This was a statement made angrily, eyeball to eyeball, with a finger in my face. Their threat was never carried out because they used a lie, unquestioned by the press (that supported their Party), to go around even my *potential* blocking. With the press in on it anyway, and my career in the balance, there was nothing to be done. It all happened just as they had planned. Kids had to change schools, people had to move out of their homes, entrepreneurs lost their businesses, and the public had to pay extra millions so that this Senator would get money from a secret deal made possible by the expense of public funds. I have rarely even mentioned this and will never remember the name of the places or the people. With Party control using the government as a tool at every level, many of these people can and will hurt you. We ordinary Americans are nothing to these people. We are like sheep that are bought and sold, moved or slaughtered as needed to support their drive for power and money. Anyone who tells you otherwise is either totally ignorant of the facts, or is a liar.

In order for any of us to choose a direction in which to move forward, we need to know where we actually are. So we all must understand that the Parties and many—but not all—of their minions are taking advantage of us. They use the positions we provide them for the benefit of their Party and themselves, all around the country and on a daily basis. Those on the inside know it, and many profit from it. To protect themselves and their profit, they don't speak about it. It is pretty much kept inside the Ruling Elite, which consists of the primary Party people and those who support them. My experience has been about money and other considerations being transferred to Party politicians in order to gain access to public project contracts. But often, information comes out about the bribes and corruption in other "political" sectors, too.

Google *"Abscam"* sometime. This FBI "sting" operation in the late 1970s netted convictions of six U.S. Congressmen and one Senator, a state senator from New Jersey, and members of the Philadelphia city council. It was based on a sham company named "Abdul, Ltd." These officials became convicted criminals caught taking money variously in a bag, in an envelope, stuffing it in pockets, or by taking $50,000 increments in stock.[3] These bribes were accepted in exchange for using control and contacts within government agencies to get something for the

---

[3] Federal Bureau of Investigation. (2010, August 3). Abscam. Online Ten Part Report of Investigation. www.foia.fbi.gov

person paying the bribe. It is called "influence peddling" and is the selling of access to the people's public money or other public assets (like citizenship or a pardon) to those who otherwise cannot get it.

In this case, a fictitious sheik was seeking asylum in America, partners for a business venture, and to bring money into the country illegally. Although the U.S. Senator was convicted and officially condemned by his peers, he was not expelled from Congress for this breach of public trust. He resigned and spent only two years of a three-year sentence in prison. Sadly, after Abscam, Congress quickly passed *bipartisan* legislation that made it much more difficult to mount any investigation against members of Congress without them knowing about it in advance. Consider this: all of the people convicted were Democrats except one, and his case was overturned. So why would the Republicans join with the Democrats to pass such legislation? Could it be because (1) both of the Parties are frequently involved in this sort of thing? Or maybe it is because (2) "the loyal members of the Congress must preserve separation of the branches of government and protect their rights in order to well serve and preserve the liberty of the people"?

Select answer number one. It is no surprise that in the thirty years since Abscam, there has been no similar scandal uncovered. Do you think that is true because the politicians have stopped their lawless activity, or is it because the Parties together used legislation to block "sting" types of investigation?

If you believe the former, you are a naïve believer and exactly where they want you to be. They want you to believe in them, just like you did Santa. Think about it. If a herd of sheep knew that their fate was uncaring destruction, would they follow their shepherd anywhere they were led? Abscam is illustrative of how corrupt these Party politicians can be. It also shows how the Parties work together to protect themselves from The People and is reflective of the structure of how ordinary People are controlled and taken advantage of.

There is a large and well known list of incidents of bribery, corruption, illegal acts, and bad behavior that comes from the very people we trust to do otherwise. All have sworn to uphold our laws and to defend the Constitution that is the basis of our nation.

The federal level has had many offenders in the past forty years, including President Richard Nixon (R) who openly lied about his knowledge of the burglary of the Democratic Party National Headquarters offices in the Washington D.C. Watergate office complex. Nixon was pardoned of all charges by President Gerald Ford (R) when he was appointed to replace Nixon as President. Nixon's original Vice President, Spiro Agnew, former Maryland Governor, had resigned earlier as a consequence of bribery charges.

President Jimmy Carter's (D) Director of the Office of Management and Budget (OMB) resigned after misuse of funds in a Georgia bank sale.

In the Reagan (R) administration, the Iran-Contra Affair was the unapproved selling of weapons to our enemy, Iran, and the diversion of those millions, via Oliver North, to rebels in Nicaragua.

The Reagan administration also had a bribery scandal at the Department of Housing and Urban Development (HUD) that resulted in five convictions or guilty pleas.

President Clinton (D) distracted the entire government from its work by its focus on his philandering and his subsequent denials and lying under oath. During the campaign against Clinton's first term, the first President Bush (R) brought up Clinton's philandering while Governor of Arkansas, but that was quickly hushed when the possibility of an affair of Bush was raised. Neither camp mentioned the subject again. As

President, Clinton was impeached, but it was not carried out since he was acquitted by the Senate. Clinton also pardoned Marc Rich, who had fled the country after charges of illegal commodity trading and trading with an enemy of America, and he also freed Carlos Vignali, an imprisoned drug smuggler. The families of both of these men gave substantial contributions to the Democratic Party and to the Clinton Presidential Library. The pardons were given as Clinton left office and after the contributions were made.

History will determine the validity of the second Bush's (R) claim that the Iraq War was truly based upon what he believed to be accurate intelligence information. During the G. W. Bush terms, six Republican officials were linked to inappropriate activity with lobbyist Jack Abramoff.

Even the current Obama administration is involved in questionable activity. There was an alleged attempt by the Illinois Governor to sell his appointment of the Senate seat vacated by the President, which resulted in the impeachment of Illinois Governor Rod Blagojevich (D). Payoffs worth millions to several states were made to get support for the Democrat-led government expansion into healthcare. In 2009, Congressman Charles Rangel (D) New York, Head of the Ways and Means Committee, and Timothy Geithner (D), Secretary of the Treasury were both found to have not paid obvious income taxes due. Even though they stand at the very pinnacle of administering tax law in America, they failed to pay. Neither earned significant admonishment, no rebuke by their peers and no penalty other than IRS fees, until more significant violations were discovered for Rangel the following year.

But Rangel had an even earlier violation that had been ignored by his peers. Congressman Rangel was also Chairperson of The House Ways and Means Committee, the primary controller of the budget in our Government, when he was found "guilty" of an ethics violation for taking privately gifted trips to the Caribbean. This is a clear violation for which he was exonerated of penalties by his Congressional Party peers. Interestingly, he assumed the Chairman's position of financial control when the Democrats took over Congress in 2006, as G. W. Bush's second term began its second half. At that point, the Republican-controlled Congress had raised the public debt to a 280 billion dollar deficit. Many were rightly concerned, and the press attacked Bush for it. The Democrats, with Nancy Pelosi (D) as Speaker, came into full control of our public checkbook then. By 2008, that deficit approached one trillion dollars, increasing by over 300% in 24 months. Part of that huge increase was money that helped to publically fund ACORN, a corrupt partisan support group for the Democrats.

The Democrats consistently blame the deficit increase to one trillion dollars on Bush because he was President at the time. This is a very usual action by Congress, no matter the Party in control; Congress will blame the past President for overspending because he is gone and they are still in office. In classic "scapegoat" style, they put all the blame on him as he leaves Washington, leaving them clean of their harm to the public. The Democrats even use the 2008 one trillion dollar deficit to blame Bush for the four trillion dollar deficit they built by the end of 2009. That is correct: Since 2006 when the Democrats took control of the House, which is responsible for the budget, the debt went from about $¼ trillion to $4 trillion, an increase of about 1,600%.

The point here is that our government is run by remorseless liars who consistently choose to act in favor of themselves or their Party, instead of The People. Yes, I am sure there are some good men and women, but the Party system they are part of overshadows them and dominates the action. And while the examples here seem ominous, they barely touch the surface of what is known to have gone on that is questionable at just the federal level. What remains unknown is likely much greater. For the entry *"us government scandals,"* Google returns more than 16,000,000 hits.

A legitimate question is, "What happens when these elected officials whom we trust with our Rights and our futures, go astray?" The answer is: surprisingly little. There is a system that has been put in place to keep penalties for misbehavior at a minimum. The Constitution's Article I, section 5. establishes that the Congress sets the punishment for its members' "disorderly behavior" and can expel with a two-thirds vote. Because neither of our major Parties wants to suffer harshly, they agree that little will be done, but it is the American People that are hurt by much of it. They want justice in such matters, not excuses.

Now, I believe that sexual relations with staff and other misbehaviors should be punished, as any employer must punish. I recognize that embarrassment and fear of voter retaliation has and will lead some to resign in such cases. But there should be a publically known set of harsh mandatory penalties for misbehavior in office at all levels of government, and especially where personal financial gain from office happens.

I have seen firsthand how pervasive the breech of public trust can be. It is inexcusable and we will address a possible remedy on other pages. We have a current structure in which questionable

> "...questionable people, doing questionable things, go unquestioned."

people, doing questionable things, go unquestioned. We cannot correct the situation if we believe the excuses or make excuses because we like a Party or a particular candidate. We must recognize that the Parties have built themselves a playground filled with our power and our money. This is a vast non-public playground in which they make all the rules and exonerate each other from wrongdoing while passing out our money to themselves and those who support them.

We ordinary People not only lose our Constitutional power and our money through such covert actions as those seen in Abscam and in other excused violations and rule bending, but also through openly-created structures. These have gradually been put in place by the Parties and have eroded the Freedom of ordinary Americans like you and me. These structures are part of the "wall" the Parties have constructed that keep The People separated from the government that *we* are supposed to be in charge of. This wall includes protection from misbehavior, lobbying, party determination of candidates, primary voting, gerrymandering, earmarks, limitless terms, unequal application of the law, nonenforcement of law, and Party representation versus People representation. There is also no structured accountability or oversight with mandatory accessible/usable reports, and government departments at all levels use "in-house" policing of ethics and legal violations.

We have a governmental structure in which people are given power and good pay, prominence and celebrity, secrecy and protection from wrongdoing and access to trillions of dollars, and then we are disappointed with misbehavior! The kinds of people that are drawn to an environment like that are the same kind that created it. Even the well intentioned are overshadowed by the way it works. This environment did not just happen; it was gradually created by the people and Parties who have been controlling it for decades, not the likes of the Founders when individual honor and integrity were revered.

Special Interest Lobbying

Among the many possible illustrations of the structures that are set up in plain sight that deliver power and money to the Parties and their politicians, one is the process that both parties have set up regarding lobbying.

Lobbying is the process by which those in legislative positions are influenced to originate, support or oppose government actions of control over the citizens. The term "lobbying" comes from the early days when "lobbyists" would actually sit in the lobbies, the public gathering areas of hotels and other meeting places. Their intent was to make contact with a circulating elected official and convey a point of view to that official which might then be considered. And that kind of made sense in the 1700s when it began, because there were millions of Americans spread out all over the large nation and within the states. It was hard to be in contact with them at all. There were no telegraphs or telephones, and huge numbers of people could not read or write. It was difficult for people to know what was happening in government centers, with no radio, television, Internet and very few newspapers outside of larger cities. Communication was slow, difficult and only gradually became the instant communication that we have today. Also, information about government was not as critical, since all government was less important and much smaller, having few offices and employees and little impact on daily life.

Perhaps I am a purist, but even then, when it was somewhat dictated by low technology, it seems that this process which allowed special access for those of a special interest or wealth, would be morally wrong, especially since there was no organized lobbying for the ordinary People. America was a democratic nation, but got off on the wrong foot, by allowing lobbying so that some of the people would have a greater influence on those that would actually decide on issues than others would have. That, in fact was the point, and it still is. The very idea is that lobbyists are *supposed* to gain advantage in getting their will accommodated despite whatever The People might prefer. I contend that most of our nation's critical decisions and policies are set by the political Parties and the lobbyists; not by The People. These two groups make the decisions, and The People are to pay for them; not only in money, but in loss of freedom. Most of The People don't realize this, and those who do don't see what can be done about it.

So how big is lobbying and how does it happen today? If one Googles "lobbying representatives," there are more than 4,559,000 site returns. Type in "lobbying techniques," more than 2,400,000 sites are returned. In California alone, just the top 100 firms paid to lobby at the state level spent $267,000,000 in the two years 1995 and 1996.[4] Remember, most people spending money on lobbying are expecting to have something of greater value coming back. The figure stated for California above included: California Professional Firefighters, $6,416; Marin County, $133,000; California Association for Bilingual Education $169,000; Apple Computer, $40,000; Association of American Publishers, $111,000; Electrical Contractors Association of California, $427,000; Avis, $10,000 and United Domestic Workers of America, $28,000. These figures are sums from only *one* lobbyist firm, but many special interests have more than one. Lobbying may be sometimes about getting a contract or its terms, a union benefit or perhaps getting some new law passed, modified or removed, but it is always about power and about money.

Yes, lobbying is big. It is no wonder that we hear about it so often. We must remember that its purpose is to have the government act in a certain way in its governing of The People.

---

[4] State of California 1995–96 Lobbying Expenditures Index. (1996). 1995–1996 Lobbying Expenditures and the Top 100 Lobbying Firms. www.sos.ca.gov/prd/lexp/top100.htm

Environmentalist, religious and other organizations, education, sex, race, age and other socially-oriented special interests, for-profit companies and non-profits, unions, the military, and even school districts and other government bodies are among those constantly working to get the government to be used as a tool on their behalf.

There is a paid cadre of aggressive and likely "connected" men and women acting as "hired guns" to deliver to a myriad of special interest groups something of even greater value than the money being paid to them. They are not only active at the federal level, but also at every level of government in every state. The money owed by us ordinary People because of politician deals for contributions and payoffs dwarfs our ability to pay. Each year, billions of dollars are being expended by special interest groups to assure that it is their will that is done in America. When it comes to assuring that The People are running things, special interest group lobbying has grown to be a large roadblock. But compared to the next structural issue in the way, it is small.

The Parties are themselves the ultimate special interest groups. Both Parties publically claim to be against what they actually are. They represent their own interests and that of those who support them, not yours.

Political Parties: The Ultimate Special Interest Groups

The Major political parties in the U.S. are the Democratic Party (the color blue, the symbol is a donkey) and the Republican Party (the color red, their symbol is the elephant). These organizations are viewed by many American people as an actual part of their government and for good reason. These Parties predate any living citizen, so, for every citizen's entire lifetime, they have always existed. They are much like an old tree in the grandparents' yard; they seem to have always been there and it seems like they should be there. For the living, they can even be like water to a fish, in that the fish was born into the water and, in a sense, does not even know the water is there.

However, in reality, the Parties are neither a planned part of our government nor have they always existed in our nation. They were created after the founding of America by men who sought to find a means of harnessing the power of the new government to achieve their own goals.

For us ordinary citizens to understand how our government works today, we need to understand how political Parties work and how they relate to our government. They have a key, no, *the* key influence on our government; the same government upon which we not only depend, but also financially support and serve, even to the point of offering our lives.

Despite their position of greater power over the American government than that of the citizens as a whole, political Parties are *not* part of the government. There is no mention of the Parties in the Founding Documents.[5] The Declaration of Independence, 1776, presents its case for breaking the bonds of The People from the "King of Great-Britain." It neither uses the word "political" nor "party." It is all about the body of the people of the American Colonies as a whole. The U.S. Constitution, 1788, written primarily by James Madison, is a carefully constructed document that established the powers that would be entrusted at the federal and state levels. It replaced The Articles of Confederation (which also did *not* mention "parties") that were adopted as the operating rules of America in 1781 but were determined to be inadequate soon after.

The inadequacies included the inability of the central government to force payment from the states. At the time,

---

[5] United States Constitution and other American Documents. (2009). New York: Fall River Press.

the central government, called the "Confederation," had no power to tax. It relied on the states, which could tax, to each contribute a proportional payment to the central government. States were reluctant and tardy, sometimes even keeping the central government from functioning for lack of cash. There were also troubles between the states. Some states were taxing goods crossing their borders, and there were also states, attempting, in effect, to be separate countries. There were rising disputes and no system in place to resolve them.

A great struggle ensued between "Federalists," those wanting a new constitutional government, and "Anti-Federalists" who did not. After years of work, the Constitution was adopted in 1791. Several of the states adopted it on the condition of the inclusion of a group of ten amendments that were to be approved after the adoption of the base document, which came to be known as the "Bill of Rights." But even in that, there was no mention of political parties.

Again, each of these Parties today is like a "super" interest group that combines all the interest groups that support it, along with the interests of the political Party itself. Each of the Parties has some support from almost every group, but, in my opinion, there are discernable groups of primary special interest for each of the parties.

The Democrats carry the special interests of government workers, unions, and those that view themselves as victims of economics, of history or of culture. This Party is called the "Liberal" Party in the U.S. and includes the recipients of desired wealth transfer from others, the "takers"[6] that we have witnessed since childhood.

The Republicans have the interests of business, free market people, and those that view themselves as personally responsible,

---

[6] Schweiszer, P. (2008, June 3). Makers and Takers. DoubleDay.

desirous of opportunity, and the more religious. This Party is called the "Conservative" Party in the U.S., generally includes the "makers," the producers upon whom the takers depend.

Many of the supporters of the Democrats have a primary connection with the past. They are oriented to *what was* and seek atonement for wrongs done to those of the past that they feel connected to, but probably do not know, even by name. For Blacks the connection is with people of their race who suffered slavery and racism. In recent decades, around 90% of all Blacks voting do so for Democratic Party candidates.[7] Jewish Americans have a connection with those who suffered in Europe from hatred of their Jewish culture and religion (anti-Semitism) and with those who are the less fortunate in society. Again, more than 90% of the Jewish vote is tradition-ally cast for the Democrats at all levels of government.[8] The Democratic Party mines this way of thinking by assigning blame to the living in the opposing Party or any others not in their own super interest group. Emphasis is on how something is done, not on the outcome.

Many of the supporters of the Republican Party have a primary connection with the future and with principals and opportunity. They are oriented to *what can be ahead* and are detached from what happened with other people in the past, although they adhere to values and traditions from the past. Their Party mines this thinking by emphasizing the dependency of opposition that holds back the promise of the future. Emphasis is on the outcome of what is done, and less on the means of getting there.

---

[7] Brazile, D. (2004. January 29). African Americans Crucial to Democratic Victory. The Black Commentator, Weekly Internet Magazine.

[8] Benhorin, Y. (2006. November 8). 87 percent of Jews vote Democratic. Israel News. Ynetnews.
http://www.ynetnews.com/articles/0,7340,L-3325529,00.html

These two camps of special interests are at war, and both attempt to use the government against the other side. It has been a long war, longer than any of us have been alive, and it has no end in sight. Both Parties are dedicated to winning, but there is no winning—just one side having more control of The People, temporarily. Since most of us ordinary People are more like a combination of both liberal (Democrat) and conservative (Republican) thinking, we are less partisan than *either* group. It seems we must reconcile ourselves to accepting the "lesser of two evils."

In America today, these two political Parties are the primary determiners of all that is government in the United States. From most town and city levels, to county government, regional districts, school districts, most judgeships—including the Supreme Court—and on to the Federal offices, the Parties cover our government with a blanket of control. At all these levels, the Parties seek to control who gets elected or appointed, who stays in a position, what that person does in office, what legislation is proposed and what is passed, what government workers are paid, and who the government does business with. Without any doubt whatsoever, it is the Parties that determine what our government is and what our government's relationship is to us.

It is not the *ordinary Americans that are welding such power, not "We the People." It is the Parties.* Most of us accept this as something that is just "as it should be," like the old tree, or like the fish—we don't even see it.

Because political Parties are so powerful and so impactful in our lives, maybe it is time to really examine and *think* about this. After all, shouldn't The People have the power? Wasn't that always the idea? Actually, that was the idea that the Founding Fathers had. The reason for the strict separation of government at the federal and state levels and the partitioning into two legislative sections was to make the government difficult to be controlled by power hungry politicians. As great as their effort was, even the Founders did not anticipate the powerful assault on the freedom they planned by the spread and allegiance to political Parties. James Madison, original framer of The Constitution, specifically noted that ". . . the accumulation of all powers . . . in the same hands, whether of one, few, or many, and whether hereditary, self-appointed or elective, must be pronounced the very definition of tyranny." With that fearful understanding in place, Madison also explained how he intended to protect the future Americans from it. "The unwanted powers of government . . . are guarded against by the division of the government into distinct and separate departments. . . . The power surrendered by the people is first divided between two distinct governments, and then the portion allotted to each subdivided among distinct and separate departments. Hence a double security arises to the rights of the people. The different governments will control each other, at the same time each will be controlled by itself."[9]

The ability of the Parties to cross over the barriers that James Madison and others erected in the Founding Documents was seemingly not anticipated. The Parties are not assigned any duties in either the Declaration or in the Constitution. It is no wonder. These documents are about the dividing and limiting of the state and federal governments, while the goal of the Parties is to achieve consolidated and unlimited control by using the government as their "power tool."

So what does this mean today? A good example of the problem created by Party affiliation can be seen in the April, 2010 state push-back after the passage of the Democrats' national

---

[9] Asmus, B., & Billings, D. (1995) *It's Tea Time Again*. Phoenix, AZ: AmeriPress.

health legislation known as "ObamaCare." Twenty-six states joined in a lawsuit questioning the constitutionality of parts of the 2,700 page law. Although this was about constitutionality issues and also included requirements that would cost each state millions of dollars, not a single state controlled by Democratic Party leadership opposed the law. The exceptions were where there was an opposing Party State Attorney General who filed without the Democratic governor's consent. In many of these States, the voters were against the federal bill's passage. But their government took no action, and it was expected to be that way and would likely have been similar if the Parties were reversed. The "solidarity" exhibited by the Parties simply thwarts the control by The People intended by the Founders and reduces the representation of The People at all levels. The establishment of this kind of blanket-like Party control and Party manipulation of voting districts ("gerrymandering") to make it difficult to vote out their incumbents are two of the Party methods that thwart the realization of freedom that the Founder's intended for the ordinary People.

Let's underscore that there is no conspiracy theory aspect to this. There was likely no group that appeared and looked at our Founding Documents and said "we can beat this." The situation we are in has resulted from the gradual playing out of a basic negative nature of some human beings. This notion that the rise of the Parties is part of a natural response to the establishment of democratic government has evidence beyond our borders. Democracies that have begun across the planet spread from the United States model, as we will detail in pages ahead. Many of them have used our very Constitution (or a version of it) as their own. Where these democracies have begun, all over the planet, political Parties have also appeared. And efforts by some to gain control over any government structure seems logical, based on what we know of the human condition.

Humans naturally seek to improve their own conditions, and for some, that seems to include having power over others.

There have likely always been ordinary, independent people who want to live their own lives and trust others to do the same. There have also likely been those people whose basic nature drives them to want to control others. This is the foundation for what we have today. You can see how, over time, these two types of people in a free society could coalesce. Over many decades, they might split into opposing groups each with strong leaders seeking power over others as well as those that don't want that. In America, some of those with a controlling nature saw that there was a place where they could wedge in and not just gain control, but also get paid well to do so, both in money and in power. Once in place between the people and the government, they could use the control they gained to get more followers, and expand, and get even more money and more power. They could use the power of the laws our government makes for us and the money it takes from us for their own purposes. Of course, they would say, and perhaps some would believe, that whatever they did was for "our own good." And that is likely similar to what all tyrants have said throughout world history. It is also what the Founding Fathers tried to protect us from in the way they drew up the Founding Documents.

So how do we account for more than one Party? Perhaps some group began with the true intention of having some positive impact for others, just as a charity might get started. It seems more likely that it happened that more than one "Party" developed because multiple groups saw the same good thing as possible for themselves. And why are they called "Parties" anyway? My guess is that many of these group leaders were attorneys, and used the same non-descriptive term that they used in writing legal documents, as in "the party of the first part." And that *would* be less negative than using more accurate terms, like "interloper" or "usurper" or "gang."

To perhaps understand better how the Parties would "naturally" come about, let's look at it in the form of a story about a small American town. Imagine that you live in "Our Town" in the U.S. in the 1950s. Life seems pretty simple; most people go to work, raise their kids, pay taxes, and look forward to retirement some day. Under the tree-lined streets to downtown, people greet each other meaningfully, and life is stable. Everyone knows the cops, the mayor and other officials and believes that they are earnestly looking out for the town and treating everyone fairly. Now imagine that a gang moves into town and one way or another gradually gets its gang members in the positions where those officials of character used to be. Slowly you realize that government actions that used to be responsive to the citizens of the town now seem to be about what is important to the gang. These new town officials all agree to pass ever-increasing salaries and benefits for themselves. The school teachers throw in with the gang and students are learning less. Then another gang comes to town, vowing to fight against the one already there, for the "sake of the citizens." But once they are in control, little changes. The speakers of both gangs seem to say the right things, but there are no plans and very few ways to make them accountable for what they say or do. If one of the officials gets caught stealing or lying, both of the gangs do little other than protect that person and minimize any penalty.

As the years go by, the gangs begin recruiting your growing children to work in the city government for them. The kids say the work days are short and the pensions are great, so why take risks in the business world? New fees and permits appear, and taxes are raised, hurting businesses and the ordinary People. The town offers programs to give some of the money back, if you will only follow new rules that they have set—or are part of groups that they favor. Then the other gang makes fanfare that they will get control back and "fight" to make things right, but once they are the gang in power, they then find new ways to control the town, to raise your taxes, and spend your money. "It's all for the good of the town," they say. Then the gangs start applying laws unequally on their friends and making different laws for themselves and for those who support them. This drives wedges between different groups of people. You finally begin to see that maybe it is the presence of these gangs that are actually causing many of the problems, despite what they say and the town flags they both wave. By taking advantage of the people's trust, and by not being accountable, it looks as if they gradually wedged themselves between the townspeople and their government. So you talk to people in your town about how this is not the way it is supposed to be, but you discover that many have given up, thinking their vote makes no difference. After all, they explain, "We only get to vote for the candidates they put up and they are all gang members, just like who they appoint." The two gangs are "two sides of the same coin," they note. When you call out to other towns and the state and even Washington D.C., you find that the gangs have affiliates in every one of these places too. Finally, in desperation, you seek counsel with others, most of whom are younger than you and find that they cannot even see what is around them, because they grew up in it. You also find that many of these people dislike those who oppose the gangs; as if the gangs are parents who give them things and you are like a selfish and mean relative that they took it from.

This is just a simple story. But by substituting the two gangs for the two primary American political Parties, it helps us to understand what these Parties are all about. The Democrats and the Republicans are like the Crips and the Bloods but without all the honesty. These gangs and these Parties use the same colors; they use rule bending, unspoken tactics, and other people to achieve for themselves. Like the gangs, the Parties are "two sides of the same coin." You may like one side better than the other, but, for most Americans, it leaves their choice as only between the "lesser of two evils."

Frequently, we ordinary Americans view our government policies and actions as "stupid" and not good for us or the country. We are amazed that our officials are so "dumb" and how their work product seems so "illogical and wrong." After all, we think, "These people are from the best schools, how can they do the things they do and say the things they say?"

We need to stop and think. If we step back and actually think about it, the truth becomes clearer; we are the ones who are being stupid and incredibly naïve. We have not seen the truth that is right in front of us; these Parties run our government. They have inserted themselves between us and our governance. They use our government as a tool to control us and to take from us. No wonder, then, that their actions seem so out of touch with us; their actions are not for *us*; their actions are for *them*. What they do is for their benefit, not ours. Their goals do not match the goals of the American people. If we hope to make a positive shift in the way our government works, we must understand that the Parties are running it, not us. The plans and programs that the Parties make are about them and theirs, not The People. Make no mistake, the Parties—both of them—are all about what is good for *them*.

We understand goals, don't we? In terms of personal goals, most of us ordinary Americans, want to use the opportunities our country provides us to control our own lives and better ourselves and our families in business enterprises or government service. Just as in the imaginary "Our Town," most of us follow the rules, work hard, take responsibility for ourselves, pay taxes, save up, dream of doing better and maybe having our own business.

We know that business goals are different from personal goals. A business has goals of expanding and making money for those who run and own it by selling customer goods and services, and also by treating employees fairly and honestly. A business is accountable to regulations and laws, to the marketplace which seeks to genuinely compare quality and cost, and to the buyer with warranties.

But what are the goals of political Parties? A political Party has a goal of expanding its power and money by selling people representation in the control of people's lives. The political Party is mostly accountable to an election in which each Party seeks to disingenuously compare, falsely promise, and to ignore any accountability for the past or for the future.

The people who lead the Parties want to control their own lives, of course, as do all of us. But they also want to control *your* life. It is their very nature and most of them truly believe that they know what is better for you than you do. By their very nature, political Parties and those in them are prone to tyranny, and the more they are involved in controlling your life, the less freedom you are left with. It is really no different than the relationship between you and your parents, you and your significant other, or you and your boss. The more they control you, the less freedom you have to do what you think or believe is best; the less they control you, the more you control yourself, and the more freedom you have. Personal control is what is known as a "zero-sum" game[10]; a situation in which there is only so much of something, and

---

[10] McCain, R. Game Theory: An Introductory Sketch. (2010, August 8). faculty.lebow.drexel.edu.McCainR//top/eco/game/zerosum.html

if one entity takes some of it, the other entity has less of it. In the situation between ordinary People and government, that something is freedom.

The Parties both work hard to portray their roots as being in the real worlds of economics, social concerns, education, and even science. There is a reality about each of these, but it is different from their political reality, which scorns truth, ridicules and attacks dissent, fosters disunity, and often seeks a worship-like following of its leaders. It seeks to increase its control—perhaps even over all aspects of life—for the benefit of the Parties and promises to use the offices of government to do their bidding in ruling the ordinary citizens.

It seems like a human defect that finds tyranny acceptable as long as the acceptors get some share; as if character and principles are old ideas that don't matter. In tyranny, the few want to control the many. These few believe that they know better than the ordinary People and also know they will reap the rewards of power and money, not from making something, not from helping produce wealth, but from controlling others. Power, as the currency of politics, is used to improve their lives and to do so at your expense. Bottom line: the tyranny of increased government control of citizens denies the citizens' basic human drive to do better for themselves and their families.

Tyranny has shown to fail with the masses, who ultimately almost always have sought freedom from its chokehold. It was the appeal of tyranny to some and the acceptance of tyranny by others that allowed slavery to exist, that brought Hitler to power, and the world to war. It was the reality of tyranny that crushed free thinking and wisdom and thrust the world into the Dark Ages, and it was also the dominant thinking behind the rise and establishment of Communism, which brought millions to poverty, hopelessness, and death.

It was the resistance to tyranny that ended the Dark Ages, caused the colonists to come to our soil, and overthrow the English in the American Revolution.

The American freedom established there, coupled with a free market economy, ultimately changed the economic system of the world. The standard of living for ordinary People had not been materially improved for some 600 years. The American formula of free People and free enterprise vaulted ordinary Americans ahead of their peers worldwide in a matter of decades. The new American nation soon surpassed civilizations that were thousands of years older—in material wealth, in innovation, and in freedom and influence around the world. We ordinary People have flourished, and today are living better, longer, and happier lives than the billions who preceded us. It is not perfect, we must contend with our impact on earth and we still have wars, but it is clear that personal freedom together with economic freedom allows ordinary People to thrive.

Unfortunately, tyranny has been the normal state of man on earth, not freedom. Freedom is anathema to those who desire to control others. Freedom is the enemy of tyranny in the same way that light is the enemy of darkness and the way that truth is the enemy of lies. Tyranny will always seek to destroy freedom, and it will use the darkness of stealth, and it will raise lying to a virtue to do it.

But tyranny is only a concept of conversation without The People to make it real, to give it life and action. And today, tyranny has its recruits and is on the move against freedom in democratic nations around the world. We have both external and internal enemies who seek to destroy our freedom and both tell us the same old story; "it is for our own good." On the outside, are the Muslim extremists who seek to control us by their religion; we are to submit to their thinking and live our lives with the limited choices that they believe are "right"

56

for us. On the inside, we have Party extremists who seek to control us by their ideology; we are to submit to their thinking and live our lives with the limited choices that they believe are "right" for us. Vainly, we expect those of the internal threat to save us from the external threat. It may be more likely they will, at some level, become allies in defeating us.

In sum, like street gangs, political Parties seek to control and gain by deception and connection. If needed, intimidation, force and payoffs will be used. The Parties are the ultimate "special interest groups," which, ironically, both will claim to be against. Tyranny is about the few forcing the many to behave in the manner that the few believe is correct; and it also happens that tyranny often materially benefits those few. Tyranny is what the "left" is about in its global march to expand central government and its control over the lives and economy of ordinary citizens. Tyranny is what the "right" is about when it seeks to push in the limits of privacy and to impose its notion of adult moral behavior. Freedom has always been the hope and desire of the ordinary People; tyranny has always been the desire of those who are the Ruling Elite.

> "The Democrats and Republicans are like street gangs, but without all the honesty."

Capitalism and Socialism: What are these "-isms" anyway?

We have a duty here to make it clear what these economic systems are about, because many Americans simply do not know or do not know enough to make a decision about what they want. In a sense, we will attempt to do in the following paragraphs what our representatives should have made sure was done for the past 200 years—to inform you, as a citizen, about an issue so that you can understand that issue and intelligently decide. This information will be presented in a rudimentary manner so that the least economically educated of us ordinary Americans can grasp the concept and its meaning to us free people.

When economists talk about an "economic system" they are referring to how money flows and how the production, development and management of wealth occurs.

As American residents, it is natural to think the system that America has is "just the way it works" or "the way it is supposed to be." It is what we know, and what we grew up with. However, we must all realize that America's system is *not* like that of all the other nations of the world, although many nations have mimicked it. Our economic system differs in some fundamental ways not only from those that preceded it, but also from some systems present in other countries today. For most of mankind's history, almost all material wealth (money) and all land was held by the few rulers of the people. Especially in Europe, these were mostly powerful families that passed down ownership and control to each succeeding generation. In order to accumulate and retain wealth, it was necessary to be able to take from others and to keep others from taking from you. That required the ability to inflict financial or physical harm on others, and the ability to block others from doing similar harm to you.

This should help in understanding why, in the places most Americans came from, the castles of old were built and why there were king's armies as well as alliances between different "royal" families. The stories of King Arthur, the walled castles of Europe, and Shakespeare's writings about royalty were all inspired by the actual social and economic systems of those times. An important point is that the ordinary People, like you and me, barely got by and had little money, security or opportunity. They lived as actual or little better than slaves to the rulers who owned most things of value and controlled for their own benefit. To be sure, there were some exceptions, but in general, for the ordinary People who preceded us, the words "economic" and "opportunity" were rarely used together, if at all.

For their time, the American Colonies of the middle 1700s did offer some economic opportunity which had been growing, encouraged by some new ideas about individual freedom from Scotland. The control center of England was distant from the Colonies, which helped provide a sense of independence. Taxes (the taking of money by the rulers to pay for whatever they wanted to spend or keep) were somewhat low, so the colonists were accumulating money. These savings allowed them to invest in new ideas, which created more jobs and money. More and more ordinary People were getting educated, learning to read, communicating, and accumulating money and wealth.

They began to realize the way in which things could work. They also saw how much their lives were still controlled by the few members of the king's royal family and their supporters. They learned that, in different forms, the world had always been something like this, where the masses were ruled by a small elite group. That small group forced the ordinary People having businesses, farms or jobs to give them their money. The ordinary People then lived poorly, while the king or other ruler and his supporters all enjoyed better food, warm comfortable housing and often, for some, the very best that life offered at that time in history.

Eventually, the King of England went too far in attempting to extract maximum benefit from his Colonies in America. He sought to impose more control over the Americans' lives and to take more money in taxes from them. The ordinary People defied their English rulers and followed their own leaders to form a country that was based on having no royalty and little government to rule over them. Ultimately, their nation was founded on each individual's freedom to control person and property. As stated in the Declaration of Independence, they asserted that ". . . all Men are equal, that they are endowed by their Creator with certain unalienable rights . . ." These rights were granted not by any king, nor any person, but rather they were granted by God at their birth, just as was their breath and their natural desire to better their life through opportunity and work. Our Founding Documents reflect this belief and the choice of an economic system that would allow hard working Americans to reap financial reward, accumulate and invest, and then create more businesses and more jobs.

Capitalism

Capitalism is defined as "an economic system characterized by competition in a free market in which the means of production and distribution are privately or corporately owned and development is proportionate to increasing accumulation and investment of profits."[11] In regular words, it is a money system dominated by a free market where individuals or groups decide what they will make or do and how and at what price they will sell it to others. It includes creating wealth by accumulating profits and reinvesting those profits to create more businesses. Jobs are created by business creation, expansion, and investment. Wealth is created only through business and profit or from natural resources. Business is the source of most of the wealth of America, and natural resources are the source of most wealth in the Middle East nations.

Capitalism is the economic system that has been in place in our nation since it began. The American Founders were

---

[11] American Heritage Dictionary (2nd College ed.). (1985).

clear in their writings that they saw it as the best arrangement for a free people to handle the production and trade of goods and services in the new country. They saw capitalism and free markets as a complement to free people; it was like chocolate to milk—or better, like icing on a cake.

Ultimately, personal freedom, along with the free market base of the economic system of capitalism, combined to create the most prosperous and powerful nation in history. This system has also changed the relationship between The People and government in much of the world today. (Yes, I know that this is a little flowery, but I am a believer; and besides, history shows that the ideas of the Founders worked like nothing before. Ever before.)

Bear with me here. This is brief and simply stated, and we all really need to know this. We ordinary People have a need and a duty to know about the world we live in. There are competing sets of beliefs about freedom, and about economics in our country and in our world. There are also groups of people in the world that support these different sets of beliefs and are willing to destroy your community and kill you and your family for not following their belief set. It is called "ideology," you had better understand what your beliefs are and what you want your children's to be. If you don't, someone will decide for you. Get this and get it now: your future and that of your family and friends is at stake. We live well here in America today, but have no doubt, the nature of mankind has not changed and the game goes on. The enemy is not just on the other side of the world or even down the road; the enemy is where you are. I don't want to scare anybody, but you need to know the facts, decide where you stand, and act on it. I'll offer some possibilities for action later in this book.

For your own good and your nation's, please read on.

Socialism

Socialism is:

1. "A social system in which the producers possess both the political power and the means of producing and distributing goods.

2. In Marxist-Leninist theory, (Socialism is) the building of the material base for communism under the dictatorship of the proletariat."[12]

In regular words, Socialism is a system that is a middle stage between the destruction of Capitalism and the establishment of Communism. It is about increasing Government control over the free market and the people that becomes a step toward a dictatorship called Communism, defined as: "A system of government in which the state controls the means of production and a single, often authoritarian party holds the power with the intention of establishing a higher social order in which all goods are equally shared by the people."[13]

It sounds great. A nation organized around all things belonging to all people. In college, I was a believer in this approach myself. I have heard it said that ". . . a person in college who is not a socialist has no heart; a person in the real world, who isn't a capitalist, has no brain." As I matured, I realized that the Founders had it right; the nature of a human is to do better and they respond well to rewards from effort that include material things likes good and plentiful food, nice housing, and also security, prestige and the sense of self worth that can only come through accomplishment. These Founders built the nation with that idea in mind.

---

[12] ibid
[13] ibid

Socialism/Communism was the social and economic system conceived by Karl Marx in 1848 and was the basis of the Soviet Union.

Capitalism had been adopted by many countries around the world in the 70 year period before the theory of Socialism/Communism was written. Socialism/Communism is the basis of government in Cuba, Venezuela, North Korea and China. It has been rejected in favor of democracy by many countries all over the world. This is especially so in the past 40 years. Socialism is a continuation of the Ruling Elite system of old, only by another name, and it exhibits the same domination of the many by the few.

Capitalism and democratic freedom have replaced the Ruling Elite systems in much of the world. That is a simple statement of fact. But now that you know a little more about it, you are better prepared to make a decision based on definitive information instead of what you might have heard.

Socialism versus Capitalism

Forget the name calling and slogans; this is what it is really about. Decide where you stand.

Capitalism rewards people who make a product or deliver a service that other people want. The makers receive something of value in exchange for providing it to those who want it and which is more valuable to them than is the cost of the product being traded away. That difference is called profit. The closer one is to the ownership of the idea or ability to make the product, the more of the profit is the reward. By creating and trading many units of product or service to others, the maker can increase profits (which accumulates wealth), use these profits to acquire personal items (which creates the need for makers of other products), or use them to increase the ability to make more products (which expands the producing business, thus creating jobs and often leads to creating other businesses). Multiplying this process by hundreds of thousands of times creates jobs, savings and new businesses which, in turn, create more jobs and savings and new businesses. Do this for 235 years, among as many as 300 million people, and you have America. The ability to be some part of this simple but successful process is what is known as the "American Opportunity," which allows anyone to reap reward from their ideas, work and skills. It is to increase the chances of doing well in this system that we are taught a common language, learn to improve our capabilities, and go to work each day.

Socialism has a catch phrase, ". . . from each according to their abilities, to each according to their need." This philosophy seeks to ultimately have the government own and run all the making of products, take all the profits, and then to distribute the profits to those they determine, based upon their definition of "need." When Americans understand this basic Socialist concept they cannot see how it can work well. They know the long hours and hard work people do to reap the rewards and so ask the question, "Why would anyone work hard when he or she gets no greater rewards than someone who does not work long and hard—or not at all?" Those who have espoused the Socialist idea in the past say they would do so out of a sense of duty. As to how ordinary People would fare in this system, the notion is that they would feel better having less material wealth and comfort because everyone would have a similar level and it would be better for the environment because there is less pollution from the production of fewer goods and services.

I stand for Capitalism. I recommend that you stand there too, and the reasoning is clear: it works. The combination of free people in a free market in America has created the largest and most wealthy group of ordinary People the world has ever known. It also has created the largest wealthy group of top earners in the world and, importantly, has enshrined the possibility that anyone could get there. It has produced most of the major breakthroughs in medicine and the sciences. It has allowed the greatest standard of living for more people than ever on earth. Capitalism has been infectious, with huge numbers of other countries emulating the American plan generally, and even adopting versions of its famous Constitution, specifically. And it is working well for most of the adopting countries too.

As for the competition? Everyone is familiar with the dismal poverty in Cuba. Decade after decade, the condition of their ordinary People does not improve. In Red China, it remains much the same, with the regular citizens struggling to live, perhaps on more than before, but still relatively low pay; the government takes most of the value of what the people produce. In a move which reflects China's own realization of the benefits of Capitalism, they have increased trade in the past few decades. China has become the manufacturer for the free world because of how relatively little its work force is paid, approximately 2.5–3.5% of comparable cost in the U.S., Japan and Europe. The Chinese economy is completely dominated by the Ruling Elite, and the Chinese government is flush with the cash it keeps out of the people's hands.

Yes, the Cuban and Chinese systems "work" in the sense that a system is in place and functioning, but they do not function well for the ordinary People. The Ruling Elite at the top live well and control everything, while the ordinary People just try to get by, and have little control over their lives. The Union of Soviet Socialist Republics, also known as the USSR or the Soviet Union, was a twentieth century effort at Socialism. It was created by the deaths and struggle of millions, and after oppressing the lives of its ordinary People for decades, it collapsed and broke apart. Tellingly, the "satellite" nations that were within the sphere of influence of the USSR, all of which were based on Socialist economic systems, changed that base to Capitalism when they had a choice. The political unit known as East Germany, including East Berlin, was part of that "Soviet bloc."

About eight years ago, I was involved in an incidental conversation with Alan Greenspan when he was still the head of the Federal Reserve, America's central bank. I was among a group of about forty business people invited to tour the Cleveland Federal Reserve Bank. As it happened, Mr. Greenspan was visiting there at the same time. There was a cocktail hour in the bank's dining room, and suddenly, there I was, standing with two others in a conversation with this legendary economist. I asked him what the greatest occurrence to date was during his tenure as Chairman of the Federal Reserve. He thought for a moment, and then replied that he would tell me instead ". . . the biggest thing that has ever happened in my lifetime as an economist." I was amazed as he explained about the fall of the Berlin Wall. "Let me point out," he said, "we economists are not interested in politics. We are about the movement of money. For us," he continued, "Socialism had always been a valid theory of economics, just as valid as Capitalism. But the tearing down of the Berlin Wall changed that. Let me tell you why. For the first time, a homogeneous population was arbitrarily divided. For nearly thirty years, one side of the wall was under Capitalism and the other side was under Socialism. When the Wall was removed," he made a pulling up gesture in front of his chest, "we economists were able to compare the results. And from that time on, Socialism was over." The details were that on the Capitalist side of Germany, the Western section of the country, ordinary People had flourished. Jobs were plentiful and the standard of living was high.

The People were well fed, happy and healthy, with low infant mortality. Businesses were modern, and many environmental controls were in place and working. On the Socialist side, in East Germany, despite all the propaganda and the waving of flags and promotion of their truly fine gymnastics teams, life was not very good. Ordinary people there struggled financially and had a low standard of living. Businesses and farms were controlled by the government, and they were not very productive or modern. The people had poor food availability and quality, were not happy, not healthy, and infant mortality was high. The environment in East Germany was a disaster.

No matter what I might have thought at any other time in my life, hearing these words from Mr. Greenspan was very convincing, and since then I have emphatically agreed that Socialism simply does not work—not for the ordinary People. I am guessing, however, that the East German Ruling Elite and their supporters did just fine.

It would be wrong to not point out that there is much that is "gray" in economic systems. While the general or primary structure of the systems is based on Capitalism or Socialism, most economic systems take on parts of the other system, as well. China, for instance, has certainly added some features of Capitalism, opening up trade globally and allowing investments by its citizens (perhaps they saw the results in Germany, as Mr. Greenspan did).

America, for its part, regulates business—sometimes strongly—and in 2009 actually took control of the Chrysler and General Motors car companies. At a cost of approximately $100 billion, the U.S. Government took 60% of the failing General Motors, while the Auto Workers union healthcare fund owns 17.5%, the Canadian government 12.5%, and the bondholders 10%. This was a major incursion into the free market.[14] The concern of ordinary Americans is not that America is Socialist, but rather it is becoming less free market, hurting opportunities and removing freedoms. And, of course, ordinary People are, and should be wary of the future.

In my stand for Capitalism, I believe that the vast majority of ordinary People in our middle class, who have done astoundingly well in Capitalism, are intelligent enough to know that and to be very wary of those who are attacking that system. They are savvy enough to be alarmed at those self-identified leftist bureaucrats who are interfering in that system's success with little substantiation, blaming the system for problems their regulations may have caused (some believe intentionally), and burdening the system with debt and taxes that will consume profits and eliminate Capitalism's ability to use them. It has been said that the larger a government is, the smaller the individual is[15]; this statement concisely reflects the Zero Sum Game that we are in.

For most Americans, the Declaration of Independence and the Constitution are significant documents that must be protected. These documents complement the Founders' establishment of Capitalism as the primary economic system for democracies and establish individual freedom for all ordinary citizens. We ordinary Americans hold our freedom and our economic system dear because this combination has served us so well. It needs improvement in how we deal with the those who truly cannot help themselves, with discerning the truly helpless from those who are lazy and want to take advantage and in protecting itself as a system from the Ruling Elite who

---

[14] King, N. and Terlep, S. (2009, June 2). GM Collapses Into Government's Arms. *The Wall Street Journal*, p. A1.

[15] Prager, D. (2009, September 1). The Bigger the Government, the Smaller the Citizen. http://www.townhall.com/clumnists/DennisPrager/2009/09/01

will always attack it. Of these three points, the latter point has become the most immediately important.

There is anxiety about the current administration, expressed by the Independents, Tea Parties, the Town Hall protesters, and 9/12 groups, among many other groups and individuals. They are concerned that the current administration seems to be more left-leaning than believed during the last presidential campaign and more than any administration in their lifetimes. They cite American car company takeovers, the infusion of tax money into both the banking industry and into a huge stimulus package as evidence of their concern. They note the manner in which these government actions were taken and it frightens them. These huge financial commitments were made on an emergency basis with little input from opposition and little transparency to the press or to The People. Those actions were followed by a focused effort toward a restructured healthcare system with more regulation by the federal government and perhaps a nationalized system. The 2,700-page bill was developed, literally behind closed doors, without opposition negotiation, and then required immediate voting. And the voting in the Senate was not done on the usual 60 of 100 to pass, but rather a simple majority. Literally, the nation was committed to embark in a direction that polls show they did not want, and may financially destroy the nation, on the strength of a few votes among more than 300 million people. Discussion by opponents and informing and interfacing with The People were mostly precluded. Those in control of the government are acting with a level of force and disregard for the American public that many view as stunning in any democratic nation, especially their own. The Party in power does not seem to realize how these actions negatively effect the ordinary People and are causing us to question their commitment to our well being. Many think the healthcare revision effort has particularly eclipsed all previous government efforts in their lifetime in terms of stealth, intentional misleading and in having a basis on stated goals that appear to be false. In order to draw together your own thoughts, consider the following information.

For most of American history, medical care services were acquired in the free marketplace. Medical needs were considered to be personal needs and part of personal responsibility. The primary doctor/patient relationship was a "one-on-one" relationship that included personal responsibility for payment during the nation's first 170 years. It wasn't until after World War II that medical insurance began to be generally offered in the U.S. marketplace. Known as "hospitalization insurance," it was stimulated by a Government mandated pay cap on how much any workers could earn and was set by the federal government to avoid inflation, once the troops began returning. What we know today as healthcare plans began in response to the federal government regulating the economic system. In the late 1940s and early 1950s the offering of medical insurance as an additional benefit to prospective employees was used to gain a competitive advantage over other employers because higher pay couldn't be. Unions in both government and non-government settings began to regularly make healthcare plans a standard demand during negotiations with employers. It expanded rapidly in the government workplaces because unions, supported by Democrats, were expanding. Non-union workers began asking for similar benefits from their employers. All levels of government adopted such benefits early on, as a means of offsetting the typically higher pay for similar jobs in non-government arenas.

During the next 20 years, non-government or "private" health insurance grew to become an expected benefit of better-paying jobs. In July of 1965, Medicare, a government program, was begun as a means of insuring citizens 65 years of age and older, and Medicaid began as another government program for the poor. Medicare was funded by a payroll tax. Many Americans began to think that they had a "right" to have someone else pay for their medical service. The Democratic Party, doubtless mindful of similar thinking in Socialist countries around the globe, had started to echo that thinking.

During the first term of the Clinton administration, 1993–1997, there was an attempt to establish a complicated Government program to replace the existing free-market healthcare system. It failed, and no such attempt was made again until the Obama administration in 2009, when the Democratic Party controlled both Houses of Congress and the Presidency once again. The details of the final bill were hard to know before passage because the bills both in the House and in the Senate were drafted in closed rooms without knowledge of the press or The People. The Republicans consistently resisted this remarkably un-democratic process for an effort that would likely put the full one sixth of the economy that healthcare occupied under Government control. However, because of their absolute majority, the Democratic Party could do whatever it wanted, and acted with an arrogance that still troubles many; they passed the largest entitlement program in America and the largest appropriation measure in the history of the world. The Democrats had long been called the "tax and spend" Party. This effort marked a seeming conversion to a "spend then tax" Party, where they force through a commitment to a costly program and then explain later that they are forced to raise taxes because of commitments made "by others."

Many ordinary Americans have shown their great concern not only for the content of this legislation but also for the manner in which it proceeded through Congress. During the development of the bill, the polls showed that a majority of Americans still opposed it and feared a potential nationalization of healthcare.

Not a single opposition Party Senator supported it. In fact, the further this bill advanced through legislative hurdles, the larger became the percentage of ordinary People against it. The supporting Party openly misled the public regarding its deficit neutrality by planning to collect taxes to support it years in advance of when program benefits are to be provided. At the time of this writing, polls indicate that nearly 60% want this legislation repealed, and the Republican Party has pledged to do so.

There is concern, too, that the goals that were stated as the basis for preparing such far reaching legislation, are not being met in the final legislation. Those stated goals were: (1) to provide healthcare for the millions of citizens who could not get it, (2) raise no taxes on those making less than $250,000 per year, and (3) those who had private insurance could keep it.

The first goal was just a story to grab the attention and a manipulation of the truth. The truth is that every American citizen has access to medical service. No one can be turned away from the emergency room. Doctors are well distributed everywhere and most will see any patient. The truth is that America has quicker, easier and better access to medical services than most Socialized systems. What the Administration meant was that there were millions who don't have an insurance company, the government, or money saved up to help them *pay* for services received. But that is not what they said, because the truth would not sell well as a reason to change all of the nation's healthcare system.

The goal of having a plan that will not raise taxes, as they said, will not be achieved in either; there is a host of new and increased taxes coming on people at all levels of income.

The goal of keeping private insurance? The intent of the plan made that unlikely; it sets the stage to make private insurance companies compete with a government option that could, and likely would, be priced below them. Come on! How does anything compete with the government who has access to all our money? That is precisely why it is not usually permitted to have the government compete with business. That is not competition, not free market, and is just a sham use of words. Indeed, the history of America has been to avoid putting government in competition with free enterprise so as not to compromise its capitalist system. But now, this Administration presents it as some sort of desirable and virtuous thing to do.

Even though the bill does not meet the goals our government stated as the reasons for changing this core element of our lives as users and the lives of millions of citizens in the health business, they ignore the goals, not even speaking of them now, and plan to impose it on us "for our own good." The process of the development was done behind closed doors without opposition or openness or a vote by The People. The legislative votes were sudden, literally within only a matter of hours after release. They used this process to keep the whole nation in the dark and to eliminate discussion or pushback for refinement. This forceful government approach is seen as reprehensible by many.

Under the leadership of the current Democratic Party, our government has arrived at a place unforeseen by us and our Founders; our government today does not care about what The People want and it is not much trusted. It will use all means to circumvent the intent of our democratic nation. They keep content to themselves, ridicule those citizens showing dissent, attack and threaten those groups that oppose them and use public money to pay off those in their own Party to get cooperation. As an example, the state of Nebraska was granted millions in non-payment of Medicaid to the Feds in exchange for casting a single Democat Senator's vote in favor of the Administration's healthcare bill. While sweeteners to encourage a legislature to go along with political Party goals is not new, three things should be noted: first if the legislative process was at all representing The People instead of the Party, it would not happen; second, such payoffs rarely have this magnitude; and three, payoffs have never had a consequence this great. For the payoff of several million dollars of our tax money, a Nebraska Senator threw all of the American people who must pay billions and billions "under the bus." It is hard not to see that if he thought the bill was good for America, he should have voted for it; if he did not, then he should have voted against it. But he did not, his approach was, in effect, "give me a payoff, a bribe, and I will vote your way. I will vote for your special interest." How disgraceful. It underscores that such "representatives" do not care about The People or our nation. It is about them. It is about their Parties. We ordinary Americans, our traditions, our values and beliefs do not matter, especially now. For the very first time, the Americans living today can see how far a Party can carry its disregard for the ordinary citizen.

The current government, run by the Party of Democrats, seems intent on forcing nationalized healthcare on The People, and that is giving rise to accusations of tyranny. They believe that they know what is better for us than we do, and think that their positions in our government are more important than the principles of democracy and rule by the People. It is legitimate to ask why those controlling the government of free people would complete such an effort in the face of such great opposition. The answer may be found in the following excerpt from an Arthur Schenfield article entitled "Capitalism Under the Test of Ethics," where he wrote:

> "All socialists are utopians in some measure or other. They propose a powerful state, but their powerful state will be caring, compassionate, benevolent. It will be incorruptible, efficient, far-seeing, progressive,

and adaptable. Its politicians will think only of the public welfare, and its bureaucrats would think only of service to the people. The rule of law will prevail, and yet the government will have wide discretion, so that it may do the utmost good. The government will control all essential sources of livelihood; yet criticism will be free and, as if by magic, also effective."[16]

Our government is now controlled by a Ruling Elite of the Socialist kind. We must acknowledge that this Party did not arrive here without the other Party. Together, both Parties brought us to this point. Over the last several decades they have worked hand-in-hand as Ruling Elites to take us down this path. Both the political Parties worked to secure a structure of government to complement their existence. Both Parties sought to increase their power at our expense. Always with false protestations, they both continue to promise to strike down pork barrel spending, earmarks and lying to The People. But neither Party follows through. Both promise openness in government, bipartisan governance and the end of lobbyists' influence. But it does not happen. Both Parties tell us they too honor our troops but then hold back our military from fighting to win and they don't fix the VA. They cry out with us at the loss of our children and our hope to the drugs and the criminals who own our streets. But their mutual War on Drugs is decades old and still more die each day. Our Parties stand up to assure the education of our children, but under them, billions are squandered, thugs and unions roam the hallways and those that want to learn and teach are either taught not to, or give up. These Parties each blame the last

---

[16] Schenfield, A. (1988). Capitalism Under The Test of Ethics. *Economic Notes Number 13: London: Libertarian Alliance.*

President and then reward all the power to their old guard members who then work to keep the Parties in full control of The People. Perhaps it is time to give up on the Parties; both of the Parties. Perhaps we should seek to remove them from their wedged in place that now keeps us, the ordinary People, from our government. And it *is* our government.

The Party in Power: Ruling Elite Gone Wild

The Party in power today is a leftist Party that hides behind the American flag of freedom. Their leader is like the Wizard of Oz—with a Socialist behind the curtain. This is not speculation. Even others in the world know that today's Democratic Party is a Socialist leaning party similar to every left wing Party in the world. Reuters reported on June 2, 2009 that during a live Caracas television broadcast, even The Socialist President of Venezuela quipped that he and the Communist President of Cuba, Fidel Castro, may not be as far left as the current American President.[17] Many people with leftist backgrounds, writings and ideas have been appointed to both the Cabinet and the ranks of "Czars." These Czars are special appointees who report directly to the White House. In an overt expansion of power in the past two presidencies, these appointments extend control of the chief executive. Interestingly, the designation "Czar" originates from the title of the Emperor of Russia, and is often used to mean "a tyrant." As in past administrations, such positions are normally filled with the friends and political allies of the President, and are complained about as expanding executive power at the expense of legislative power. President Bush had 15, and President Obama has 38

---

[17] Pretel, E. A. (2009, June 2). Venezuela Chavez says "Comrade" Obama more left-wing. Reuters, Caracas.

Czars.[18] This threatens the balance of powers planned in our Constitution, since "Liberty consists in the division of power."[19] Most Americans do not yet seem to realize that truth about these actions of the White House.

Many things go unrealized; that is not by accident. The political Party in power works hard on their disguise. Just as a celebrity might use a name change to create an image or to manipulate ethnicity, this Party seldom calls themselves "left." In further disguise, they even had their complicit media change the color used in referring to them. In the last decade, the Democrats have been called the "blue" party. Most Americans do not realize that they used to be called the "red" party, which was automatically attributed to them because of their similarity to all groups worldwide that promote the Socialist ideal of big centralized government in control of production and distribution. Throughout the world, virtually every major leftist organization and the related socialist and communist parties are proudly termed the "red" parties; Stalin's communists, red; Hitler's national socialists, red; communist China, red China. However, in the United States, with its history of standing in opposition to Socialism in the Cold War against the Soviet Bloc, against the North Koreans and against the "Reds" in Viet Nam, the left has decided to not be open about it.

The 1950s experience of anti-left McCartyism in particular, likely helps drive the disguising we see today. That was a less tolerant time and today we are a much better nation at hearing all voices. Favoring more Socialist policies is the privilege of any American. Nonetheless, pure Socialism is an economic

---

[18] May, C. (2010, June 25). Do Obama's Czars Rule America? Daily Caller. http://dailycaller.com/2010/06/25

[19] Acton Institute for the Study of Religion and Liberty. (2010, August, 4). Lord Acton Quote Archive.

system that is radically different and in direct opposition to the system of Capitalism, which is one of America's proven founding concepts. If we, as a nation, are to change in ways that impinge upon our long-proven Capitalist economic system, then we, The People, should be directly involved in the deliberations. Such a huge change cannot be allowed to be put in place by stealthy manipulation or force by any political Party acting in its own interests.

There is no real choice in the election from the major Parties. Whoever is on their ballot is a handpicked Party believer who is thought by the leadership to be a follower. A candidate simply would not be endorsed by a Party if the Party leaders believed the candidate actually would, if elected, represent The People; candidates are endorsed by a Party because they will represent *the Party.* They only say they are going to represent the interests and view of the People. As just one simple bit of evidence, consider the Obama Administration's offer of appointments to two Democrats planning to compete with the candidates these Party leaders wanted in the 2010 primary elections in Pennsylvania and Colorado; if these candidates would drop out of the primary, the Administration would reward them with appointments to positions that it had the power to control. This is illegal. When found out, and admitted to by U.S. Rep (D) Joe Sestak in Pennsylvania,[20] the excuse was, "It happens all the time." Note that there is a federal law that prohibits offering things of value to affect election outcomes. It seems that nothing will happen to those behind this breach of law because these Party people are "above the law."

---

[20] Condon, S. (2010, may 25). White House Wards off Questions about Alleged Sestak Job Offer. http://www.cbsnews.com/8301-503544_162-20005850-503544.html

So that it is clear that both the Parties are run similarly, I will offer another true story. I had lunch with a friend at the end of his first of several terms as a Republican in the U.S. House of Representatives. He grew up in the town next to mine and was from an ordinary family. I asked him what he learned in his first term. He replied, ". . . to get along, you go along." He explained that if you do not follow what the Party leadership expects from you, you will not get highly visible or desirable things, ranging from a good office facility to a good committee appointment. The Party leaderships use such things to control their members. A bad committee appointment means no press and no importance, which lessens the opportunity to get good press, lobbyist attention, and campaign donations. Yes, that is the way it works, and *both* Parties behave the same way. There really is little difference when it comes to the Parties representing the voter; neither will. They both are out for themselves. But both have an ideology, and that is where, especially today, you need to make a consideration and choice. The individual candidates don't really matter much.

To use a sports analogy, the political Parties have made elections like a big-time boxing match. Before the match, there is some verbal sparring and commentary in the press. There may be a TV showdown and a flurry of figurative "punches." The more publicity and hype, the more money the fans gamble on each side. At the match, the fighters go to the center of the ring appearing as proxies for all those supporting them, to fight on their behalf. In reality, the combatants are representing mostly themselves and those in their corner at the edge of the ring. While the fans around the ring eagerly watch to see the victor, the promoters and both of the opponents and their managers get piles of money and celebrity status, which will assure more money through endorsements later. No matter which combatant wins, those on both sides of the ring divide

up the spoils and send the fans home. Sometimes there is corruption, sometimes a good fight, but always, always the match
is played for the benefit of the *players*, not the audience. If you
still cannot see how it works, it is not surprising, because we
all tend to see what we want to see, it is our human nature,
and we have a resistance to realizing the facts instead of seeing our desired view.

Perhaps this will help: It is like when a loving spouse
wants to believe that those special looks between two people
are just imagination, or those late hour hang-up calls are
accidental. Or perhaps like when a father brushes off blades
of grass from his daughters back as she returns from a spring
evening walk by the lake with her boyfriend and the father
says, "What happened, honey, did you fall down?" We tend
to be blind to what we do not want to see, what we do not
want to see true. But facts are still facts, whether we choose
to believe them or not.

And the fact is, our government is run by two groups who
jostle for position; but, like the fighters above, they are both
fighting for the same thing: victory for their own benefit; victory over us. Once we realize this fact, we may want to do
something about it.

So what do we do? We really cannot expect the Parties to
represent us unless we change the existing rules of the game.
While it may be unwise or impossible to destroy the game
of government and politics, we can use our people power to
change the way the game is played.

Today, the political Parties present a danger to our traditions
and our future. With the rise of closed process, forced issues,
and the intention of government control over all healthcare
when they cannot even run Amtrak well, we can see that they
are a danger to our very lives. They are the public's enemy.
Our Founding Fathers knew that such a day would come.

In the second paragraph of the Declaration of Independence they wrote, "We hold these truths to be self evident, that all men are created equal, that they are endowed by their Creator with certain unalienable Rights, that among these are Life, Liberty, and the Pursuit of Happiness—That to secure these Rights, Governments are instituted among men, deriving their just powers from the Consent of the Governed, that whenever any Form of Government becomes destructive of these ends, it is the Right the People to alter or abolish it, and to institute new Government, laying its Foundation on such Principles, and organizing its Powers in such Form, as to them shall seem most likely to effect their Safety and Happiness."

So I ask you: Do you feel safe? Do you feel happy?

Power from Favor: The Weapon of Unequal Treatment

Unequal treatment under the law may be the least recognized—but most harmful—issue in our nation today. This is a strategy used against the citizens by Party leaders to increase their power over us. Most ordinary People have just accepted it because it has existed in various forms for so long. Unequal treatment of citizens through our government stands in violation of our nation's principals, causes great harm, and is at the root of two of the most important issues we are dealing with at this time: the continuing financial crisis and illegal immigration.

Conventional wisdom regarding the financial crisis is that it was caused by greedy people in business and on Wall Street. We need to revisit this issue, because we may discover that this common belief is a falsehood. First, let's think about why we all believe that business and Wall Street caused the 2007 financial crash. Was there an open study done? Did independent economists from around the globe gather to carefully consider the matter? Has it really been studied at all? What we think about this issue reflects statements from our government and primarily from the political Parties. We were told that capitalists seeking profit sold us out because of their greed for money. But there is evidence to the contrary. The truth may well be that the politicians who provided this explanation were actually the ones who were mostly responsible for the debacle. Even the four non democratic members of the Financial Crisis Inquiry Commission (FCIC) were dissenters to their report.

What if the primary cause was that these misleading politicians, pandering to get votes, were the ones who sold us out because of their greed for power? Both Parties seem to have encouraged bad financial conduct in the housing industry for that very reason. President Clinton (D) initiated the idea for this special treatment with the 1977 Community Reinvestment Act, mandating banks to provide loans in their geographic areas to minorities who could not meet financial standards for loans. As President, the second George Bush (R) later set a number of 40,000 such loans a year for his 2003 limited American Dream Down Payment Act, which was targeted to Hispanics who could not meet the primary protection against loan default, the 20% down payment. Then the 2006 Democratic House seemed to drop number and racial limits on the numbers of risky loans backed by public money. All these efforts intended to give special treatment to some, and they ignored common knowledge and long held standards for housing economics. The result was that it collapsed the market, costing hundreds of billions, and probably hurt far more people who had nothing to do with it than the number it favored.

So we have all these Party leaders risking our public money behind people with bad or no credit to permit them to live in homes they did not qualify to have, in order that these people would vote for them. These Party politicians were pretending that a house was a Right instead of the result of personal responsibility, work and saving. They rewarded those who did not do these things and penalized those who did. That is the conclusion of many, including the three credible sources below.

An article appeared in *The Wall Street Journal* in March, 2010, authored by a former chief credit officer at Fannie Mae, one of the federal agencies directly responsible for financing our housing crisis.[21] He claimed that, prompted in part by Acorn lobbying, congressional leaders gave directives to the agencies to buy bad credit mortgages. As a result, 5% down or less loans soared from 9% of their total in 1991 to 29% in 2007, and to $1.5 trillion with a 10.3% delinquincy rate in 2009. The instruction given by these congressional leaders informed mortgage lenders that these agencies would back highly risky mortgages if they were granted to applicants who were members of minority groups. Apparently, like the support for the Community Reinvestment Act, loans were to have race as the primary factor of the loan applicant, and less so his or her ability to repay the loan.

Applied to the entire nation, this policy resulted in hundreds of billions of dollars of public money, put at unacceptably high risk. When those loans predictably failed, having seven times the default rate of conventional loans, the collapse began.

In the book *Meltdown*, bestselling author, Thomas E. Woods Jr., who studied many documents and interviewed many of those involved, comes to a similar conclusion. He asserts that, along with artificially low rates by the Federal Reserve, our government agencies, directed by the Democratic congressional leaders, assumed great risk by providing "affordable housing" for people who would normally be unable to get

---

[21] Pinto, E. (2009, November 12). Acorn and the housing Bubble. *The Wall Street Journal,* op ed.

a housing loan. Because these loans were available and more based on the applicant being a minority or poor than having the ability to pay, the housing market became highly stimulated.

Many weak buyers flooded into the marketplace. Homebuilders reacted to that demand and begin building more homes—many more homes. Their suppliers began to import and produce more products for the builders. Because demand was greater than the supply, the price of housing exhibited a strong, steady rise. Homeowners responded by selling their homes at a large profit and buying newer and bigger homes. In short, the American housing market acted like all markets do when demand increases greatly. But this American housing demand was increased by providing public backing to people likely to not pay their mortgage, rather than by careful buyers making down payments and risking their own money. The leaders in government knew the directives they made and did not change them; their actions caused the default rate to soar.

What many don't know is that the financial institutions overseas considered the American mortgage market to be among the safest of investments. American mortgages were routinely traded in bundles among the world's financial institutions. Their longevity and safety had earlier convinced some on Wall Street that mortgages could be leveraged, meaning that the original risk was so low that they could add more risk on them, and they did. But the mortgages being supplied in 2006 and 2007 were weaker that those of the past because of the inclusion of government-sponsored, below standard mortgages, so they were already risky. In fact, they were much less likely to be paid back by the home "owner" than the constant stream of mortgages that had preceded these years. When that stream was found to be defective, the trading stopped. But nearly all those involved, including AIG, which insured these mortgage instruments, were overwhelmed. There were more mortgages going bad than ever experienced. The bad mortgages that our congressional leaders encouraged or directed our government agencies to accept were so numerous, that they overwhelmed and brought down the whole system. The people who were in the houses that had special loans often just walked away; they had little or nothing of their own invested. This was a program of Party favoritism for many uneducated, economically unstable households, some of whom were not even American citizens. These mortgages were frequently provided with little or no documentation about assets or employment, or residency. They required no money down and at no cost or "points." In some cases, the mortgages were well above 100% of the appraised value. At the same time, mortgages were being provided to many of the educated, well-qualified borrowers at the secure traditional loan maximum of 80% of the home's value, with 20% cash up front. There was nothing of favor for them. Even worse, they were going to be hurt by the favoritism offered to others.

Another of the many sources with a similar viewpoint is Fox News Channel journalist Bret Baier, who provided a report with dated video after video of congressional leaders of the Democratic Party who controlled the housing finance agencies saying they were just fine and claiming that Republican critics were attacking the administration of the housing agencies unfairly.[22] Baier even showed the then-chairman of the Federal Reserve Bank, Alan Greenspan, warning of the magnitude of this threat to our economy. It was not a secret, it was a Party protected issue, and the Republicans failed to stop them. The fact that most Americans did not have this explained on the major national news networks, ABC, NBC and CBS is a

---

[22] Baier, B. (Narrator). (2008. September 24). Fox News Special Report on the Banking Crisis, Part Two. [Television Broadcast]. New York: Fox News Channel.

travesty. It underscores the reality of a very political mainstream media, which some speculate is the reason for the continuing reduction in the viewership of these networks.

So why would congressional members have directed public agencies to operate in such a potentially dangerous manner? It appears that it was for political gain for their Party. In 2006, the Democrats took control of Congress. The House of Representatives directly controls the housing agencies involved, Freddie Mac and Fannie Mae. It appears that Democrats were pandering to the poor and "minorities" who are two of their Party's primary demographic constituents. This was an effort that favored minorities and poor and disfavored those who were not, completely ignoring the realities of finance and of world markets. It appears that the Democrats, trying to increase their voters' support, destroyed a large part of America's wealth during their effort. Ironically, those favored by the Democratic leadership lost little or nothing and many thousands of innocent responsible ordinary People without their favor lost both the down payments they had to make—and often the home equity that had built up over time.

Perhaps worse is that the very Democratic leaders, including Barney Frank, who have been at the helm of the mortgage agencies since 2006, remained in charge, and endorsed more regulation on the financial industry until after the 2010 election replaced them with Republicans. This issue certainly requires more study, as quickly as possible and by the best independent minds. Partisanship cannot be allowed to permit either cover-up or inaccurate accusation. The American people deserve immediate protection and to know the truth, and that truth is required in order to protect our future. Regardless of whether or not these Party efforts were the core reason for the financial crisis, the very fact that they happened points to an even greater issue and relates to illegal immigration as well.

The continued flow of illegal entrants into America is a major issue. In mid-2010, Arizona's Republican Governor, Jan Brewer, having lost confidence in the federal government's desire to control their Mexican border, signed Arizona State Senate Bill SB 1070, under which Arizona would itself begin to enforce federal immigration law. Remarkably, the United States government, under Democratic leadership, sued Arizona to block this effort. During the appeals process in that lawsuit, an internal Obama Administration memo was disclosed confirming that the Democratic Party intends to protect illegal immigrants coming from Mexico. Protecting the flow of illegals appears to be the reason Border Patrol agents were seeking out Mexican bandits who were attacking that flow 15 miles into Arizona in December 2010. In the ensuing gun battle, Agent Brian Terry was killed. He died because he was ordered to protect the incoming illegals, not the border and American citizens. The reason for this protection of non-citizen illegal presence appears to be to secure voting rights for these people. They are known to normally support mostly Democratic candidates, sometimes even by voting illegally. The Democrats are willing to grant special favor to Latino immigrants by allowing them an illegal presence in our country instead of bringing them under the same laws as all other immigrants. In a nation of immigrants, they are offering special favor to one group and disfavoring and insulting the rest of us whose home-country applicants must comply with present law. If the Democratic Party was not willing to treat Latinos specially, there would be no border issue.

How can we be a nation of equality when Party leaders in our government act with favor? The very idea of equality and fairness begins with equal treatment under the law. It is time to draw a line by blocking anyone in any position in American government the ability to treat anyone unequally. The Democrats are using our government to import foreign voters to support its control of us. They are willing to corrupt the base of American voters, essentially canceling out votes of lifelong Americans by trading special treatment for Party votes. It is time for anyone who expects to be favored in a land of equals to be ashamed. Those Democrats, and others who are complicit in this plot of greedy favoritism, are selling out our country's central purpose of equality to those of another country in order to accrue more power over us. That may be worse than those who would sell our military secrets for money. Make no mistake, by this favoritism for some immigrants, the Democrats are acting against the base interests of this entire nation of immigrants.

It is hard to mentally process this, but it appears that Democratic leaders have already risked our economy and assisted our financial meltdown by trying to get more voting power. Now they are manipulating our immigration laws in order to secure more power and calling concerned Americans who oppose it "racist!" Every American, every person in a democracy, every person who reveres freedom, must declare these acts astonishing and unacceptable.

As a NonPartisan American, I must conclude that we have come to a time when we have leaders who pose an actual danger to our country. They are creating the problems that confront us. We must rid ourselves of them and destroy the weapons they use against us.

This situation underscores not only a failure of a Party to enforce the laws of the land, but also a greater danger: they are willing to ignore the intent and words of the Constitution that protects our Liberty. The economic crisis we are suffering may not have happened and the illegal immigration issue would not exist if the Parties would just treat everyone according to our purpose; i.e., equally under the law and blindly in the courtroom.

Our government should be operating under the same laws that control The People. It is not. Our government now operates under the rule and intent of the Democratic Party. Our government is run by Party politicians who seem to ignore the Constitution they are sworn to defend. We consistently see that these Parties use our government as a tool for their benefit, not for the People's protection. While both Parties have ignored our Constitution, using varying excuses, the recent actions by the Democrats make clear the danger of uncontrolled political Parties.

This is the issue that must be named: For many years now, these Parties, when it suits their purposes, openly and purposely enforce our laws or refuse to enforce them, as best benefits *them*. This brazen disregard for equal treatment has brought disunity, distrust, and even hatred between different parts of our citizenry. We have suffered the use of our government by the Parties to favor one group over another many times and to the detriment of our nation.

After the Civil War, which was fought to end the slavery of Blacks, it was the Democratic Party in the South that utilized governments there to continue to favor Whites in their law making and in the hiring of public employees.[23] One group cannot be favored without disfavoring another group, any more than it is possible to favor one child and not have another one *dis*favored. You cannot feed one and not another and explain away the thin body and the disappointed mind.

So while Southern Whites happily received favorable laws and public jobs (as recipients of gifts always do), Blacks were treated unfairly and did not get public jobs. The excuse was that Blacks "could not learn" and/or "were not trustworthy," so it was "best for the state" to have these laws, called "Jim Crow" laws. It took many years before Republicans (along with some Democrats) at the federal level were able to rectify

------

[23] Davis, L.F., Ph.D. (2010. August 4) Creating Jim Crow: In-Depth Essay. http://www.imcrowhistory.org

the situation, and, in fact, the stigma of unequal treatment remains in our country today. Just since the 1960s, governments controlled by one Party or the other, have established hundreds of quotas for jobs and schools, devised complicated special action plans, and reserved set-asides for groups that can exhibit some characteristic of color or sex. Disregarding our government's guarantee of equality, the Parties, like all Ruling Elites, have institutionalized the policies of favor and disfavor as a tool to garner support. They have passed out money and built agencies, stressing dissimilarity and encouraging class envy and racial hatred. Their continued efforts have brought us to where we are today. We are divided in every way that they have wanted us to be. Our prosperity is threatened. Our equality is questioned. We are ruled by a Party that entertains excuses from Mexican foreigners that a border Americans died to determine does not matter; right is wrong and wrong is right.

> "...the Parties, like all Ruling Elites, have institutionalized the policies of favor and disfavor as a tool to garner support."

I cannot tell you in this space why this has happened, there is more in the book. But this I can say briefly and for certain: Favor to one, has always meant disfavor to another, whether in our homes, in our communities, or in our nation. It makes us vulnerable to great harm, like we are experiencing now. And a government of special favor is the opposite of what our Founding Documents guarantee this nation to be. No excuse for unequal treatment by any Party or any person can any longer be tolerated, nor should it *ever* have been. The Parties, particularly the Democratic Party, have used this tool to divide and control us for decades, and it has brought us to the brink of disaster. We must take this tool away. That repeating cycle must finally end. No excuse, however filled with emotion and earnestness, is acceptable; our entire history shows it does not work; our Founding Documents declare it is wrong, and our common sense confirms it.

If the other nations before ours was founded would have committed to the wisdom of our Founders that "all people are equal under the law," there would have been no slavery in the world. If the governments of the South would have followed our Founding Documents, there would have been no period of Jim Crow laws. If our Parties today lived up to the intent of this country and to the words of the Constitution, there would have been no financial collapse and no issue on our border today. Lacking this clarity, we have caused our own burdens.

While the outcome of American lives should and will doubtless be as different as our abilities, it should be for no reason more than that. This is the guarantee of our Constitution. *Favoritism by reason of natural human characteristics and culture is the enemy of our Constitution.* Citizens must never claim to deserve such favor from our government nor allow our government to bestow favoritism; history shows that one day we will all be the victims.

> "Favoritism... is the enemy of our Constitution."

We must at last cleave to the hard truth that our Founding Documents have always been right: our greatest freedom, prosperity, and happiness will come from treating all as *one*.

Taking Back Our Sandbox

My fellow ordinary Americans, we have no choice. We, The People, have the responsibility to assure that our government operates according to our consent and not according to any political Party's claim to power over us. Their claim is not valid. The political Parties are usurpers of our crown; America is *our* nation, not *theirs*. Our Founding Documents are the proof. Review the commentary provided next in the "Documents of Democracy" chapter. And read the actual documents that are in the back of this book, too. They are readable and confirming. You will likely agree that these Parties have now gone too far.

Yes, one Party has driven these recent actions, but both have been constructing their cocoon of control for decades. And doesn't each Party bear responsibility because it could not or would not stop the encroachment on our Freedom by the other Party? In today's onslaught, has the minority Party even satisfactorily put up a fight? Have they, in absolute rejection of a remarkably undemocratic process, acted to join with The People in protest or encourage noncompliance? Have they pursued without accepting business as usual in trading off our offices and our money for their power? Have they invoked the traditions or the Constitutional rights of us ordinary People? Have they rebuked the opposing Party? Did they truly even confront the Democratic Party frontrunners for what they were in the last Presidential election? They have done none of this. They are either too weak, or they also want the additional power it will bring them when they may again be the majority Party in power. Either way, we cannot allow a structure to remain in place that allows *any* political Party the ability to take away our freedom, either by mutual consent of the political Parties, or by one Party's weakness. Such fundamental and far-reaching changes that get to the heart of our freedom must be decided solely and directly by The People, not by some few and their Party supporters who seek change for their narrow benefit.

As many have said and written, all powerful governments have invariably turned out to be anything *but* benevolent. They are controlled by humans and humans just do not work that way. This is not news. In 1887, Lord Acton wrote, "Power tends to corrupt and absolute power corrupts absolutely."[24]

Even more to the point, in a speech to the House of Lords in 1770, William Pitt said, as rebellion was in the air of the American Colonies, "Unlimited power is apt to corrupt the minds of those who possess it; and this I know, my lords, that where laws end, tyranny begins." (As cited by Melton, 2004)[25]

A structural fence of laws must be put in place that will restore our freedom and block more freedom-taking attacks that are sure to come. And that structure must be watched over by The People, or new routes around them will be established.

The People must not be fooled with claims of powerful benevolence—it does not exist. Those powerful governments of Idi Amin, Stalin, Hitler, Castro, Mussolini and the Taliban seem to show exactly the opposite of omnipotence with benevolence, and there is no example of such a government to be found in the history of the world.

Only the arrogance of the Ruling Elite, who just feel that they know what is good for us ordinary People, can believe such a thing; it is their arrogance that allows them the belief that history is not meaningful and the belief that they are the best ever; they will do it "right." In a sense, the recent gluttonous efforts at using our government as a tool to take large bites of our freedom has done us a favor. We can now understand—through their effort to reform our healthcare, for example—that what we really need is to reform is how *Parties* work. They talk about "comprehensive immigration reform," but what we must seek is *comprehensive government reform.*

---

[24] Acton Institute for the Study of Religion and Liberty. (2010, August, 4). Lord Acton Quote Archive.

[25] Melton, Bruckner F. Jr. (2004). The Quotable Founding Fathers. New York: Fall River Press.

The Parties, whose very business is power over others, cannot be expected to reduce their power on their own.

The recent actions by America's Democrats are rightly seen as steps too far, and they show that the system the Parties have established for themselves puts us in peril. This cannot stand; we must assert ourselves; we must demand change in the way our government works for us.

Its structure must change, both to destroy today's tyranny and to never permit it again. We can do this and we will do it, forcefully, but peacefully. There is no revolution wanted here. That is unneeded because our Founders framed our Constitution to avoid it. Revolution would do to our nation what these usurpers are wanting to do to our healthcare—throwing all of the good away to achieve their end. No, there is no need for revolution, and may God ever keep America from it.

Our arrival at this point has been long in coming, but today it is clear; it is time for a new Evolutionary Point of Change, a time for the American *Evolution*: a move to something better, a move up, a positive change in the structure of our government that puts The People more in control of government. Our government. Not theirs. Our government. We need an Evolution that diminishes the power of the Parties over us ordinary Americans, an Evolution that allows we ordinary People to use the American ideas and the American natural and human resources to create jobs and the greatest prosperity yet known on earth.

We will climb back onto the road to the future that will actually eliminate poverty in our nation and, for the very first time in our history, will truly have the government not discriminate against any citizen; a nation not drowning in the disharmony wrought by the derision and deception of the Parties, but a nation deeply committed to unity, to the overriding vision of our Founders.

We must question whether it is possible for us ordinary People to do this and what tools we have or could create to achieve this outcome.

An examination of our Founders and the Documents they prepared for us reveals that they left us the tools. In the next chapter we will become familiar with the thinking of the Founders, their motivation for making the effort, the uniqueness of their solution, and the true nature of the country they created. A brief study will add much to any American's greater understanding of his or her nation.

I believe that the Founders understood then what we confront today. They saw their problem not just in terms of King George of England, but rather in the eternal condition of mankind that he represented to them. They recognized that the real problem, was much larger than any single king. Its roots were in the eternal existence of some few who were compelled to control the many, a Ruling Elite that would seek to dominate over ordinary People, externally or internally. That was their problem then, and they knew it would return in some form in the future. They wrote the Founding Documents for their use then and for our use now. They left the tools for us in the Documents of Democracy.

FOUR

The Documents of Democracy

As we know today, any complicated thing comes with a set of instructions from those who created it. Whether computer or car, toy or appliance, instructions for its use are provided as a means of disclosing what the maker intended and how the user will gain its full benefit, satisfaction and enjoyment. Such "instruction sets" are particularly important when there are details that are not plainly evident or conditions that could accidentally render the creation useless—or perhaps even destroy it.

Every nation is a human creation. Most have been fashioned by—and for the benefit of—the wealthy or powerful families that controlled the wealth at the time the nation was founded, and these establishments usually included the religion of those founders.

Unlike those other nations, in America, a group of men of European decent pooled their minds and means, their hopes and particular Christian beliefs of God, and fashioned agreements and rules which would allow disparate groups of their time to organize into a single, functioning nation. The Founding

Documents that they prepared are the basic "instruction set" for the users of the nation they created. They are augmented and clarified by the written and spoken words that these men, like George Washington, left behind.

To many, it seems legitimate today to question the validity of applying the documents and thoughts of these men of so long ago, to what we do now. After all, they reason, much time has passed, and people and situations have seemingly changed, as well. But even with a cursory review, we see that the thinking of these men at the time our nation was founded was actually thinking for *all* time. The documents that they carefully crafted were focused on the timeless nature of humankind rather than on some fashionable political thought of the day. Indeed, their documents established a nation unlike any then existing. These men were to nationmaking what Frank Lloyd Wright would become to architecture and what the Wright Brothers would be to transportation—far ahead of their time. Rather than develop an instruction set that would simply institutionalize the control of their own mostly powerful families, which was the norm of world history, these men of the American Colonies instead, reflected deeply upon the very nature of man and the role of God in life. They pondered about the peaceful transition of power from one group and one generation to the next. They deeply concerned themselves as to how to establish and institutionalize Liberty in a manner that would reflect the natural state of humankind.

They also sought to secure that Liberty, despite the possibility that future people might be determined, like a pack of wolves, to dine on that freedom and to control the ordinary People for their own advantage. With their knowledge of history and their thoughts of the Scottish Enlightenment, they believed that the ". . . running hounds of Tyranny forever nip at the heels of Liberty." They worked not only to establish a nation that would deny themselves immediate tyranny over The People, but also would deny the tyranny of those that would surely be born into the generations to come. Difficult enough and totally exceptional, they even went further to allow for future changes that were beyond any possibility at the time: the end of slavery and the equalization of all men and women under the law. These two evils of slavery and sex/race discrimination, which is how we see them today, had been universal and the normal way of the world for thousands of years prior to 1776. The Founders' bold acts in developing this nation established it as a frighteningly different place to the Elite of their time, sowing the seeds of a transition that would allow the ordinary person equality and a strong say in governance. Instead of domination by a Ruling Elite using governance as a primary control tool, they sought to empower ordinary People; this was a radical notion in their time. Even today, some 235 years after they developed this daring nation, a significant part of the world remains much as it has always been: controlled by a governing Ruling Elite; institutionalized discrimination favoring those supporting or resembling the Ruling Elite; no freedom of religion; and pursuing unequal treatment of others, including certain races, classes or cultures, as a means of dividing the masses and garnering support from the "favored."

The new direction that the American Founders took, basing their work on the timeless nature of man, while noble and courageous, was an unproven theory of governance. Its intention was to free the ordinary common People from the clutches of the Elite that had always shackled their potential and confiscated the value of their efforts. It seems that life for the common people had been not much different than life for common livestock—both were assets to be used for the gain of those who controlled them. The validation of the Founders' work would become evident in the coming decades. Over time, the success of their creation established a compelling case for all nations to become a similar combination of freedom of person and property within a free market economic system.

In a little more than 100 years, the nation they created became an economic, military and political force that over-shadowed all the nations of the world, past or present, and changed the face of the globe. Millions of inspired people from every part of the world relocated to become part of its dream of freedom, prosperity and security. They made their original culture, along with its particular prejudices, mindsets and stratified classes, secondary to being "American." They became followers of the Declaration and the Constitution and the promises that flowed from them. Although still not perfect, but a work in progress, the resulting nation that they all helped move forward became the greatest force against evil and tyranny ever known. It has abolished slavery, equalized instead of marginalized women, and led the world to destroy the tyranny of the National Socialists in Germany and the International Socialists of Russia. The history of the United States of America shows that it eclipsed nations that were founded hundreds and even thousands of years before it.

The Founders' theory proved that with little fetter from the Ruling Elites, ordinary men and women could truly prosper, that they could be allowed to reap the benefits of their work instead of turning over the fruits of their labor to the royalty or to other Elites who claimed control over them, and that the entire society would be catapulted forward. In America, they could own land, accumulate wealth, and build lives for their families. Instead of being subject to the whim of a few who could redirect or destroy their plans or efforts, they enjoyed the distinct possibility that by following the rules of their new country, they not only could, but perhaps even likely would, succeed. America became paradise for the ordinary People.

The world took notice of this fledgling nation as soon as it issued its now famous Declaration of Independence on July 4, 1776. This document contained words that shocked not only the government of the mightiest power then on earth, Great Britain, but likely every existing nation that read them. This document declared that "all men are created equal" in a time when no nation would support such a statement. It stated that "they are endowed by their Creator with certain unalienable rights" at a time when any right for ordinary People was what a human Ruling Elite allowed it to be at the moment. ". . . that among these are Life, Liberty and the Pursuit of Happiness" they said; this, when any life and freedom were usually at the mercy of one's "betters." Although less vulnerable in England, the lives of most ordinary citizens of the world seemed really just a different form of slavery, where most still had little possibility of achieving prosperity or security, but where the "master" was the Ruling Elite. This Declaration put the ordinary American Colonists into direct confrontation with the British Royalty who ruled them. It must have embarrassed the British Royals before their peers, who were the Royals, as well as other Elites throughout Europe and the world. This affront almost guaranteed that military action would be taken and that those responsible for, or in support of, the Declaration's statements would be sought out for destruction.

In the Revolutionary War that followed, the United States would go on to win its independence from Great Britain, establishing itself as a separate nation. But it was at great cost to the Founders.

There were 56 signers of the Declaration of Independence. In the turmoil that followed the signing, 12 of them had their homes destroyed because of the stand they took. Nine were killed by gunshot or hardship. Five were tortured to death, many had their families destroyed, and most lost their wealth and died in poverty.[26] Although the Founders saw little from their hard work and sacrifice, the hundreds of millions who have followed them have been blessed by their legacy.

Part of that legacy is the inspired Documents they left us and the words they wrote and spoke. Although I am neither a constitutional scholar nor a colonial historian, I offer the following pages about the Founding Documents and the Founding Fathers. These pages are my thoughts as an ordinary American who believes in the amazing substance of these Founding Documents. Part of their greatness is that ordinary Americans can read them and understand. It is true, that such an understanding would perhaps not mirror that of the scholar or the historian. But consider that the understanding of an ordinary American just might be a more correct understanding; an understanding that mirrors what the writers actually meant as viewed from the perspective of the ordinary Americans whom their words were intended to empower and protect. And think about this: if we allow the Ruling Elite to interpret the documents that protect us against them, what kind of answers should we expect?

* * *

The American Founding Documents

The Founding Documents include the Declaration of Independence, the Constitution, and the ten amendments, introduced during the adoption process and known as the "Bill of Rights." Seventeen additional amendments have been added to the Constitution, with the last one, Amendment XXVII (which was originally suggested, but not adopted, as a part of

---

[26] Harvey, P. (1956). *Our Lives, Our Fortunes, Our Sacred Honor.* Waco, TX: World Books.

the Bill of Rights) having been adopted following the vote of the State of Michigan on May 7, 1992. Together, this group of documents began and have continued to guide the United States of America on its course. They launched the Ship of State, and we are the maintenance crew, the passengers and the officers in charge of that ship today.

Like all of the previous American generations, we have taken the helm from those before us and it is our responsibility to handle it well and to deliver the Ship of State to the generations that will succeed us. We arrive at this point of responsibility with the training we were provided, with the understanding of history, and with the great Founding Documents as proven controls on our behavior.

Although it is distasteful for detractors, we should all realize how great these Documents are today, how unique they were at the time of their writing, and the major impact they have had on the world as we know it. They codified a new way of thinking in the late 1700s and, as stated before, they were earth shaking in their very nature. They called for ordinary People to control their lives as intended by the Creator, not as allowed by powerful other people, which was the prevailing way of life in the world. They also established a process that would permit changing the rules over time—and for the peaceful transition of one set of leaders to another—at a time when such occurrences normally included contrived alliances, chaos and bloodshed. They combined the ordinary People's control over their government and their property with a market economy where prosperity could be achieved when prosperity was not normally possible for the ordinary People of the world. These were and remain great Documents because their essence is to offer ordinary People the possibility of having an extraordinary life.

In 1788, the Constitution established the United States of America as the first democratically styled government since

Rome, about 2000 years earlier. Some consider that it was the first since the Greeks, whose political system peaked some 500 years before the Romans. The type of national structure the Founders chose had almost never been seen on earth, let alone in the time of any person then living. Thanks to the fantastic nature of these Founding Documents, our nation grew and prospered like no other and established a model for successful nations that has since swept the planet.

The establishment of the United States as a democracy provided a model for what a country could be for its People. It appealed to that part of the intrinsic nature of humans to control their own person and their own property.

After the United States model prospered, other nations began organizing as some form of democracy[27]; for example, Canada, then France—through its revolution—and Switzerland. New Zealand, Australia, Norway and Belgium became democracies as the nineteenth century came to a close. The twentieth century brought a great explosion in democracies. The early half included much of Europe as well as India, Japan, Fiji, the Philippines, Malaysia, Lebanon, Israel and Sri Lanka. The Americas added Costa Rica and Cuba. The middle decades added Uruguay, Ecuador, Brazil, Columbia, the Dominican Republic, El Salvador, Guatemala and Guyana, Jamaica, Panama, Peru and others. In 1789 the United States of America was the one and only democracy on the entire planet, and the first one established in some 2000 years. By 1974, there were 41 democracies among 150 nations, about 27%. Another wave of change then occurred, and Spain and Greece became democracies. Military and one-party dictatorships had been

---

[27] Muhlberger, S. compilation, Chronology of Modern Democracy, Vanhanen, T. (1984). The Emergence of Democracy. http://www.nipissingu.ca/department/history/MUHLBERGER/histdem/vanhanen.htm

the dominant model in Latin America, but that changed as nine countries exchanged military rule for elected civilian rule in the period from 1979 to 1985.

Democracy has enemies, and the democracies in Cuba, Costa Rica and Panama floundered and reverted to dictatorships, but Costa Rica and Panama soon returned to elected civilian rule. The Philippines had become essentially a dictatorship under Ferdinand Marcos, but then became a democracy again in 1986.

In the 1990s, many nations of Africa exchanged dictators and royalty for democracy, and by 1987, about 40% of all the world's nations were democracies. These democracies stood in alignment with the United States and the other democracies. They were in opposition to the socialist block of nations, which were mostly controlled by Russia. Communist China and the monarchies that had dominated the Middle East also stood separately outside the democratic sphere. The socialist countries, communist regimes and democracies spent the more than 60 years since the end of World War II in what may be described as "pre-war tension."

Some of that tension was reduced when the Russian bloc disintegrated in 1989.

The Berlin Wall had stood as a physical barrier between the free people of Democracy and the captives of Socialism, many of whom had wanted to escape for decades. As the long established "shoot to kill" policy on the Socialist side of the wall dropped its grip, hundreds of thousands voted with their feet and poured across in a rapid mass migration to the West. The Wall itself was attacked and torn apart. As the control of Socialist Russia continued to loosen, even more democracies were then created. Today, about 60% of the world's 193 nations are democracies. But democracy, seemingly victorious, cannot claim victory.

Tyranny is control of the many by the few and is the constant opponent of democracy. Tyranny is the enemy of freedom, and history shows that tyranny should be considered the natural state of man. The Ruling Elite have taken many forms in history's long battle to keep the common man down and under their control for their own benefit. There have been kings and queens, military strongmen, dictators and sheiks. They have assumed the roles of man-god, religious icon, Party leader or czar. By whatever name they arise, and regardless of whatever uniform, robes or disguise they make for themselves, their intention is the same; more for them and their supporters and less for the ordinary person. It is always claimed to be for the good of some vision, some goal, and some entity larger than humankind itself, and it always entails great cost to the wealth and the freedom of the most productive humans that these great visionaries can affect. Without a single exception in the entire history of the human world, every effort that reduces Liberty has cost the ordinary person opportunity, success, freedom, justice, and many have lost their lives.

Although the recent modern record is encouraging, the uniquely American freedom of the common man has enemies and democracy can be lost. Fourteen modern democracies that have been established later succumbed to tyrants. Five of those have not returned, including Cuba. The failure of Germany with the rise of Hitler and his National Socialist (Nazi) party is a notable example of a democracy lost. Not only did the German people come under the control of a tyrannical and vicious few, but also their government was used as a tool to externally attack and destroy the freedom of other democracies as well. This German example shows that democracy can be lost, not only from external attack, but also from internal attack by elected officials who seek to increase control and thus reduce liberty "for the people's own good."

In a review of the 2700 years for which we have a fairly good record, we can see two things clearly: democracy was tried before and failed (Greece and Rome); and then it was absent for some 2000 years. In the intervening centuries, it is hard to imagine that democracy as a form of government was forgotten about. After all, two of the handful of the past great civilizations had been built around it, and their art, culture, material success and governmental organization had long since been well known in the world. Instead, it is more likely *that the world has always been a hostile place to elected civilian rule*. It remains so today. The tyrants are still present among our democracies and within them. They want the power from the free people, just as mythical vampires want to feed on the blood of the unwary; it is their nature. Where they are not in control, they will seek once again to regain control. History has shown that they will use every deception and every guise to control the common People. The tyrannical never give up; they simply regroup. And we common, ordinary People, whose nature is only to control our own lives and our own property, must always remain skeptically vigilant and recognize those who are tyrants for what they truly are. The Founders knew well the human condition and the tyrant rich world into which they were introducing our nation, and they sought to write our Documents so as to protect us.

✳ ✳ ✳

Notes on the Declaration of Independence

As a result of the spread of democracy, the Declaration of Independence is among the most well known documents of the world. Some might argue, more accurately, that because of the increasing knowledge about the Declaration, democracy spread. It is a document of that much gravitas. For admirers of the written word, its demonstration of the remarkable writing skills of Thomas Jefferson make a visit to his former Virginia home, Monticello, almost a spiritual event. John Adams and Benjamin Franklin were involved, but it was primarily the then thirty-three-year-old Jefferson's work.[28]

As an addendum to this book, the original words of the Declaration of Independence and the other Founding Documents are presented exactly and in their entirety. These documents are owned by every one of us. No American home should be without its copy of them, and no American should fail to read them. That is why they are included in this book.

We all know that if we do not care about something that we own, we should expect to lose it. These documents make three things clear: (1) that each of us is the beneficiary of the greatest experiment in governance the world has ever known; (2) that each of us has both rights and responsibilities as a citizen; and (3) that the Founders knew that those who seek to destroy freedom will lurk just outside the door—and inside it, too.

The thinking of the Founders in preparing the Founding Documents was influenced by the teachings of Christianity. To believe otherwise is simply foolish. Not only were nearly all of the Founders Christians, but they readily identified themselves as such. It was because of their own religious beliefs that they made America a place for diverse religious beliefs. They also prohibited any religion from being officially endorsed by the government, a tactic that was often used in history to set up government leaders as worshipful figures, which, to Christians, was idolatry. The Founders often referred to the divine in their speeches and writings, and many had formal education in theology. Many acts of the Founders support this

---

[28] Jefferson, T. (1776). The Account of the Declaration. Jefferson's Story of the Declaration. http:/www.ushistory.org/declaration/account/index.htm

fact, including their call for a day of "Fasting and Prayers" by all supporters of independence on June 1, 1774, the day the English Parliament's "Boston Port Bill" was to close that famed harbor. None of this means that Christians generally made any claim then—or now—as to some sort of ownership of this nation. The opposite has been shown to be the case.

These men were also heavily influenced by growing up under English traditions and laws. Much of that influence was generated by the Magna Charta (Carta), a 1215 document originally intended to save the barons (the wealthy landowners) of northern England from over-taxation by England's King John.[29] The King had destroyed the economy with debt from war and then ordered higher taxes to pay those debts. The rebellious acts of the barons forced him to document the traditions that had long been observed. These written words acknowledged his limited ability to tax, required him to follow recognized protocol, or "due process," in his royal work, and put a kernel of the theory of "majority rule" in place via a council that was created. The principles of this document would expand and improve during the reigns of the following kings and would eventually come to apply to all freedmen. After the American Founders use of these principles, and their subsequent successful rebellion, these ideas were also written into a new constitution for England and were eventually applied to all of its people.

The confluence of this background and the situation that arose in the American Colonies in the mid 1700s, was world-changing. England's King George III was ignoring the American Colonists' traditions and their requests for redress for grievances.

---

[29] National Archives & Records Administration (2009. November 6). Magna Carta and Its American Legacy. http:// www.archives.gov/exhibits/ featured_documents/magna_carta/legacy.html

He was striking down the colonists' laws, raising taxes, and refusing their representation in "Parliament," the representative body seated in London, England. In America, the discussions and writings of the day turned to focus on a government that had become tyrannical and abusive to the people. In time, those people sought freedom from the King's control and prepared to become a separate sovereign nation in order to control themselves. The Declaration of Independence was the written notification of that intention. The following comments are intended to put in the simple wording of today what has been entrusted to us for our safekeeping. Please feel free to look at the original documents placed in the back pages as you continue. All ordinary Americans need to know how these documents make *us* the rulers of this nation and call *us* to stand up and protect our Rights as citizens. And please do continue; the words here are the only words that make us ordinary Americans free of control from a small group of Ruling Elite. Hundreds of thousands have died for them and every one of us needs to know about them.

The Declaration

Paragraph One

In a concise set of words, The American Colonists seek to eliminate their submissive stature to Great Britain and instead to become a nation of their own. They state that the natural way that God set up the earth entitles all human beings to make this choice. It also points out that, out of respect, an explanation for why they intended to separate was owed to Great Britain and to the other nations of the world, whose ranks they sought to join.

Paragraph Two

Here, in the most memorable prose, Jefferson makes the point that all people possess Rights that come with their very existence, provided by their Creator. These Rights are depicted as "unalienable" Rights, meaning that they cannot be impinged upon or removed. This stood against the global norm; because the usual way was for people of power, wealth and connection (the Ruling Elite) to decide what the ordinary People could do, what they could own, or what they were allowed to believe. These notions could change with the country, the royalty, and over time. The common People were left at the mercy of the Ruling Elite, with little hope of doing better in their lives.

The paragraph goes on to say that government's primary duty is to protect the written Rights of the People. So at a time when most governments were whimsically busy determining what the rights of ordinary People might be, the Declaration assigns their government the specific task of protecting the Rights that the Founders clearly state and that they claim People already have and were born with. They declare that People have the Right to their own *Life*—in a time when most nations' rulers could take your life indiscriminately and absent of cause. They declared that all People have *Liberty,* which means that they may control their own lives and their own property—at a time when millions were enslaved around the world and millions more were not allowed to own land. They even state that a birthright is the ability to *Pursue Happiness*— at a time when ordinary People were considered to be subjects, not people, let alone happy people.

The paragraph further declares that if a government fails to protect the Rights that the People have by their very existence, those People have a seriously considered duty to "alter or abolish" that government and establish a government that *will* protect those Rights. The framers go on to accuse Britain of establishing Tyranny, meaning absolute and arbitrary control, over the People of the various States of America. They then introduce a list of abuses as evidence to the world that the Colonists were acting out of the need to protect the basic Rights that are granted to every ordinary person.

Paragraphs Three through Twenty-Nine: The Grievance List

These paragraphs offer a list of twenty eight abuses, directed to the then King of Great Britain, King George III. These allegations include his refusal to allow laws that the Americans have passed in their local legislative bodies, his dissolution of entities that have opposed his directives in the Americas, and his control over the pay and tenure of the colonial Judiciary.

Among the laws disallowed by the King were those passed in the Colonies to allow a currency to accommodate their growing commerce, representation in the Imperial Parliament, and a law forgiving the colonists involved in an anti-England incident in Boston, Massachusetts. This "Boston Tea Party" was a tax protest demonstration that had occurred in December of 1773 as a public response to a series of very restrictive British revenue laws, including the "Stamp Act" (1763) and "The Townshend Acts" (1767). Public ire had been further aroused in 1770 when a group of armed British soldiers killed five colonists in what has become known as the "Boston Massacre." This insurrection was perhaps the first precursor to the American Revolution and, along with the Boston Tea Party, certainly motivated the Founding Fathers to compose and issue the Declaration of Independence.

Although the King originally indicated that he might pardon the participants in the Tea Party group, he reneged by issuing the punitive "Intolerable Acts" statement that closed the Port of Boston in March of 1774.

Other complaints listed in these paragraphs, therefore, include condemnation of increasing British bureaucracy and having military stationed in the Colonies.

British soldiers present in the Colonies were not subject to the local civil authorities and were protected from punishment for wrongdoing. There were also military attacks on the citizens and property of the Americas. It seemed that there was no extension to the American Colonists of the basic English system of justice accorded to other British subjects.

This section of The Declaration also calls out the issues of forced recruitment of colonial citizens that required them to take up arms against their countrymen, interfering with trade, encouraging American Indians to attack them, and also taxing them without their consent.

The sum of the complaints is that King George had set aside English and American law and was attacking them to force compliance with what he wanted.

This is an example of the Tyranny that persists among people. Despite the more advanced state of man and government in Great Britain, potential Tyranny was just below the surface and became very evident in the Americas. The Founding Fathers wanted out of this situation, and sought to set up a government that would eliminate Tyranny and discourage its future reappearance.

Paragraph Thirty

The writers state here that they have respectfully pointed out these abuses for some time, but without a corrective action in return. They then conclude that the King is a Tyrant, not a leader of free people.

Paragraph Thirty-One

Since they have asked their British oppressors to stop aggressive acts and have warned of consequences for failure to do so, they now must reconsider Great Britain and view it in the same manner they would any other nation, as ". . . Enemies in War, in Peace Friends."

Paragraph Thirty-Two

In this section, the writers establish that they now see themselves not as a group of Colonies under the control of Great Britain, but as "Free and Independent States" that will govern themselves. They name the new nation "The United States of America" and announce that in this Declaration they speak for this new nation as a united group of representatives. Further, they announce that there no longer exists any relationship between them and Great Britain and, as in any nation, they claim the right to wage war if needed. In the last line before the signatures of those who agree to support this document, they assert that they rely upon the care and guardianship of God to protect their efforts and they pledge to support one another with "our Lives, our Fortunes, and our Sacred Honor."

Signatures

There are 56 signatures placed upon the document, provided by representatives from each of the thirteen Colonies that are now states. It is an impressive assemblage of leaders of the day which includes John Hancock, Benjamin Franklin, Thomas Jefferson, Benjamin Harrison, and John Adams. Although the remaining 51 men signing the Declaration of Independence are not as widely known today, they were recognized leaders in their day. A few scattered but interesting examples follow.

Button Gwinnett was the first to sign. That name is often recognized by those in Georgia because of the 430-acre county that is named after him.[30] Gwinnett was born in England, the son of a pastor and came to the Colonies as a man in his twenties. Gwinnett settled in South Carolina, became a successful merchant and then a plantation owner. He was elected

---

[30] Deaton, S. (2009). Button Gwinnett (1735–1777). The New Georgia Encyclopedia. http://www.georgiaencyclopedia.org/nge/Article.jsp?id+h-2543

to that colony's Provincial Assembly, then to the Continental Congress. Meeting in May, 1776, that group finalized the Declaration that bears his signature. He traveled to the new state of Georgia and used the model developed by John Adams for a State Constitution for that state. He then served in the Georgia Assembly and became the second Governor of Georgia. He died in a duel of honor with a political rival in May of 1777.

Signatory Lyman Hall was also the son and the nephew of pastors, and from Connecticut.[31] He graduated from Yale in Theology and later in Medicine. He had come to have a plantation and practice medicine in St. John's Parish in Georgia, which was a very pro-British "loyalist" part of the state. An outspoken critic of Britain, Hall was appointed to represent Georgia at the 1775 Congress. He went on to help supply the Continental Army of George Washington. The British military destroyed his home and plantation, and he became a fugitive, escaping to Philadelphia for safety. After the Revolutionary War, he returned to Georgia, served in its state legislature, and helped found a religious education state university that later became the University of Georgia. Lyman Hall was named a Chatham County judge, and died in 1790 at his plantation near Augusta, Georgia.

John Witherspoon was a signer for New Jersey. He was a theologian from the University of Edinburgh and St. Andrews in Scotland.[32] These schools were considered the finest centers of education in the world at that time, and many of the supporters of the democracy in America had been exposed to such ideas from their Scottish educators. Witherspoon became

---

[31] Deaton, S. (2002). Lyman Hall (1724–1790). The New Georgia Encyclopedia. http://www.georgiaencyclopedia.org/nge/Article.jsp?1d=h-664
[32] Kindig, T. (2009, November 5). John Witherspoon (1723–1794). Representing New Jersey at the Continental Congress. Signors of the Declaration of Independence. U.S. History.org. http://www.ushistory.org/declaration/signers/witherspoon.htm

a Presbyterian minister and later President of the College of New Jersey, a school founded as a seminary and place of higher learning in 1748, which is known today as Princeton University. At that time, Witherspoon was also elected as a delegate to the Continental Congress. He closed the college and evacuated as the British attacked New Jersey and destroyed much of the campus. After the war he returned, rebuilt the college, and died in 1794.

Francis Lewis, signing for New York, was from Wales, raised by a wealthy aunt.[33] He too was educated in Scotland and then graduated from London's Westminster School. As a successful merchant, he would later supply uniforms to the British during the French and Indian Wars. He survived being a prisoner of both the French and the Indians and retained his wealth to become a member of "The Sons of Liberty." He was elected in New York to the Second Continental Congress and moved his family to his Whitestone estate on Long Island. Soon after signing the Declaration and returning to his home, Lewis found himself attacked by British troops, who destroyed his estate and took his wife prisoner. His fortune and his wife were both lost in the war that he helped to bring about. He died in 1802.

In sum, of the fifty-six men who signed, as detailed in earlier pages, almost all suffered greatly as a result. Many had their homes taken over, looted or destroyed. Some were captured by the British, were tortured and died, or had members of their families captured. Others lost their lives in military service, and some of their sons died, too, in the war that followed the signing.

---

[33] Kindig, T. (2009, November 9). Francis Lewis (1713–1802). Representing New York at the Continental Congress. Signors of the Declaration of Independence. U.S. History.org. http://www.ushistory.org/declaration/signers/lewis.ht

The key thing to note is that these people represented some of the most accomplished and widely known families of that time. These educated, wealthy merchants, theologians and professionals could have become the new American royalty, but they would have none of that. Instead, they were Founders of our great experiment in freedom, spearheading a movement that produced the most economically and militarily powerful nation from the diverse masses that migrated to its opportunities. They devised a remarkable formula for Freedom and Prosperity that has spawned imitators all over the globe. The United States of America is an amazing story that some have said only a loving God could write and only evil men could destroy.

> "They devised a remarkable formula for Freedom and Prosperity that has spawned imitators all over the globe."

The Declaration of Independence changed the very nature of what the relationship could be between the government and the governed. It inspired millions, sowed the seeds of freedom, and established goals not yet achieved even in its home country.

Today, the United States of America is well on its way, and it is an impressive work in progress.

* * *

Notes on the Constitution

There was a time gap between the adoption of the Declaration (1776) and before the Constitution was prepared and ratified by the ninth ratification vote of the State of New Hampshire on June 21, 1788. During that period, the new American nation was operated on a frequently overlooked document called the "Articles of Confederation."

This perhaps may be referred to as the "Pre Constitution." The document had no power over individuals, no taxing power, and no allowance for an executive branch or a judiciary. It was drawn up hastily and allowed the various new states to establish a rough working relationship. It had glaring problems that became burdensome and evidenced the need for the more definitive and well reasoned successor document which we now know as the Constitution of the United States.

Among the major negative issues in the Articles were the trade barriers between the States and the inconsistent financial support for the central government. Tariffs were often imposed to protect certain industries or the agriculture of a State, which suppressed trade between the states and caused enmity. Also, the central Confederation government relied on each of the States to pay to the Confederation an annual share to cover the operating costs of the central government. Some states did not pay, others paid late, and these conditions often crippled the central government.

There were also issues of payment to Britain for its claims of war debt, as well as some new disputes related to the western areas that the British were to vacate, and with frontier areas where settlers proposed new states.

Those and many other issues were addressed in the Constitutional effort undertaken by James Madison and others. There was a Constitutional Convention organized in Annapolis, Maryland in 1786 to draft a new Constitutional framework for the young nation, but it failed. A Second Constitutional Convention began in Philadelphia in May, 1787, and it resulted in a signed draft to take to the states for approval in September, 1787.

The Constitution is the most important document in America. It is the foundation of all legal authority for the nation. It is an eternal agreement between The People and the government, between each of the States with one another, and between the central government and the States. Most importantly, the Constitution established, in written form for all to see, what responsibility and control was granted to these government bodies from the American public. This is so important you need to read it again; "what responsibility and control was granted to these government bodies from the American public."

That is the way it was and the way that it actually remains today. Yet most of us ordinary citizens believe that our situation today is about just the opposite: what the government allows *us* to do; what freedom the government allows *us* to have.

If that is what we believe, then it is no wonder that this is the way we behave and the way the government will treat us. Simply read the document for yourself.

Most Americans have likely not read it, because if they had, more would understand that most of us are accepting much more control over our lives than was expressed in this document. We have not ceded additional control to our government really, but rather to the people who supposedly serve us there; and they are people having one Party ideology or the other. More control is happily accepted and selfishly wielded by the two major political Parties for their own benefit.

I have contended above that the Founding Documents were written for the ordinary person to understand. Yes, it was written for our equivalents in the mid-1700s. Those Americans used a more formal and older English than we are accustomed to using today. But it is still the same language, and the vast majority of the words used then have the same meaning today. It is very readable, and it is a *necessary* read.

If one stands as a Christian, then he should have at least some familiarity with the Bible—at minimum, the basic belief ascribed to the Ten Commandments—just as self-identified Jewish people should have the basic knowledge of their faith book, the Torah. A Communist should know the works of Lenin and Marx, and an American should have at least a general familiarity with the Constitution, the "Document of Freedom." Again, its full text appears later in this book.

The following pages will look at the Constitution from an ordinary citizen's view.

As I mentioned about the Declaration, I am not a professor and I am not a constitutional lawyer, but I will offer the following as a sort of layman's guide for understanding the most important non-religious document in your life, and of all of our lives. Just look at the original words, along with the simple explanations provided here. I present plain words and include some history so that it is easier to fully understand the context of the original document and the amendments. I also note places that were amended and relate what currently applies instead of what once did, which can be seen in the exact original document.

Before we begin, please understand that a lawyer, especially an experienced constitutional lawyer, will criticize this as over simplistic. That person would likely tell us that we just cannot understand it on our own because of the way that lawyers have established meanings today based on results of court cases, which they call "precedent." We would be cautioned that judges' writings and court briefs have detailed meanings and have determined much. I would agree with such remarks if we were going to court, but that is not the purpose here. We are going to an understanding about how our nation works, not to court.

Some might also say that this Constitution is a sort of guideline with less meaning today. I will say more later on that, but for now, I would reply that legal interpretations have all been made after the Founders wrote the document. They have been made with a specific point of view and perhaps one thing in mind that was used to support another and then another and have become like an overly complex building that has been built over a simple foundation; I would reply that perhaps many of these overlaying thoughts came about purposely to take the Constitution further from The People while their pocket full of freedoms was being picked.

The simple and critical features remain as clear in the Constitution, which was written 224 years ago, as do the simple and critical features of the Bible, written from more than 3,400 years ago. In the case of the Bible, millions of words have been written interpreting it, three great but differing religions were spawned from it, and tomes have been issued explaining each of its books and even the specific lines and words it contains. But the basics are still there in the original and can be generally understood by ordinary People. At a base level, the meaning of the Bible's Ten Commandments, despite hundreds of their specific scholarly studies, remain the understandable Ten Commandments, and the Constitution's original stated rights and responsibilities remain an understandable statement of our rights and responsibilities today.

THE PREAMBLE

This opening paragraph contains only a single sentence, but it has become one of the most recognized and revered group of words in world history. It is beautiful and recognizable. I request that you turn to the original right now (page 313), and read the Preamble's words, the revealing and powerful words written with a quill pen by the caring and daring of those who preceded us, composed for our protection today.

The Preamble states clearly that is on the behalf of the American People that this Document has been prepared. It points out that its purpose is to improve the union that already exists. We recall that The Constitution came about as a result of the failings of the Articles of Confederation. Part of the problem of the Articles was that they left too much undone, which gave rise to rancor among the states, as well as between the states and the central government.

The words ". . . insure domestic Tranquility" seem to convey the intended end of the unworkable period of the Articles.

The next phrase, ". . . provide for the common defense," specifically points out that the duty of all governments is to focus on providing security for The People.

". . . promote the general welfare" expressed in words that the burden of acting in the public interest is at the forefront of all government consideration.

Those who prepared and signed the Constitution, as they had done in the Declaration of Independence, confirmed their belief in this premise.

The phrase ". . . secure the Blessings of Liberty" without question relates to the Declaration's claim that the right of Liberty, our freedom, comes from a divine entity, rather than from man. The particular Christian words "Blessings" and "ordain" are words of spirituality that we commonly recognize today. The intended permanency of the work they prepared was summed up in the reference. " . . . to ourselves and our Posterity."

The author of these famous words is not well known today. His name was Gouverneur (his name, not a title) Morris, whose brother, Lewis Morris, was a signer of The Declaration of Independence for New York.[34] Gouverneur was a close friend of both John Jay and George Washington. Morris was a key player in defending Washington from a character attack—which was actually a grab for the power—by his competitor for control of the Continental Army, Thomas Conway, of

---

[34] Eddlem, T.R. (2006, April 3). Meet the Author of U.S. Constitution's Preamble. America.gov. http://www.america.gov/st/pubs-english/2006/April/20060403118203pssnikwad0.6276056

Maryland. Morris was opposed to slavery, concerned about too much democracy, and a man of faith. He once wrote that the future ". . . is still in the hands of that Supreme Intelligence which mocks the prudence of man, and his cunning which we presume to dignify with the name wisdom."

ARTICLES

There are seven Articles in the Constitution, four have Sections, but Articles 5, 6 and 7 have no Sections. The Articles are given no title in the actual document, but for readability, they are listed here by what they refer to:

- Article I – Congress
- Article II – President
- Article III – Courts
- Article IV – The States
- Article V – Amendment
- Article VI – Debt, Supremacy and Oaths
- Article VII – Ratification

Article I – Congress
Modified by Amendments XVII, XX, XXVII

This Article establishes the existence and operation of the first of what is commonly known as the three "branches" (or basic functional parts) of our government's structure. The "legislative" branch is about Congress, the "executive" branch concerns the President, those who report directly to the President, and staff of the White House. The "judicial" branch is about our courts and judges. These same three branches are, in general, the scheme that government uses at each State level—and often at the county and the municipal (city) levels.

This opening Article of the Constitution is its longest. I will offer a simple summary of each of the sections in the following paragraphs:

Section 1, The Legislature, one sentence in length, simply establishes that at the federal level there is to be a legislative (law writing) branch called "Congress," which is composed of two parts (bicameral), called the Senate and the House of Representatives.

The next two Sections detail the composition of those two parts:

Section 2, The House, establishes the House as a body of officials elected by The People of each respective state for two year terms of office, called "Representatives." They must be at least age 25, a U.S. Citizen for seven years, and inhabit the state they represent. The number permitted from each state is based upon the number of Citizens living in that state. It sets the number of persons per representative to be 30,000 and creates a formula whereby a free person and contracted slaves be counted as one each, excludes Indians, who were not taxed, and every other type of human was to be counted as three-fifths of a person.

Apparently, most of those who did not participate fully in the post-colonial society had less than full representation in its government, but actually the three-fifths clause would reduce the number of repre-senatives a slave state had in Congress. This, as we will see, was later changed by amendment. This Section also establishes that a count of Persons, what today we call the "Census," is to be taken every 10 years.

At the time of this writing, in 2010, that process is being repeated once again. This provision, setting the number of qualifying inhabitants, determines the number of representatives from each State. This Section established the original number of representatives from each State and outlines that the body will choose its own "Speaker"—the leader who presumably "speaks" for the others—and additional officers, and also allows each State executive, now commonly called the "governor," to fill vacancies that may arise.

Section 3, The Senate, similarly details the Senate as a body, with two elected representatives from each State, called "Senators" and chosen by each State legislature for six year terms of office (later changed). The Article provided that the first Senate to be seated would be staggered by thirds into two, four and six-year terms so that all subsequent elections for six year terms would affect only one third of the Senators.

The electoral scheme in the House of Representatives offers citizen protection from the entire body rotating at one time, thereby allowing for consistency and minimally disruptive change. Senators must be at least age 30, a U.S. Citizen for nine years, and inhabit the state they represent. Senators were originally elected by the State legislators, but Amendment XVII changed that to be directly by the vote of the citizens of each State. Senators choose the officers of their body also, but the Vice President is assigned as the President of the Senate and votes only if there is a tie vote. The "President pro tempore" officer of the Senate replaces the Vice President if the office of the President becomes vacant. The Senate is considered to be the "upper class" or "upper house" of the Congress. While the House of Representatives considers bringing an action to impeach, or remove, the President, they must pass their positive majority "articles of impeachment" on to the Senate. Upon receipt, the Senate has the duty to actually hold a trial of the President. If that occurs, the Chief Justice of the Supreme Court, head of the judicial branch, presides, and two-thirds of the Senators must agree on the verdict. If they convict the Chief Executive, the President is removed from office, and becomes subject to indictment and trial in the criminal courts.

There is a great interest in impeachment among American citizens today because many have lived during one or two of the only three full impeachment actions in our history. In 1868, President Andrew Johnson was impeached for several reasons.[35] He came into the office when Republican Abe Lincoln was assassinated. Johnson was a Democrat whom Lincoln put on his ticket to garner at least some Democratic Party support for the Civil War, which Lincoln was preparing to fight in order to abolish slavery in the South. Most Democrats were protectors of Slavery, but Johnson was a critic. After the Civil War was over and the victorious Republican Lincoln was assassinated, Johnson became President with an all-Republican Congress. He would not consent to the later repealed Tenure Act, which required appointees confirmed in Congress to have their dismissal confirmed there, too, as he was removing Lincoln's appointees. He also was against giving Blacks full

---

[35] Linder, D.O. (2010, May 2010). The Impeachment Trial of Andrew Johnson. University of Missouri-Kansas City School of Law. http://www.law.umkc.edu/faculty/projects/ftrials/impeach/imp-account2.html

citizenship and voting Rights and would not require the former "Confederate States" to provide these Rights as a condition of reconstruction and regaining full State privileges after their loss in the Civil War. He also vetoed the Republicans' Civil Rights Act. In addition, on July 30, 1866, there was an attack at a New Orleans convention of Republicans and newly freed Blacks, as a result of which 48 people were killed and 166 were wounded.[36] It was determined by congressional investigation that this attack was planned by New Orleans Democratic Mayor John Monroe with his city officials and likely agreed to by President Johnson. Johnson was therefore impeached by the House, then acquitted in the subsequent Senate impeachment trial by a single vote.

In July, 1974, Republican President Richard Nixon was impeached by the House for abuse of power and obstruction of justice ("high crimes and misdemeanors"). In order to avoid the likely conviction in the Senate, he resigned, was replaced, and then pardoned by his Vice President and successor, Gerald Ford. Nixon had a Democratic Party controlled House, and Senate.[37] After his House impeachment, enough of his fellow Party members planned to vote with the Democrats to reach the necessary two-thirds majority to convict him in the Senate. The impeachment came about because of his involvement in a burglary at the Watergate Building offices of the Democratic National Committee and for his subsequent lying and covering up of his knowledge of it. It would be reasonable thinking that the Constitution would not allow Ford to pardon Nixon because of its prohibition of the use of pardon. However, Nixon was not pardoned from impeachment, because he was

---

[36] The New Orleans Massacre. (1867, March 30). *Harper's Weekly*, p. 202.
[37] The History Place, Presidential Impeachment Proceedings. (2010, August 7) Impeachment: Richard Nixon. http://www.historyplace.com/unitedstates/impeachments/nixon.htm

not tried and found guilty in the Senate. Nixon resigned from office and was pardoned of any potential wrong in the matter that might have brought criminal charges against the disgraced former President.

In 1998 President and attorney Bill Clinton, a Democrat, after a lengthy investigation filled with legal, political and public relations wrangling, was formally accused of obstruction of justice, abuse of power, and perjury (lying under oath) related to cases with two different women, Paula Jones, when he was governor of Arkansas, and Monica Lewinsky, during his second term as President.[38] He was impeached by the majority Republican controlled House, but acquitted by all 45 of his fellow Democratic Party members in the Senate where the two-thirds rule to convict was not met. He continued to the end of his second term.

Now, returning to **Article I**:

> **Section 4, Elections and Meetings** states that Congress is to meet annually and the next Section establishes rules regarding record keeping, behavior, expulsion (two-thirds), and adjournment. 1933 Amendment XX modified this Article to set the beginning of the terms of President and Vice President, as we know it today, at noon on January, 20 after the previous November election. It also requires that Congressional terms should end at noon on January 3 and the new Congress be assembled at that same time.

> **Section 5, Membership, Rules, Records and Adjournment,** allows each section of the Congress to make its

---

[38] Wikipedia.org. Political Scandals of the United States. (2009, December, 28) 1993–2000 Clinton Administration. http://www.wikipedia.org/Political-scandals-of-the-United-States

own rules for procedures and for the misbehavior of its members, but it requires that a two-thirds vote for expulsion in either the House of Representatives or the Senate. It is this section that is referred to when the news covers the "House Rules" or "Senate Procedures." Both Houses are required to make a record of proceedings and votes, historically available in the printed "Congressional Record," but today, all this is viewable and reviewable on CSPAN and the Internet. This section also prohibits one House from adjourning for more than three days without the other House's approval, nor can either House conduct business in any place where they are not present together.

Section 6, Compensation and Arrest, establishes that members are not subject to arrest while attending legislative session and that no national office may be held simultaneously with an elected post in Congress. The former point was likely made so that a critical or close vote would not be disrupted by coincidental—or perhaps intentional—intervention by the power of law enforcement wielded by those seeking to influence the vote.

Section 7, Revenue, Legislation, and Veto, establishes the House of Representatives as the place of origination for all revenue legislation. It also is about overriding a veto by the President. Each half of Congress must pass a bill, normally by a simple majority in the House. Today, however, due to a Senate procedural rule, a three-fifths majority (60 votes) is required in the Senate to avoid a "filibuster" that can allow endless debate on a measure, effectively halting the bill from passing. After both Houses have passed a bill in identical form (sometimes requiring a "reconciliation" within a joint House-Senate Committee that resolves language and content differences between a House Bill and that of its equivalent Senate Bill), it must be sent for the approving signature of the President. If the President disapproves, then with a decision called a "veto," Congress may reconsider it, and it can become law without the President's approval if it passes again with a two-thirds majority in each House.

Section 8, Powers of Congress, encompasses such general powers as borrowing and coining money, running the Post Office and the Patent program, declaring war, raising and supporting an army, a navy and an organized militia. It also states that it is the role of Congress to execute all the powers set forth in the Article and elsewhere in the Constitution.

Section 9, Congressional Limits, contains some legal prohibitions, including not being able to act against slavery prior to 1808, about nine years after the signing. Some more general legal issues are mentioned, including the principle of Habeas Corpus (which blocks illegal imprisonment by requiring the accused to appear before a judge) and prohibitions against the issuance of a bill of attainder (a historical precedent from English Common Law that allows persons or groups to be singled out and punished without a trail).[39]

---

[39] Technical Law Journal. (2010, August 7). Bill of Attainder. http://www.teclawjournal.com/glossery/legal/attainder.htm

Section 10, Powers Prohibited to the States, the final section, prohibits some State actions like coining money, making treaties with another State or a foreign nation, and engaging in war unless invaded. It also prohibits the States from levying duty on imports and exports, which was one of the main problems with the preceding federal organization document, the Articles of Confederation of 1778.

Article II – President
Modified by Amendments XII, XXII, XXIII, XXV

This Article establishes the duties and power of the President. Along with the Vice President, his staff and appointees, they are considered the "executive" branch and often referred to as the "Administration" or the "White House." The latter, of course, comes from a reference to the white building located in Washington D.C. which is both home to the sitting President and his family and offices for the President (his personal office is called the "Oval Office" due to its unique shape) and many of his direct-report staff.

Section 1, the President and the Electoral Body, establishes that the term of elected office for both the President and the Vice President is to be a simultaneous four years. It then sets out a separate body of "Electors, appointed by each State and equaling the then current number of House and Senate representatives from each State. These Electors are empowered to cast the final votes that elect these offices. This Article was amended in 1804 by Amendment XII and again by Amendment XXII in 1951. The most recent was Amendment XXIII in 1961 which established the process of using Electors today. This method of election is often commonly referred to as the "electoral college," but that term is not used anywhere in this Document or its amendments. The purpose of the body of Electors is to be a compromise between having Congress itself elect the President and direct election by the popular vote of The People. Each State has its own method of appointing the Electors, generally through the political Parties. Most States have a "winner take all" approach that the candidate with the most popular votes in that State receives all of the electoral votes of that State. Only Maine and Nebraska are different, with a proportional allocation of their votes according to their State's popular vote.

The Electors meet in Washington, D.C. on the first Monday after the second Wednesday in December of the electoral year. The candidate receiving 270 or more votes from this group wins. Although it does mandate that Congress controls the time schedule of electoral activity, there is no mandate in the Constitution that the Electors vote according to the popular vote, and it is their vote that decides who will be President.[40]

The Section continues with a paragraph indicating that the President is to be compensated at a constant rate during the entire term of office and that compensation for executive service must come only from the United States and in no part from any individual State.

It concludes with the exact words of the President's oath of office, a single sentence swearing to "preserve,

---

[40] Longley, R.(2010, August,7). About.com. The Electoral College System. http://www.usgovinfo.about.com./od/thepoliticalsystem/a/electcollege.htm

protect and defend the Constitution of the United States." In its simple and direct form, this oath clearly states and, because it is the only duty mentioned, seems to reinforce the singular role of the President. If the President doesn't follow this oath, only Congress can do anything about it. Today, Congress is often dominated by those in the President's own Party, which seems to have a gang mentality, making The People vulnerable to a single person's whim.

Section 2, Civilian Over Military, Pardons and Appointments, makes the President "Commander in Chief" of our military forces and allows the President to pardon people for offenses against the United States. These are two huge powers. Making the President the Commander in Chief clearly puts a non-military civilian in charge of the American military forces. This was carefully crafted to underscore and assure that the power of the military serves The People. It is to be a protector *for* them rather than a dominator *of* them. The powers allowed here mean that the President can wage undeclared war and can also pardon those who are convicted criminals, including friends and donors. The presidential pardon power is thought to be necessary because neither our justice system nor that of any country is perfect and yet it is "fundamentally political."[41] By court cases over the years, it has been established that presidential pardons can be issued at any time, for nearly any reason, can neither be refused nor be

---

[41] Dodd, G.G. (2009) Law and Politics Book review. Review of *The Presidential Pardon Power.* Crouch, J. (2009).

overridden by Congress, and may be conditional. Court cases that raise questions about what the Constitution means may be accepted for review by the highest court, the Supreme Court. It is here that case law, as in pardons, elaborates on the meaning of the Constitution and also where past cases (precedents) are used in determining future cases, just as in other court levels. It is here in case law that this Document falls into the province of specialist attorneys for detailed application, as does all law. Still, the basic understanding of its guarantees may be understood from its reading by ordinary People.

Section 3, State of the Union and Convening Congress, gives the President the ability to convene Congress as well as to adjourn it, and to give Congress information regarding the State of the Union when judged necessary. The tradition is to provide a State of the Union message annually. The office is also given the authority to receive Ambassadors (representatives of other nations), monitor the execution of laws passed, and to commission all Officers.

Section 4, Disqualification and Removal, is a very simple statement that the President and Vice President as well as all Officers may be removed or Impeached for "Treason, Bribery or other High Crimes and Misdemeanors." Therefore, acting in a manner that violates allegiance to our country by helping our enemies—especially waging war, taking money in exchange for doing something for the source of the money, as well as other unspecified illegal acts—are grounds for removal from office.

The term "Misdemeanors" does not equate to the word used commonly at the State level as a lesser criminal category than a "Felony."

The office of President is the most dear and honored position that a person can hold in our nation. It is an office greater than any person who may be elected to it, for that person represents us all to each other and our nation to all other nations. The man or woman who occupies the Presidency must realize that this is a place of high trust and honor that not only retains much of the operational control of our country, but also is the primary place of guardianship for the aspirations of the more than 300 million Americans of today, and for those future millions of tomorrow who will follow us in the pursuit of Freedom and Equality. We depend on our President to meet or exceed the oath of office of this Constitution.

Article III – Courts
Modified by Amendment XI

Section 1, Judicial Powers, establishes one Supreme Court and other secondary "inferior" courts, as decided by Congress.

Section 2, Jury trial and Jurisdiction, lists the types of cases to which the Court's power will apply, which includes those "arising under this Constitution," the laws of the nation, to treaties and those that make them, to our international representatives, such as Ambassadors, and to those of this nation versus other nations and of one State to another State.

The 1795 Eleventh Amendment prohibited the nation's judicial power from extending to any case prosecuting a State of the United States by citizens from another State or by any citizens of a foreign nation. The section concludes by setting all criminal trials being by Jury and set in the State where the crime was committed.

> **Section 3, Treason,** is about acting against the United States and is narrowly defined as warring against them or "adhering to their Enemies." This is one of the only terms that the Founders undertook to define in the entire Constitution. The perceived need for a definition probably resulted from the long history of varying claims of treason by the Royals in England and the harsh punishment that resulted. Typical punishment for traitors included hanging and disemboweling while alive. This Section allows Congress to set the punishment for Treason but limits the punishments to not be applicable to family members simply because they are blood related, and when the crime is punished that persecution ends. Conviction is only possible with a confession or by two direct witnesses of the act. The narrowness of the definition was likely a reaction to the broad and punishing persecution of the Founders and their supporters at the hands of the British after The Declaration of Independence.

There are many cases of treason in our history, including the famous and not so famous, and the penalty determined by Congress has varied. Aaron Burr was tried for treason in 1807, for his alleged attempt to fight to take the west and Mexico for an empire of his own. Burr had resigned as Vice President to start the undertaking. The plot was foiled, and he was acquitted of the charges but disgraced. Burr is most remembered for killing Alexander Hamilton in a dual.

During the Mexican War (1846–1848), which established the southern American border, hundreds of Irish American soldiers deserted to fight alongside Mexican General Santa Anna after his appeal to defend the Catholic Church. Fifty of them were later executed by American General Winfield Scott for treason.

Castner Hanway was tried and acquitted of Treason regarding his alleged violence against a U.S. Marshal who was enforcing the Fugitive Slave Act. Iva Toguri D'Aquino, known as "Tokyo Rose," used her well-spoken English to constantly deliver morale breaking messages on behalf of the Japanese Imperial government during World War II. She was convicted in 1952, fined and served prison time.[42] Tomoya Kamakita, was tried for treason for his acts in that war. He held dual citizenships in Japan and America and had tortured captive Americans in a World War II Japanese Prison Camp. After the war, he enrolled in USC and worked at Sears. He was discovered by a former prisoner, convicted of treason, served 16 years in prison and then was deported.[43]

Article IV – The States
Modified by Amendment XIII

These four sections must have been difficult for the States to agree with. At the time of its writing, the very basic

---

[42] United States V. Iva Toguri D'Aquino. (2010, May 27) http://www.justice.gov/criminal/foia/records/tokyo-rose-p8.pdf

[43] Rosenzweig, R. (2002, September, 20) POW Camp Atrocities Led to Treason Trial. *Los Angeles Times.* http://articles.latimes.com.2002/sep/20/local/me-onthelaw20

problem between the States was that most of the southern States wanted to protect slavery and expand to the new States that would be formed, while most northern States wanted to end existing slavery and not allow it anywhere. Added to that were the struggles of commerce that were happening throughout the new country, and differing religious opinions, even though Christianity was almost universal. As it turned out, the Founders did a fine job and accomplished getting agreement on the base new document. Part of that effort included mostly agreeing to the first ten amendments to the Constitution (often called the "Bill of Rights") in advance of the Constitution's passage.

> **Section 1, States Honor Others Equally,** pronounces "full faith and credit" mutual acceptance by each State for all the acts, legal cases and records of every other State. This allowed each State to proceed in its own way, but required them all to be respectful of each other in a kind of a "do unto others" approach.

> **Section 2, State Citizens and Extradition,** which requires each State to return a charged criminal to the State where their crime was committed when requested by its authorities. While this Section eliminates a lot of controversy in advance, all States are permitted to have different laws about what is a crime and how it is to be punished. This Section originally applied to slaves as well, but was later amended.

The 1865 Amendment XIII modified Article IV to make slavery and involuntary servitude illegal in all States. This was accomplished at the very end of the Civil War, which was fought between 1861 to 1865, primarily over the issue of slavery.

The presidential election of Abraham Lincoln was a catalyst for war. Lincoln was a well recognized leader of the anti-slavery Republicans. The Republican Party was new and was formed primarily as an anti-slavery Party. He was victorious over the Democrats, who were pro-slavery and equated the intention to end it as a State's Rights and Property Rights intrusion by the Federal government. As a result, South Carolina and ten other pro-slavery states established the separate Confederate States of America, and the nation moved to war.

> **Section 3, New States**, sets limits on how new States will be admitted to the Union, which block a new State being formed out of an existing State or from parts or combinations of others, without both State and Congressional legislative approvals. The section concludes by stating that Congress will make all rules regarding the Territories or other property of the United States.

> **Section 4, Guarantees by Federal Government,** requires the Federal government guarantee that any State will be a *Republican Form of government.* (This in no way relates to a political Party, but rather to the form of government in which the people elect representatives to vote on their behalf.)

Most nations commonly referred to as "democracies" are actually a blend of governmental types, essentially "democratic republics," under which the citizens vote for those who will represent them in the various government structures.

The Section concludes with a statement that the central government will defend the States against invasion and against domestic violence, when requested.

Article V – Amendment

The Constitution may be amended by a specific process outlined in this single section Article. That process begins with either a proposal for an amendment from a two-thirds majority in both Houses of Congress or by two-thirds of the State legislatures requesting an amendment. Once presented, if three-quarters of the State Legislatures or State Conventions agree to a proposed amendment, it becomes part of the Constitution. This process was originally limited from action related to slavery stated in Article I and from depriving a State of Senate votes. Note that there is no direct involvement by the President in the amendment process.

The manner of amendment has normally been passage by two-thirds of both Houses of Congress and then ratification by three-quarters of the State Legislatures. However, a State constitutional convention approval, instead of by the legislatures, which would have a different body of people deciding, may be used. State constitutional convention methods vary according to the laws of each State. This state convention method was only used once, in the passage of the 1933 Amendment XXI, which repealed the prohibition of alcohol products that had been passed in the 1919 Amendment XVIII. This method and a seven year period within which to accomplish ratification were specified in the wording of the approved Amendment XXI.

Article VI – Debt, Supremacy and Oaths

These words document that all obligations of debt that were valid under the Articles of Confederation would remain valid under the Constitution which was replacing it. It clearly states that the Constitution, along with laws of the United States made to support it, comprise the "supreme Law of the Land" and all judges shall be required to support it. It expands on this in its final sentences, requiring that all governmental representatives, executives, and officers are to be bound by oath or affirmation to support this Constitution, but a religious test for any such position is barred from being a requirement. This barring seems to make sense, given the Founders intent not to have a nationally endorsed religion as many had experienced in their European backgrounds.

Article VII – Ratification

The approving, or "ratifying," of the original Constitution required nine States to vote for it in state conventions. It then would be established as the basic structure of our country.

The Signatories

The document draft was the result of the Second Constitutional Convention begun in May 1787 in Philadelphia. It was approved on September 17, 1787 with thirty-nine signatures. There had been fifty-five who attended from twelve of the States, Rhode Island sent no delegates. Of the seventy-four that were invited to attend the gathering, nineteen refused or were unable to attend, four left in protest, nine left early, and three refused to sign. This underscores the occasional complaint that "democracy is messy."[44]

The Constitution was ultimately ratified when New Hampshire was the ninth State to approve it—on June 21, 1788.

* * *

Notes on the Amendments

Since the Amendments to the Constitution actually have the same weight as its original words, it is appropriate that we contribute some words about them here. There are 27 Amendments, the most recent ratified by the states in 1992. The first ten are collectively known as "The Bill of Rights" and were all ratified about two and one half years after the ratification of the Constitution, in December, 1791. The ideas in The Bill of Rights were refined during the State Conventions held for the Constitution and, as is expressed in the Preamble to the Amendments, intended to further restrict government. As permitted in the original Constitution's Article V, the Bill of Rights added new Articles and changed others. The Bill of Rights was authored by James Madison, who had originally been opposed to it, but then, as a new member of the House of Representatives, he realized the need. This group was about increasing limitations on the Federal government by specific statements. Nine of the Amendments relate to individual rights, and one is about States' rights. It was not until the addition of the 1868 Amendment XIV, that the Bill of Rights was extended to include the States as well as the Federal government.

---

[44] USConstitution.net. http://www.usconstitution.net/index.html

Amendment I, 1791—Freedom of Religion, Speech and Press

This is the best recognized of the Amendments and perhaps the most important, so I will provide some more expansive notes about it.

This amendment prohibits Congress from establishing a religion. Part of the history of humans is that the Ruling Elite have often sought to have the power of deity behind them. To encourage people to have faith and be worship-like to leaders has often been used as a means to quell dissent and to accumulate more power and money from ordinary People. This has been accomplished by: demanding or endorsing a religion (as the King to the Church of England); by being in a very close symbiotic relationship with the religious leadership (in Venice, the leader was called the Doge, and his palace on St. Marks Square abutted the St. Mark's Church); or even positioning to be a God (as Julius Caesar did in Rome).

The Founders sought to separate the nation's government and religious organizations to block this abuse and from endorsing one religion, which would put others at a disadvantage and perhaps limit the freedom of religion. The Founders likely sought fairness, freedom, and tolerance, as we do today.

Amendment I also makes the freedom to speak our minds a Right by prohibiting the government from stopping the speech of any citizen. As in all Rights, it has been modified for a reasonable application. One cannot just speak anything, for example, threatening someone, yelling "Fire" in a theater or libeling another all remain limited here. Freedom of Speech is the freedom to share your opinion with others and to those with whom you differ, as well as they to you. It was provided primarily as a means to openly disagree with those who rule, whom we in the U.S. refer to as our leaders. For most of human history, that has not been possible. Rulers could, and often would, harass or even physically hurt their subjects with torture, maiming, and even death for disagreeing with them. Our Founders have been revered for centuries as being the first to establish that the Right to state opposition to government is guaranteed.

Free press, uncontrolled by the government, is a closely related Right for The People. It allows the media to always seek to find the truth and tell it. Most realize that the press today seems like a tool for one Party or the other. Unfortunately, that seems to be a growing condition. It is important that we discourage such bias, wherever it exists, and that we compare, verify and think about the information we receive.

Ask yourself such questions as: Is the information logical? Who, what or where is the source? Might that source benefit from misleading? Why would a leader, politician or Party do or say such a thing? Such questioning can help us discern and choose sources that are more likely to provide multiple sides to a story and not just the side of the Party they favor. Using more than one source is an even better way to get to the truth. Recently, the Democratic Party seems to be using phrases like "alternate truth" and "my truth." I had a discussion with a left-leaning political cartoonist who had published a cartoon related to the 2010 Arizona illegal immigration law. He characterized the law as an anti-mmigration law and its backers as white men who opposed people of color, which, bluntly, I knew was a lie. I called him, giving him the benefit of the doubt, and asked him his source. He did not name one. I told him that I had attended multiple rallies, read a lot, including the actual bill, and had gone to meetings about it, and it is solely about illegal presence by any person and specifically prohibits racial profiling. I also mentioned that polls showed the majority of the legal Hispanics support it. I suggested that if he does not know the truth, as a cartoon journalist, perhaps that it would be good for all if he sought it out. Stunningly, he said "that is your truth; mine is different." He clearly believes that whatever he thinks is truth; he thinks his political belief to be truth. I pointed out to him that (for roughly 10,000 years of human history) there is only one truth. The definition of truth is "Conformity to fact or actuality," or better, "Reality; actuality."[45]

This experience re-awakened for me discussions I had years ago with a close friend (interestingly at many levels here is that he is a native of a Hispanic country) who offered some interesting thinking. He told me that if I was going to understand the Democratic Party, I would have to think of it as a religion. It is not based on fact, but rather on belief, he told me. The leaders of the Party are kind of worshipped and seem to be believed just because of their position. And so, I suppose, are its journalists and its economists—and maybe its judges.

> "In the modern world, truth is what we seek to reconcile with our beliefs, not avoid *because* of them."

I am proud of the fact that I am a spiritual man, but living life in the earthly world is based on facts and the truths that we have come to know or establish. The world is round, there are 24 hours in a day, the liquid covering most of the planet we have agreed to call "water," all, of course, in different languages. One may believe that the earth is flat and that "water" is "a bus," but neither is true. There is fact, there is truth. In the modern world, truth is what we seek to reconcile with our beliefs, not to avoid *because* of them.

Like most of us, I have a belief about where we came from and where we are going and about how I should live. I believe that someday that belief will be borne out as true. But in the

---

[45] American Heritage Dictionary (2nd College ed.). (1985).

earthly world, aside from our particular religions, whatever is not based on facts is called "opinion" or "theory" but not "truth." To assume otherwise simply stops human communication, and for some, perhaps that is the purpose intended.

I was once told by a person very close to me, during a lively discussion, "I don't need to know the facts, I already know the answer." Perhaps that is the crux of it. People who just automatically believe their opinion to be truth don't have to labor with those pesky facts. They do not have to evaluate the real world or the accurate situation or the other people in it. Whatever these apparently very special people think, is just "right." It must be comforting to have such a grand confidence about your mind. But couldn't it also be considered very arrogant? After all, it dismisses unheard (or un-listened, at least) not only what the opinions of others might be, but what is actually true, as well.

With this approach in mind, it fits that we constantly see interviews where a question is asked but the answer given is not an answer at all. The politician does not even listen to the question usually, and if it is listened to and involves a fact or truth, it becomes unworthy of consideration because the answering politician already just knows *his* "truth," so he (or she) just states that. It seems to happen so thoughtlessly and automatically, with a pre-understanding that such questions originate in some alternate reality that is unrecognized by the politicians and the Ruling Elite; a place called "truth."

The interviewer and the audience would like to know how an opinion or a fact fits in with the politician's position, but they are righteously dismissed. Oh! Now it makes some sense; maybe my friend really did have it right, Party Piety is the problem.

To be accurate and fair, both Parties seem to exhibit such thinking. This accounts for the ability of the best politicians to spontaneously say things that you know are not true, to attack opponents and to not do a thing they say they will and then to blame that on others, including us for misunderstanding! Is it any wonder, then, that government sort of lumbers along, ineptly doing its tasks?

We need to have complete and accurate knowledge in order to make well-informed choices in our personal lives, at work, and in our democracy. Yet we must understand, not only that there are many who cannot deliver truth because they are excused by the Party line from realizing what it is, but also because there are many who do not want us to have the truth, for if we did, we might not be willing to consent to their viewpoint or to make a choice that they benefit from.

To be successful in all areas of our lives we must be truth seekers. Freedom of the press is a key to the freedom of the ordinary Person. We ordinary People must become more discerning and constantly sort through our information sources, removing the ones who deceive. Personally, I believe, all three of the major networks have been compromised.[46] Perhaps those on the major U.S. television networks really don't recognize their monocular vision, since many have been raised, schooled and steeped in the leftist world. It is past time for them to look over their wall. That bias was clear when CBS anchor Dan Rather reported the content of what he likely knew was a fake, damaging letter on evening news, in order to hurt the re-election campaign of a President he opposed. It is a glaring example of the biased reporting of these networks. We can remember when they all led with the Iraqi and Afghan wars every night. That stopped when the Democratic candidate they

---

[46] Vernon, Wes. (2004, December 4). CBS's Goldberg Exposes Leftist Media Bias, Newsmax.com. http://archive.newsmax.com/archives/articles/2001/12/3/215106.shtml

coddled during the election became President. Our nation is still involved years later, but these former critics are all but absent, since their guy is now in charge. The list goes on, but I do not go on with them.

Hundreds of thousands have been leaving these "Legacy Media" behind and have moved on to BBC, Fox and the Internet to get news. You should, too. "Stop the Brainwashing. Think!" If any source is going to not be close to neutral in reporting, but pretends it is, quit it. We should all drop these big three networks for news and consider turning them off for everything else, as well. Go to other sources, and send a message that makes them change to being for The People rather than The Party. I urge every ordinary Person to simply switch off the major networks until their reporting of the news is neutral.

There are other assaults on our Rights that need mentioning. First, I was personally alarmed when former President Bush pushed through the Patriot Act, which diminished our privacy. At least it was considered by Congress and not just by him and his closest "Yes" people. The Administration now has continued that and much worse. Democrat Nancy Pelosi and others have discussed putting in place the "Fairness Doctrine"[47] legislation that will destroy talk radio that opposes them, but not other media which does not. The President, a Democrat who has almost complete support from every union, giving him millions of dollars and pressuring thousands of votes, has mentioned his desire to remove secret balloting for employee votes to bring unions into a company and also counting the votes in a way that regards those who do not vote at all, as a "yes" vote for the union. He wants to change the way voting is done to help assure that those who support him will win and

---

[47] Fletcher, Dan. (2009, February 20). A Brief history of the Fairness Doctrine. http://www.time.com/time/nation/article/0,8599,1880786,00.html

expand their hold over companies. For decades the ordinary People have voted against having the unions in free elections, so what does our President want to do? Surely, we ordinary People think, it must be to represent all of The People and his Constitutional Oath of Article II, Section 2. No, he wants to rig the voting so the unions that support him can more easily win. If these changes are made, unions can win more simply and can intimidate opposition who will be exposed to them. We require secret voting everywhere to avoid voters being threatened or hurt by others! Among our rights is privacy, and this group, who vociferously attacked Bush about Privacy issues in the Patriot Act, has renewed that Act and also wants to eliminate voting privacy in this case! Will other voting situations be next?

However, the most threatening action against Freedom of Speech I have seen in my lifetime occurred in October of 2009. At that time, President Obama's Administration removed the Fox News network, which often is critical of them, from being in the White House News Pool. He/They actually *did* this. Fox was reinstated after the other networks unanimously refused to be in the News Pool unless Fox was also included, which is clearly to their credit. In America, this act by a President is alarming, and, not withstanding any other thing, this act alone makes me very frightened of the people that our structure has currently allowed to rule over us. This will be expanded on later in this book.

Amendment II, 1791—Right to Bear Arms

This Amendment has also been interpreted to have reasonable limits, like yelling "fire" in Amendment I. A citizen cannot have whatever weapon exists. Having a pistol is one thing, but an atomic artillery piece is not permitted. While the Federal government is very limited in action in the absence of a new court case, the States may, and do, regulate. Of course, efforts by those who feared that placing any limits would encourage some to increase those limits, or to functionally emasculate this Right, totally continue today. Despite—or perhaps because of—the fear of the limit-pushers, or of crime, more ordinary citizens are becoming gun owners. And more permits are being issued allowing ordinary citizens to carry a concealed weapon (CCWs), which have proliferated in many States in the past decade.[48] At this time, only two States prohibit CCWs, while 8 may issue them, 37 shall issue them, and 3 have virtually no State mandated restrictions at all. The topic of gun ownership has become more intense in the past fifty years or so as proponents point out the 220-year-old Right and their need for a means of defense. Opponents point out accidental deaths, murder rates, and that other countries have banned their possession. They also make the argument that there is no need for citizens to have weapons. Consider this quote from the co-author of the Constitution, author of its Preamble and creator of the line "We the People," Gouverneur Morris of New York: "Americans need never fear their government because of the advantage of being armed, which the Americans possess over the people of almost every other nation."[49] Opponents do not want the Right for themselves and wish to take it away from everyone. There is a process for that, as we saw in Article V. While there does seem to be a number of Rights that one portion or another of The People wish to take away, there appears to be no momentum to discard this or any Right of the Constitution by a majority.

---

[48] Concealed Carry News. (2010, May 27). http://www.moccw.org/map.html
[49] Gouverneur Morris (n.d.). BrainyQuote.com. Retrieved October 4, 2010. http://www.BrainyQuote.com/quotes/quotes/g/gouverneur197488.html

Amendment III, 1791—Quartering of Soldiers

This was an issue of the Founders during the Revolutionary War, when troops forcefully took over people's homes. It has been a non-issue in modern-day America. This amendment permits it but is allowed to do it only according to law.

Amendment IV, 1791—Search and Seizure

This establishes our right to control ourselves and our property, essentially to be left alone, unless there is "probable cause" to violate our sanctity, which normally requires a judge to decide based on the situation and, in agreement, to issue a warrant that instructs law enforcement officials as to specifically what they can do. Not only is this what you have seen on "cop" shows for years, but it is a wonderful right to limit the government interference by whim in our lives, something that the Founders experienced themselves and wanted to protect ordinary People from in their new country.

Amendment V, 1791—Trial and Punishment and Compensation for Taking

This is the "double jeopardy" restriction that assures Americans that they cannot be subjected to more than one trial for the same offense. It is also the famous "Plead the Fifth" amendment that protects defendants from having to testify against themselves. It also protects citizens from suffering losses by the government without "due process." That legal concept is not defined here and is mentioned in Amendment XIV, as well. "Due process" is about how laws are enforced, procedurally—meaning fairly, understandably, and that laws apply to all entities in the U.S.; i.e., citizen, alien, or corporation, alike. It also is about substance, such as why those laws are made; for example, taxes and property can only be taken for legitimate public purposes, and abortion is regulated for the health of the mother.

Amendment VI, 1791—Right to a Speedy Trial and to Confront Accusers

This sets the trial location as normally being held in the State or district where the crime occurred. It also defines the process of a trial, allows us to confront witnesses against us, and permits us to assemble witnesses for us, while assuring an unbiased jury and the use of a lawyer in our defense.

While we sometimes complain about the long trial process of accused people, it is evident that it is because of these Rights about trial that our Founders insisted upon; their idea was to judge people fairly and honestly and to be as correct as possible. These are Rights we all share.

Amendment VII, 1791—Civil case Trial by Jury, 1791

This amendment allows trial by jury in non-criminal cases.

Amendment, VIII, 1791—Cruel and Unusual Punishment

This limits bail (the ability to put up money so that you can leave jail during the wait for the trail to occur). It also establishes that fines and punishment must be reasonable compared to existing law and subject to review. In practice, accused who are deemed to be likely to flee or create more harm have higher bail set or are denied it completely, although it is considered by a judge.

Amendment IX, 1791—Constitution Construction

The list of The People's Rights listed in the Constitution is clarified here to indicate that there are others that are not listed.

Amendment X, 1791—Powers of the States and the People

This is known as the "States' Rights Amendment." The boundary line of power has always been a major issue in our combination of States under a single Federal government. This Amendment says that any power not specifically granted in this Document to the Federal government remains the power of the States and, if not assigned there, then it remains with The People.

The ten Amendments above comprise the Bill of Rights, all passed together in 1791. They were actually planned as a group of clarifications to the Constitution during the process of its writing. However, including them in the Articles of the original document might have delayed or derailed its passage. After passage and ratification of the Bill of Rights, there were seventeen more Amendments ratified over the next 199 years, the most recent passed in 1992. There were others that failed, but our focus is on what is, not what might have been.

Amendment XI, 1795—Judicial Limits

As mentioned above under Article III, this Amendment changed that Article.

Some Amendments added mostly new words about rules and Rights, while others added to or modified existing parts—like this one. This keeps the Federal courts from being involved in cases where citizens are bringing suit against a State not their own, and it has since been construed to include bringing their State of residence to the Federal court.

Amendment XII, 1804—Choosing the President and Vice President

This Amendment modified Article II, Section 1, providing additional details about the Electoral Process. Electors today are considered pledged to the candidates of their Party, but the Constitution states nothing about this. Some States do, and these require Electors to vote as pledged. Most have a "winner take all" policy under which the candidate receiving most of the popular vote gets all of the Electoral votes of that State.

Amendment XIII, 1865—Abolishment of Slavery

The XIII, XIV and XV Amendments are known collectively as the "Civil War" or "Reconstruction Era" Amendments. They were all adopted just after the Civil War to restructure the U.S. to mirror the resolution the war had brought. Amendment XIII to Article IV, superceding Section 2, was the official abolishment of slavery and involuntary servitude put in place after the Civil War. This was a follow on to Lincoln's Emancipation Proclamation and an increased interest in ending slavery with words in the Constitution. The words allow for incarceration of convicted criminals, but make it clear that slavery was over in the United States of America. The existence of these few words reflect many years of struggle and more than six hundred thousand American fatalities from the Civil War. They also reflect the victory of the intention of the Founding Documents and the duty of all Americans to treat all humans fairly and fellow Americans equally.[50]

---

[50] Rosenzweig, R. (2002, September, 20). POW Camp Atrocities Led to Treason Trial. *Los Angeles Times*. http://articles.latimes.com.2002/sep/20/local/me-onthelaw20

Amendment XIV, 1868—Citizenship, Equal Protection, and Due Process

Modified by Amendment XXVI

Section 1 of this Amendment is one of the more controversial. It was passed to make certain that the Republican led end to slavery was completely accomplished. The Democrat controlled states of the South had continued to resist equally treating Blacks after the end of the Civil War. This Amendment granted automatic equal citizenship to all former slaves in every State. It defines that a person is a citizen that is born in the nation or is naturalized. The notion of birth establishing citizenship was questioned and then clarified by the amendment's author, Jacob Howard, (R) Senator from Michigan, 1862–1871. Along with other key supporting Senators, this "citizenship clause" intended to exclude American Indians with tribal ties and "persons born in the United States who were foreigners, aliens who belong to families of ambassadors or foreign ministers." In U.S., v. Wong Kim Ark (1898) the Supreme Court decided that it did apply to citizens of China with a permanent domicile and residence. Other cases in 1982 and 1985 decided it applied to all foreign nationals.

Along with establishing what a citizen is, this Section specifically adds words that a person is both a citizen of the United States and of the "State wherein they reside," making a citizen responsible to the national laws as well as those of their particular location. In its "due process clause," it prohibits these local laws from impinging upon the Federal law or upon the individual person's Right to Life, Liberty or Property without following correct legal process. This clause has been used over time to strike down maximum work hours. It has allowed intervention in a strike and to allow Federal narcotics regulation. It is the basis of judges needing to recuse to assure a fair trial. It is the source of protection of our privacy and the need for a public hearing to terminate government employees.

This Section completes with the "equal protection clause." Another one of the groups of Constitutional words of frequent focus, it mandates that no State can "deny to any person within its jurisdiction the equal protection of the laws." There are only thirteen words in the clause and it seems very clear to many, but as has been seen above, the courts and attorneys may add more than what appears. It seems to say that the States must apply all laws equally to all people. This would also seem to actualize the Declaration's claim "that all men are created equal" (paragraph 2, line 1). Interestingly, this word group 100 years later began to be interpreted in the Courts *as if* it included the words "unless there is some substantial reason that some persons should be treated differently." And that seems exactly what many laws of the South that favored White people had been doing and what this Amendment was meant to stop. We examine the magnitude of this issue in detail elsewhere in this book.

In Section 2, Amendment XIV also penalized any State for denying the right to vote to any adult male reaching age twenty-one who are not rebels or other criminals, excluding Indians who are not taxed; it reduces representation by the same proportion of the State population whose voting rights were denied.

Section 3 disallows former members of Congress who took the Confederate States' side about the Civil War from holding office in Congress or the State legislatures, but allows Congress to overturn this provision by a two-thirds majority vote in both Houses.

Amendment XV, 1870—Vote Regardless of Color

This Amendment was aimed once again at the Southern States and modifying the outcome to reflect the results of the Civil War. It would be interesting to imagine the number and content of the amendments that would have been required if the South had conquered the North, and to speculate about the resulting differences in America and the world. This Amendment declared that the Right to vote is granted to all men regardless of race, color, or former servitude. It would be another fifty years before women would gain the Right to vote in the Constitution.

Amendment XVI, 1913—Income Tax

As the Federal government began to grow, it needed more money and had been struggling to find sources. This Amendment permitted them to begin taxing income, which had been considered a direct tax and off limits prior to this time. The first rates were the same for all, beginning at 1% of the first $20,000 and ranging up to 7% on all above $500,000.[51]

Amendment XVII, 1913—Direct
Election of Senators

Originally, Article I established that Senators were elected by the State legislatures. This Amendment changed that to direct election by the voters in each State. It was designed to match the timing of the election of members of the House of Representatives, and was considered to be more democratic by bringing the vote closer to The People.

Amendment XVIII, 1919—Prohibition

This Amendment resulted from the work of the Anti Saloon League, primarily a group of women who opposed the gambling and prostitution that accompanied the expansion of

---

[51] Top US Marginal Income Tax Rates, 1913–2003 (2010, July, 28). Truth and Politics.org. http://www.truthandpolitics.org/top-rates.php

bars after the end of World War I. Working from Westerville, Ohio, this group set up a publishing house and went to work. They endorsed their own candidates, and ultimately this effort prohibited alcohol product consumption, manufacture and transportation. This was an impressive grassroots effort and is still honored today in a museum at their original site on Main Street in Westerville.

Amendment XIX, 1920—Women's Suffrage

Women had never had the ability to vote in a national election, as was underscored in Section 2 of the 14th Amendment, which penalized any State that would deny the vote to any man, and in the 15th Amendment, regardless of color. Most of the history of the world had excluded women from such participation and some still do today. By 1918, most of the States had begun permitting women at least some ability to vote, and this Amendment made it official throughout the nation. This accomplishment had been assisted by the support of women in World War I and by the success of the effort in passing Amendment XVIII.

Amendment XX, 1933—Lame Duck and Succession

The period between the time of an election in which an incumbent official loses and the date on which he/she actually leaves elected office is termed a "lame duck" period. It is often a time for very political or partisan activity by those that are leaving, because any accountability to the voters is missing.

People of low principles seem to be at their worst when they have a position of access or power and little possibility for recourse from others. It is for this reason that companies who fire someone often escort them to the door for departure immediately.

This Amendment sought to shorten that lame duck time period from over a year to two and a half months, responding to better and faster communication and transportation technology than was available to the authors of the original Constitution. It also clarified succession for President-Elect and/or Vice President-Elects about to take office.

Amendment XXI, 1933—Repeal of Prohibition

Prohibition was very unpopular in many States, as it was seen as an intrusion on personal rights by the Federal government and moralists. The momentum for repeal came with the Depression and with the realization of the rampant illegal activity that thwarted the intent of Amendment XVIII.

Amendment XXII, 1951—Presidential Term Limits

The tradition begun by President George Washington had been a maximum of two terms for the office of President. That stood for 164 years until the Democratic Party decided they wanted to run Franklin Delano Roosevelt for a third term in 1940. They knew the desire for consistency would be popular as the Second World War was unfolding, and they were correct. There was no law against it, so they ran him and he won. With the same idea in 1944, he ran and won a fourth term but died a few months into it, and Vice President Harry S. Truman took over as President. During the Truman Administration, a drive began to set a two term limit by this Amendment, which was ratified in 1951.

Amendment XXIII, 1961—Electors for Washington, D.C.

The District of Columbia, the seat of the Federal government, was provided voting rights for Electors by this Amendment. The District was not intended to be a large population center, but it had grown to be one. It was granted the same number of electoral votes as the least populous State and thus has the ability to increase its power at every census.

Amendment XXIV, 1964—Right of all Adult Citizens to Vote

A strategy of the Southern States to minimize the Black vote was to issue a poll tax, requiring a payment to vote. Even into the 1960s, five states retained this requirement. Although usually the same dollar amount was required from all, it "de facto" reduced the number Black voters, who were mostly among the poorest citizens. This Amendment established the Right of every qualified citizen to cast a vote for Federal offices regardless of the non-payment of any tax.

Amendment XXV, 1967—Disability or Death of the President

If the President is declared to be unable to fulfill his duties, the Vice President will take that position until the President declares by document that he is able and receives no dis-agreement from the Vice President or others in the Executive branch within four days. In the case of disagreement, the Congress will decide the matter by a two-thirds vote in each House. This Amendment also states that if there is a Vice Presidential vacancy, the President shall nominate a candidate and the Congress will vote on it with only a simple majority in both Houses required for the motion to pass. The concern for more detail arose because of the assassination of John F. Kennedy in 1963 and the realization that he may have survived because of new medical technology—but would likely have been incapacitated.

Amendment XXVI, 1971—Voting Age Eighteen

The age for voting in national and state elections was lowered from age 21 to 18 years of age by this Amendment.

There was a great deal of activism around the voting age issue at that time. The fact that many under the age of 21 were being drafted into military service in Viet Nam but could not vote was a primary driver.

Amendment XXVII, 1992—Varying of Congressional Salaries

This simple Amendment, requiring an intervening election before a pay change for Senators and Representatives, stands as the most recent Amendment. It also took the longest to pass. It had been originally part of the Bill of Rights in 1789. Having no expiration date attached, it took 74,003 days to be ratified by three-quarters of the States.

*　*　*

Timelessness of the Founding Documents

After this review, it seems valuable to repeat that there are those who point out that these documents are now well over 200 years old and should not be vigorously adhered to, since people, culture and technology have all changed so much. That is a point that is occasionally brought up, even by some government officials who are sworn to uphold and defend the Constitution, so let us consider this assertion.

It is obvious from the previous pages that the Declaration of Independence is a written Document based on the timeless nature of all human existence. While it specifically addresses the wrong treatment of the American Colonists in the mid-1700s at the hands of King George III, it frames those wrongs not within the period in which these wrongs were committed, but rather against the permanent condition of humankind.

The Founders purposefully broadened the scope of their complaint to not be about just themselves and the King, but instead they made it a complaint about all ordinary People and those who ruled them. Instead of framing it as a smaller issue about the times in which they were confronted, they enlarged it and complained that the core issue they faced had always existed and seemed eternal.

They compared the King's collected record of wrongful acts to the abuse by a Tyrant of free men. They compared his actions to an attack on the basic rights owned by all ordinary humans of all times. They claimed that the issue they had with the King was similar to the issue of governance that had always existed for ordinary People; The Founders sought not only to have that issue recognized before the world, but they also proposed a remedy applicable to all people and for all time.

Similarly, the Constitution of the United States appears to be written without a time boundary and as a document applicable to all people, notwithstanding that it was not then possible to treat slaves and women as full citizens and have the original document be accepted. And that speaks to its flexibility. It established the principle of applying to all people and allowed, through its amendment process, the potential to be modified so as to achieve those principles, and indeed, it was subsequently modified—twenty-seven times to date.

The Thirteenth, Fourteenth, Fifteenth and Nineteenth Amendments to the Constitution gave all rights to all citizens, regardless of race or gender. Today, there is no one alive who has known it to be any other way in their adult life. The Founders wrote to overcome the timeless issues of people and governance but allowed amendments to deal with issues beyond their ability to accommodate at that time. And the process they included has been used in passing the amendments that have kept the Constitution applicable to today's world.

The Constitution is based on the unchanging nature of people of all backgrounds, on the permanent condition of State unity, on declared permanent Values, on expressly written power distributions, and it has a proven amendment process. It has allowed for the peaceful change of government dozens of times. It has been the engine that propelled this nation to the forefront of history. It arguably has created the greatest force for good the world has ever known. It has been copied as a base for national governments around the world. Millions of foreigners have sought—and still seek—to live their lives under its words of protection.

But today ordinary people do not feel safe nor happy. Our property is being transferred to others, our values questioned and ignored, and our future prosperity is promised away. The mechanism that assures our Rights is broken; Parties use our government to assure their power, not our Rights.

*　*　*

Political Parties and the Constitution

Now you have had the opportunity to go through the Founding Documents. You possess a copy of the Declaration, the Constitution, and the Bill of Rights and other Amendments.

The astonishing thing that you may have noticed is not something that you have read; it is something that you did not read. It is important to notice, so I will point it out; there is *nothing* in these Documents of Democracy about political Parties. There is not a single reference, not one word. From what you now know of these Documents as the determining guides and instruction set for our nation, you would likely agree that if the Founders had thought they would be critical to our success or perhaps just be somewhat good for us, they would have at least mentioned them, perhaps even developed a framework for us to follow. But they did not.

However, the Founders did leave some words about political Parties outside of the Founding Documents. George Washington, the first President of the United States took office on April 30, 1789. He became the first leader under the new Constitution approved in June of 1788, when New Hampshire became the ninth state to ratify it. (There actually had already been sixteen "Presidents of Congress" under the organizing Articles of Confederation of 1781 that had preceded the Constitution.)

Washington served two terms, declining a third. At his Farewell Address in 1796, George Washington, leader of the American Revolution's soldiers, Founder, first and long-time President did not just say "goodbye." He delivered carefully thought out observations and left his deep knowledge with us in his words of that occasion.[52] Washington said he wished:

". . . the free Constitution, which is the work of your hands, may be sacredly maintained; that its administration in every department may be stamped with wisdom and virtue; that, in fine, the happiness of the people of these States, under the auspices of liberty, may be made complete by . . . use of this blessing . . . to the applause, the affection and adoption of every nation which is yet a stranger to it."

Washington is clear that the Constitution is to be held as "sacred," a thing of a diety, and as a "blessing" available to other nations. I know this flies in the very face of those who

---

[52] Washington's Farewell Address 1796. (2010, July 28). The Avalon Project, Yale Law School. http://avalon.law.yale.edu/18th_century/washing.asp

would have you believe that the notion of America is devoid of the Creator, but here is more proof. And he hopes here for the "blessing" to be received by other nations as well.

He then says that he wants to offer his well reflected thoughts for "frequent review" because they are "all important to your felicity as a people." He says that to keep America strong, the bonds of unity are a key. Many times he mentions striving for prosperity for the peoples. He reminds us that "The basis of our political systems is the right of the people to make and alter their constitutions of government."

Washington also Warns Us to Avoid Political Parties:
He warns several times that *we should specifically avoid political Parties,* saying, "I have intimated to you the danger of parties in the State, with particular reference to the founding of them on geographical discriminations. Let me now warn you in the most solemn manner against the baneful effects of the spirit of party generally. The spirit is part of human nature . . . it exists in all governments generally . . . and is truly their worst enemy."

At another moment he warns us that "the common and continual mischiefs of the spirit of the party are sufficient to make it in the interest and duty of a wise people to discourage and restrain it."

Elsewhere, he says, ". . . it serves to distract the public. . . . It agitates the community with ill founded jealousies and false alarms, kindles animosity. It opens the door to foreign influence and corruption."

Yet another admonishment: ". . . it is a spirit not to be encouraged."

And finally, "A fire not to be quenched, it demands a uniform vigilance to prevent it from bursting into flame, lest, it should consume."

The "spirit of party" that George Washington referred to as "part of human nature" and government's "worst enemy" is the innate drive of some people to control others. That powerful need has caused the organization and rise of the political Parties in response to democracy, just as it caused the rise of controlling royalty, emperors and dictators of history; Parties are the current expression of the desire of the few to control the many.

The Parties were not part of the self governance plan prepared by our Founders. George Washington detested them and warned against their negative influence on our Liberty and welfare. We can see the disunity that they cause, and we are experiencing how far away from the traditions and intent of America one dominating Party can take us. They are highly controlling *consumers* of Liberty and have wedged themselves between us and our government. It is our need, and it is our duty, to correct that.

> "Parties are the current expression of the desire of the few to control the many."

Constitutional Critics of the Party Kind

Today we have the Party to which we have entrusted our nation criticizing our Constitution and seeming to ignore it. They claim that people and culture and technology are different now.

What, then, supports their criticism? What system has a similar record of success? Where can you point that demonstrates that ordinary People have ever fared better? Under what system have they been more prosperous or more secure?

If there is a better system, then you critics must prove it to the owners of these Documents, and of this nation. Show us and we will decide. But we will not follow you beyond the rules before us. You are free to criticize and present your case.

But you are not free to mislead, to misinform, to go beyond the powers that it limits, to choose which laws to enforce on whom, to stack our courts and honored positions with the fraudulent lapdogs of Ruling Elites, and to lead us back to the shackles of old that you claim is a new freedom.

We have the Documents. We have read them and read about them. We know they are the truth. The Constitution is permanent. We can see that Parties are not part of our structure. We can see that perhaps it is the *Parties* that "we should not adhere to, since the people and culture and technology have all changed so much."

Other than the stilted, more formal manner of writing, I just do not agree with American political Party critics that our Founding Documents are antiquated and not easily understood. And because they mean so much to us ordinary People, I am suspicious of those who would seek to ignore them. On what basis can it be earnestly said that our Founding Documents are out of step with the present? Has the nature of humans changed? Should the States not have unity? Is the ability to amend wrong? Is the distribution of power wrong? Wait. Perhaps we are on to something there.

To those that seem to want more power for their Party and less for The People, these Documents would be a problem, because The People are not likely going to want to give that up, and trying to amend the Constitution just might have the reverse effect: The People might just question the motive of those promoting such a "change."

Now, don't just close your mind to the point I am going to make because of conditioning that you have experienced. I am reminding us of history as a nonpartisan individual.

The history of the German democracy comes to mind. Adolf Hitler wanted to change the constitution there, too, but there would be opposition, so "for the good of the people" he ignored their constitution and stacked the courts so that judges changed the basis of law; his judges were directed no longer to base judgment upon the traditions, the principles of law, or the constitution of their country—or even common sense—but rather on what his *Party* thought was best for the people. "The abuse of law has been the trademark of world tyranny."[53] Read it for yourself in excellent detail in the 848 pages of University of Exeter Professor Richard Overy's book.

That's correct and well documented. The National Socialist German Worker's Party (Hitler's Nazi Party) said that they just *knew* what was best for the German people, and it was not old laws and old documents, and certainly not any religious based ideas of right and wrong. Hitler and his Party were "just," he said, and therefore, any thought or laws they made up were "just," as well. And the results? They are history. Liberty was lost, and they made scapegoats out of non-supporting people, especially the prosperous and Jews. Without the rule of law, the Party was able to steal from opposition as well as the nation. The government apparatus became the tool they used to plunder the country's wealth for their own use "in the name of the people." Millions of their countrymen were at first ridiculed, then destroyed for opposing their Party. And then they used the confiscated wealth and power to build weapons and attack other countries to get more wealth and power from them.

I am not accusing anyone of being a Nazi; that would be absolutely wrong. But to ignore any part of history is stupid. I am saying something far larger than any narrow, worn-out

---

[53] Overy, R. (2004). *The Dictators, Hitler's Germany, Stalin's Russia.* Saybrook, CT: Konecky & Konecky.
or W.W. Norton & Company Ltd.

attack such as that. I am saying that taking freedom from ordinary People and funneling it into control by a few is the oldest repeating occurrence in world history and Hitler's Germany is an example. I am saying that those who seek to reduce the ability of ordinary People to make choices in controlling their own lives and their own property must be the suspected enemies of those People; no matter what clothes they wear, what language they speak or what flag they wrap themselves in.

Perhaps even more suspect if they are countrymen.

PowerShifting: Moving Power from Parties to People

Before you are introduced to the following proposals, you need to understand that is exactly what they are: proposals, a place to start.

I do not claim to have all the answers, but what follows seems a common sense direction to consider. With more input coming from others, these ideas can, I am certain, be improved and modified to maximize the possibilities. Let your thoughts be known at our website, NonPartisanAmericans.com.

In order to throw off any Party's ability to continue to take the power and money of ordinary citizens at will and to selfishly distort the meaning of our Constitution as a means of reaching their partisan goals, we are proposing to proceed in a manner similar to that of our Founding Fathers in breaking free of the Ruling Elite they faced; the royalty of King George III.

Here is a five phase strategy consisting of:

1. **Realization (Read it and Weep, Together)**

2. Consolidation (Togetherness to Win)

3. Declaring the Problem (Keep Your Tyranny, We'll Take Tea)

4. Proposing a Remedy (Get in the Huddle)

5. Executing Plans (Kick Their Butts over the Curb)

Realization

We have read through many words to gain an understanding of just where we ordinary People stand today in the United States of America.

To sum up, we remain financially better off than most of the ordinary People in history and also in the world today. But we know that we are back-pedaling in the very freedoms that have allowed us that prosperity: the right to control our person; and the right to control our property. Let's review the issues involved.

Recent government actions make it clear that the Parties are "two sides of the same coin" and act almost always in their own interests: The Bush Republican leadership overspent and the following Democrats have quadrupled the spending despite great outcry from the People.The previous administration of Republicans helped somewhat to bring the mortgage meltdown upon us, they put in place the Patriot Act, which removed privacy protection that had been in place for more than two centuries, and they sent our children off to drawn out wars costing us lives and many billions of our property.

Before the 2008 election, the current Democratic Party administration promised to stop the wars and to end the Patriot Act. But after the election, that act was then extended and the wars were expanded. Although they have denied involvement, documents, video and audio make it appear that Democrats were more responsible for the mortgage meltdown than their opposition or the corporate greed they blame. The Republicans had the presidency and its "Bully Pulpit" at that time, but did not stop the Democrats from directing Fannie Mae and Freddie Mac to buy even more bad loans that were sub-standard. Like the Democrats, when they controlled the housing loan agencies they, too, encouraged the granting of home loans to people who could not afford them. Although at a *much* smaller scale than the Party of the Democrats, they seemed to want these loans especially made to minority groups so as to garner more votes and support for their Party.

Even if these Parties were mostly motivated by good intentions to help poorer people rather than to reward those who support their Parties (which is doubtful), how could they just ignore long-known economic realities that even school children learn? Didn't we all learn as kids that you just don't loan your bike to someone you don't know well? Didn't we know, even as kids, not to trust our allowance to the cousin who had never paid anyone back? Surely, common sense alone would tell adults that loaning money to people based on the color of their skin and not on their ability to pay it back is nonsense. Certainly they knew that our laws and our Constitution prohibit discrimination against the other people who were not provided such favor as a result of the government's racial profiling against them. But both Parties did it anyway, and they did it to benefit their Parties.

They abused The People's rights, they misused The People's trust, they put The People's financial well being in jeopardy and they even used The People's money to do it.

The Parties may argue that what they did was only part of the problem, but they should never have been any part of the problem, but rather they should have stopped it from ever happening. They gave away our retirement money, our jobs, and our happiness to people who earned little and perhaps, in many cases, were not even American citizens. They have lied about it, blaming everyone but themselves.

The uncomfortable truth is, that essentially, they put out a sign on the front lawn of our Treasury that read "Free Money for Those Who Will Support Us." And without any limit under the Democrats, it is no surprise that so many came to get it. Ultimately, almost half of the total loans at our key institutions became sub-standard "bad" loans. They were weak, and when they crumbled we all got pulled down.

The Democrats seem intent on expanding their Party's control by transferring the wealth of the country from the responsible and industrious, the educated, the risk taking and the hardworking people who earned it. They want to provide these rewards to those who have not earned it and who happen to be their supporters. Apparently, these are their actions to "fundamentally transform America," as President Obama announced five days before his inauguration.[54] This is a transformation that will pay off the ignorant and the less capable with other people's money, and commit them to vote for "the hand that feeds them." It will encourage prideful thoughts about their specialness and hateful thoughts about the "wealthy" taxpayers who actually support them. This is the norm for transformation to a more Socialist society. History clearly shows that Socialism does not work to bring everybody to a higher level, but rather it brings everybody down to a lower level, excepting the few in control.

The "better for all" idea is the utopian myth that is used by the Ruling Elite to sell the "makers" and "takers" on the plan, as if it is a near-religious calling. The middle class largely

---

[54] Obama, B. (2008, October 30). YouTube.com. http://www.youtube.com/watch?v=_cqN4NIEtOY

disappears and only the Ruling Elite who are in control do well. This big picture is uncomfortable to confront, and we would all rather turn away, but we need to discuss openly what they are doing. We cannot hope to correct any situation if we will not be clear about what the situation is. If the Democrats' goal for our nation is to greatly expand rewarding the less capable and the least productive, and to reduce or eliminate rewards for the more capable and more productive, it is reasonable to expect that our nation as a whole will, over time, become that which it has rewarded; *a less capable and less productive nation.* It seems likely that the transformed "Left" America will be a nation left behind.

> "...the transformed "Left" America will be a nation left behind."

The Democratic leaders also have plans for "amnesty" for millions, perhaps as many as twenty million (which is twenty thousand thousands) illegal aliens, plans for new, heavier taxes, for raising the prices of necessities in our lives, and for sharply reducing the opportunities and prosperity of our nation. It is hard to know the numbers of illegals present, because neither Party wants us to know, but this, as we will certainly see, is far in excess of the 12 million figure that they use. Even that is a *huge* number. There are just over 100 million Mexican citizens. With 10 to 20 million here, that means that between 10% and 20% of all Mexican citizens actually live illegally in the United States. Such a condition is unmatched in history, and for good reason. It means that the nation being occupied is being cheated and taken advantage of. It means that America has no national loyalty from many millions in residence and should be in fear of America's continuance as a nation.

And what would be the reasons that someone or a group would attempt to do these things? It could be due to belief in the philosophy similar to that of Marx, or it could be the arrogant elitist drive for control in which one believes that they "just know the best way." Establishing either of these as the guiding philosophy of a nation would likely make the outlook for that nation bleak.

Establishing the theories of Marx [55] has been attempted in the past and has failed miserably. Millions under Stalin's effort at "International Socialism" were led into squalor, and more millions died. Surely, the messianic "National Socialism" ideology in Germany demonstrates the need to avoid that approach to Socialism. There, too, millions of people's lives were reduced to squalid conditions, and more millions died. *History* is the world's greatest teacher, *not* its current leaders. Study the past; for *history does not lie, and politicians seldom tell the truth.*

In any event, we should understand that such change is not without limits. Surely, however far left the Party currently in power in D.C. wants to take the country, they would not want to intentionally destroy it, would they? We want to assume not, but the ideologues of other nations in the past have done so.

The past has taught the world that overburdening the means of production with taxes and regulation while lowering the potential rewards from risk will reduce the creation of wealth. That reduces the potential to produce new jobs and additional prosperity. The past also shows that discrimination for or against any group by the government causes harm to national unity and worse. That is why this nation has rules against it. But these rules are frequently ignored by the Parties so that they can use our Treasury to "buy off" segments of Americans to get or keep control over us; this

---

[55] Kreis, S. (2008, January 30). Lectures on Modern European history, Karl Marx, 1818–1883. HistoryGuide.org. http://www.historyguide.org/intellect/marx.html

costs us our money and our unity. Overall, we know the internal destruction of nations has happened and its causes are devout ideology, ignoring constitutions, and demonstrating stunning arrogance in the face of reality. This is not to say America will fail, but we should be concerned that our leadership has been faulty for awhile.

The Democratic Party Leadership knows history, and they are not stupid. However, their level of arrogance and selfishness may be their most dominant influence, to the detriment of us all. Think of the teen driver in a hurry who just "knows" he can make the light but ends up killing everyone in the car. That teen's unbridled confidence, mixed with ignorance of the actual circumstances, is disastrous.

No, these individuals leading the Democrats are not stupid, but they may be blinded to reality by the religion they call their Party. And worse, they just do not seem to listen or to care about those who are not one of them. The silent comment that those in power have been making to us ordinary People consists of two very familiar—but here unspoken—exclamatory street words. These are the same two words *often* used by those who take advantage, who attack, and who offend with arrogant disregard. They are likely similar to the words used by King George when he was levying the tea tax in Boston, and heard from the pilots as they attacked Pearl Harbor. You know these two words. You know them, and they need no printing here. We ordinary Americans know what they are, and we see it in the amazing insolence of Party-backed government officials today. Fellow ordinary Americans, we are the sheep in a pen with feces up to our necks. *If you are ready to take a deep breath, bleat back defiant words to them, and then act to end their control, please read on.*

Again, the political Parties are like political gangs; they are like the Crips and Bloods but with less integrity. They operate with the intention of controlling the ordinary People to achieve their own goals. They seek to avoid any accountability to their constituents. They make no plans against which a comparison is possible.

In the town hall meetings on healthcare and in public statements during the summer of 2009, it was evident that the current administration is no different, in a positive way, than those of the past. Anecdotally, many believe that today's Democratic Party leadership is the most aggressively anti-historical America group they have seen in their lifetimes.

When many of these alarmed people are among our more senior citizens, that speaks volumes; these people have seen more than most of us, and have a broader perspective. Many who fought in World War II and others who immigrated here lived through the real and cold wars against Communists and are particularly alarmed; they know what they are seeing and are not blinded by broad smiles and new names for the same old thing. It is incredibly uncomfortable to hear concern that the very thing many risked their lives to save the nation from is now in the corridors of our capitol in Washington. I have heard one former Marine who served at Iwo Jima say that this situation makes him "happy to be near death." Happy to be near death! These are our elders—who worked, defended, and ran this nation before! Happy to be near death because of those in control of our government today? Think of this. This is America! It just seems impossible, but it is *real*.

Even if ignoring this end of the spectrum of concern over the current Democratic Party leadership, it is evident that they consider themselves Elite controllers rather than public servants. During the 2009 town hall meetings to sell their healthcare plan, ranking Democrat Representative Barney Frank of Massachusetts publicly told a constituent that conversing with her was like "speaking to a dining room table."[56] Nancy Pelosi of California, the Speaker of the House, called opponents speaking out against her Party's healthcare proposals "un-American" and "an angry mob." She also claimed to misunderstand the presence of some signs bearing swastikas as some sort of opposition banner rather than the indictment of her own Party's behavior that it was intended to be. In the end, they did not convince The People, but the Democratic Congress passed it anyway, forcing through the largest, most expensive legislation in history, even though a large majority of the ordinary People who were to be forced to pay for most of it clearly objected to it. They "just know the best way" and The People are stupid.

Even the American President has shown open disdain for the ordinary taxpayers, usually in the "fly-over states." He ridiculed the ordinary People for "clinging to their guns and religion," a revealing remark about his disregard for the fear and faith of his countrymen.[57] A remark like this has no place on a democratic leader's lips but could easily be expected to come from any dictator in history.

In the days after the 2009 April 15 anti-tax demonstrations, the President said that he "didn't know anything about them." Really? I doubt the truth of that remark, as would any ordinary person who thinks about it. Everyone knows that there are intelligence agents around the world constantly detailing what is going on for his specific use. If they managed to miss presenting the 2010 American April 15th protests in the daily security briefings, we have even bigger problems.

---

[56] Franks, B. (2009, August 18). YouTube.com. http://www.youtube.watch?v=nYIZiWK2Iy8

[57] Pilkington, F. (2008). Obama Angers Midwest Voters with Guns and Religion Remark. New York. The Guardian. http://.www.guardian.co.uk/world/2008/ april/14/barackobama.uselections2008

We are stuck for now with yet another misleading leader, a *"Misleader,"* for our nation. His Party generally derided the April 15 and 9/12 citizen protests, and many used sexual innuendo in their derision of the Tea Party people.[58] The legacy media, which consistently supports the Democrats, misreported what little they did report. We all know that one can judge others by what they do and say as well as what they don't do and say. Perhaps the media should be judged similarly and considered by the derided as a propaganda tool to be neither watched nor subscribed to. The legacy media is lost; they are simply a bullhorn for one of the Parties. It is time to unsubscribe, to turn them off, and to permanently set them aside as you must an old acquaintance who you realize has lied and misled you for someone they like better; much better.

Most of the American media seems tantamount to the press agency of the Democratic Party. As is not only clear through observation, this is well established by reports and covered in books like that of former CBS reporter Bernard Goldberg.[59] Actions like the Sarah Palin candidate interviews by NBC's Charlie Gibson and CBS's Katie Couric in the 2008 election cycle provide more evidence. If you are a Democratic Party supporter, perhaps these things make you pleased. If you are only a supporter and not a zealot, you may realize that a non-aligned press and media are vital to democracy. Imagine your outrage if the press was as partisan as it is but in the *Republican camp*. That may help you to get the idea that it is wrong.

---

[58] Poor, J. (2009, April 4). MSNBC: The Place for Low-Brow Teabag Humor, Business & Media Institute.org. http://businessandmedia.org/articles/2009/20090414140746.aspx

[59] Goldberg, B. (2002). *Bias, A CBS Insider Exposes How the Media Distorts the News*. Regenery Press: Washington, D.C.

Sustainable democracy requires a media that seeks to disseminate truth for a citizenry, not a viewpoint for a Party. In their desire to trust the democratic process, The People depend upon the media to be a sentinel for *all* their interests. This is even more important today, as Americans are increasingly defining themselves as non-aligned with a Party. As nonpartisans, they will be more inclined to base their votes on fact rather than blind Party loyalty. While more voters will be seeking information upon which to cast votes, our press will be only able to deliver a Party point of view, similar to all press in history and in the world today that is controlled by a Ruling Elite.

Realistically, we have two Parties that act similarly but seek different groups of support. On one side, we have the group that generally believes in Freedom from government domination, Liberty with control over self and personal property, both equal opportunity and equal treatment under the law for everyone, and personal responsibility. Generally, and there are certainly exceptions and overlaps, these are the business people, the professionals, and the self motivated who trust in historical fact, recognize the validity of the Founding Documents and who mostly drive the making of wealth in our economy.

This group is being confronted by those who believe in using the government to dominate and take from others on their behalf, using a range of excuses. They are a combination mostly of government workers, unions, special interests and the "Victim Class" that denies history, questions the validity of the Founding Documents, and mostly represents the taking of wealth from our economy. This situation is reflective of author Ayn Rand's Objectivism contention that essentially there are only two types of humans: Takers and Makers. The middle of America, that former uninvolved "silent majority" is going to have to decide which side they are on, for a battle that will long define America is now underway. The opposition to the "Makers" is formidable. It includes the major legacy media which pretend not to be aligned to the Party of the "Takers." It has powerful representatives that openly disdain The People and a President who, at best, ignores the desires of the producing citizenry and, at worst, derides them.

In our current situation, there are Democratic Party efforts to have government take over healthcare, which represents the control of about 16% of the Gross Domestic Product and promises to deliver more people to being dependent—and therefore supportive of the Parties' expanded control. Interestingly, similar healthcare systems are identified throughout the world as "socialized" or "nationalized" systems, but not by the American legacy media. That might be too negative and might make more citizens realize what is happening before it is too late.

We have a President who has openly pled with churches to support his political agenda, which can cause violation of tax law; an administration that has almost no members with business experience; an Executive branch that has vilified insurance companies as the primary culprit of rising health insurance costs for the privately insured when the federal government itself is a primary cause; a Democrat Attorney General and his hirelings who prosecuted the State of Arizona for defending itself from their perceived invasion but does nothing to government entities that do not enforce immigration laws as sanctuaries and nothing when Black Panther members with uniforms and sticks intimidate voters at the polls, calling the Whites "Crackers."

Adding to this, we have a Republican Party that is unable or unwilling to mount a fact-based opposition strategy to counter the so-called first "Stimulus" package that seemed mostly a slush fund of over $800 billion that used 4% for infrastructure and much more for political payouts to pay off old and secure new voting blocs; a one Party controlled government that overrode established bankruptcy laws to give a union that supports that Party control of a car company instead of its investors; and a situation in which our nation's major energy sources are off-limits to production while we send our cash to buy oil from others who want to destroy us. And on and on.

Common sense is ignored. Definitions and truth, as well as those pesky laws and the Constitution, seem to be just weeds to be trampled on the path to Party—or perhaps personal goals of power and money. It is no surprise that ordinary People see indications that cause us to fear for our Freedom as established in the Founding Documents. We know that we must act. Consolidation is a key to acting *successfully*.

Consolidation

Consolidating those who are without solid "Big Two" Party allegiance, the "NonPartisans" is the critical first step needed in order to accumulate the power required to take the steps that follow.

Among the many sources of these NonPartisans are millions of people who have spent decades being a "silent majority" but are becoming activated by what they have seen in the last few years. There are also former or marginal Republicans who have seen the basic principles of America go wanting while their Party overspent, did not control our borders and burdened the taxpayers with debt. There are also former or marginal Democrats with a family tradition for that Party who have seen their leaders leave them; they moved too far left and are threatening America by expanding government control and diminishing motivation and personal responsibility. And there are tax protesters who are stunned and worried about the radical spending that they know cannot create wealth but does create a heavy saddle of debt that could hold them, and their families, down for generations. There are Libertarians who are seeing that smaller common sense government may be achieved by moving outside yet another Party setting. And now there are the Tea Party people who recognize the wisdom of our Founders and the folly of Party promises. Along with them, we have the town hall protestors, who witnessed the evil of lying Party hacks right in their hometowns and eye to eye. There are the newly alarmed who have not had much interest in "politics" in the past but now believe it to be of critical importance. And finally, there are millions of Independents who have specifically chosen to have no Party allegiance seeing themselves somewhere in between and having a belief in their *nation* and the capability of its diverse, ordinary People.

Of course, there are also other groups from which we can hope to add to our NonPartisan ranks that span the generations. There are the young and very motivated, like the college kids who secretly taped ACORN employees volunteering to help them by lying on tax forms, advising on setting up a brothel for illegal immigrant 13-year-olds, and getting aid from the government by calling them "dependents."[60] Aside from exposing ACORN's irresponsible assault on our tax money, they made many of us question why *any* organization that supports *any* particular Party should be getting *any* of our public money.

Yes, there are also the Baby Boomers, many of whom were active in the '60s. The Boomers early on questioned the authority of the government and its veracity. They questioned its control over our lives, over our futures, and over our

---

[60] ACORN officials Videotaped Telling "Pimp," "Prostitute" How to Lie to IRS. (2009, September 10). FOXNews.com. http://www.foxnews.com/us/2009/09/10acornofficials-videotaped-telling-pimp-prositute

choices. As they aged, their numbers and ideas and productivity propelled America into its most prosperous period. Each day, thousands of these Boomers are entering the ranks of the retired. This will leave them with the time to reactivate for the *Evolution* we need.

There are the older people, too, often called the Greatest Generation, who fought in the Second World War and Korea, folks who had a firm trust that if they behaved well and worked hard, their nation would not only allow their success but *revel* in it. Now they see what can happen when leftist policies, similar to those they fought against abroad and defended against at home are promoted or embraced by mainstream political Parties. They see the freedom and achievements of our nation, which they worked for, being berated, threatened or taken away, and they worry about the futures of their children and grandchildren.

The power we need will come from gathering all of these possible forces together as a cohesive group of "NonPartisans." We must become one large, powerful body, united in our common interests. Yes, we will have differences, but we will solve them or put them aside for now. Whether turf or ethnicity, religion, age or focus be our issues, we must move together according to the *commonality* of our being concerned intelligent Americans, first and foremost. We must focus on what we have in common as ordinary citizens and find our unity here.

This is not unprecedented in America. In fact, this is precisely what the *first* Americans did. The 13 American colonies were made up of people from different backgrounds, from different parts of Europe, and practicing different religions. Like us, they were not a homogeneous lot, either. They found *unity* and forged it into a steely opposition to those who threatened their freedom, their property, and their opportunities for the future. If the first ordinary Americans could find unity when they had little education, low prosperity, difficult communication, and no proven Constitution or successful history to guide them, surely we ordinary Americans of today can unite in opposition to our common internal enemies. Let us begin by referring to all of our diverse groups with a common name.

The NonPartisan Americans (NPA)

The NonPartisan Americans is a new term referring to all of the ordinary People that belong to or support the many conservative rights-based groups that exist outside of the Parties. We seek to end the ever-expanding control that political Parties exercise over our lives. We cannot expect the Parties that control us and operate our government so poorly to give up control on their own. The NPA are those who recognize that it is the duty of ordinary People to demand that the Constitution be followed, their Rights be protected and that the Parties cannot or will not do that.

The Parties have no legitimacy vested by any of our Founding Documents. They are not even mentioned. And yet, today they stand between us and our government as if they belong there, deciding who the candidates will be, shaping policy behind the scenes with each other, and overcoming the separation of powers that our Founders devised and placed in our Constitution. They accept millions in campaign donations from special interests that ask them to pass laws or to set policy that will assist those interests in accumulating power over us, or in taking money from us.

The Parties are the twenty-first century American version of the Ruling Elite that has always, and in all places, sought control over the masses of ordinary People. The NPA seeks to join the voices of the majority together, overpower the Parties and take control for the Constitution and the ordinary People that it protects. Yes, that *is* a big order, but what choice do we have? Should we accept their projected guilt about success and surrender to the tight control that the Ruling Elite want over us? How can we allow them to ignore the Constitution and use our government to dispense, collect and distribute our national and personal wealth and power to those who support their take over? How can we submit to their vilification of opposition and distain for anyone that is not one of them? These seem like the early choices that people made during the rise of Stalin, Hitler, Saddam Hussein, and the Muslim clerics of Iran.

Like our Founders, we must throw off the shackles of the Ruling Elite and proclaim our Freedom. And, like Martin Luther King Jr., we must do this without violence. Truth is on our side. Our common sense tells us, and our Founding Documents confirm, that we are in the right. The Democratic Party leaders have exposed their true selves in their arrogance, allowing many more of us to see them for what they are and what any Party can be. They have essentially "begged the question" that ends the debate and brings it to a vote. And make no mistake that today it is the Democrats, but at any time it could be *any* Party that could be aggressively acting to change our nation as *it* deems. We must change the mechanism of our governance not only to stop today's Democrats, but also to protect The People from any future Party leaders acting similarly. The essential question that now must be answered is this: What is America to be?

> "Like our Founders, we must throw off the shackles of the Ruling Elite and proclaim our Freedom.

Will it be a nation controlled by a Party of the Ruling Elite and their supporters, where history shows the leaders do well and the ordinary People lose prosperity and their drive to achieve? Or is it to be a nation as it was founded to be: a home for individuals with Freedom over person and property, a country of personal responsibility and a place where there is the chance for ordinary People to better themselves?

The Democratic Party approach matches the first of these two choices. Based on Socialism, a theory that has never succeeded, but rather has always led to sorrow for those that have taken or been forced onto that path. The latter, the traditional American way, imperfect as it is, has historically proven to improve the lives of ordinary People on a scale never before known.

The answer is obvious. We would not want to gamble the lives of more than 300 million Americans on any theoretical system proposed by its primary beneficiaries. And really, if they thought the American People wanted their system, they would allow us to vote on it openly.

The Constitution prescribes voting by the States as the process to make big changes in its Article V. But that is not going to happen, not while they know that most would vote against it. The political Parties would rather stack the Courts with judges who judge not blindly, as per the Constitution, but according to their Party affiliation. The Parties would rather create disunity by favoring some Americans into viewing themselves as "more equal than others" and continue to support them in that belief. That, of course, is against the "equality" guarantee of the Constitution, but the Parties have and will continue to ignore that. They would rather pay to "import" people, with your money, from Mexico or anywhere else to cancel out your vote—so they can control you. The Constitution assigns the duty of protecting our borders to the Federal government, which they will continue to mostly ignore while importing foreign voters, providing protection and attacking and prosecuting people and States that oppose them. These Party people are the same evil force of history returning to put the ordinary People back in their cage. And they will certainly not let you vote about being caged, not fairly; until they know they can beat you.

I hope that you see these smiling, lying, misleading, ideological and paid-off, anti-Americans for the terminal cancer that they really are. They are willing to destroy most of America in order to control what is left. The damage they are doing to the good people of America and the world each day is huge, and it is *us* that must stop them. Much like our nation needed all The People against Great Britain's King George and to join the effort to turn back the Axis powers in World War II, we now need a commitment to win *this* conflict. We must overpower them with numbers, challenge every aggressive action they make, and ignore the media siren song that is intended, like Tokyo Rose, to ruin us. They are like a highly aggressive disease, and we have this one time to stop it. Our Founding Documents light the way. We can do this by having the numbers. Every adult member will vote and every vote will count. Make a commitment. Go to the next meeting of whatever NonPartisan group that you belong to or are joining and tell them about our need to consolidate around our commonalities; show them this book and tell them to get a copy at NonPartisanAmericans.com; set up a book club to go through it with them or your friends and neighbors and discuss it over a few weeks. And think of the power that we can harness by understanding the ongoing attack on our Rights and seeking to secure them through the *Citizens' Rights Movement.* We must *claim* our freedom. This is what the first American ordinary People did against those that controlled their government and we must do the same. Theirs was royalty, ours are Parties who *think* they are royalty.

If this book and the social networking efforts that will go with it garner enough interest, we intend to arrange a **NonPartisan Americans Convention** to affect the 2012 election and beyond. We plan to request that the leadership from each one of the organizations including those mentioned above make contact at the NonPartisanAmericans.com and join the roster of groups and people committed to the first great cause of the American 21st Century, reaffirming and securing the Rights of the ordinary People. We will arrange a leadership forum for the exchange of ideas and the preparation of agreements that will begin to establish us as a cohesive association of nonpartisans, and begin establishing a national presence. We will seek agreement with a draft of specific demands from the ordinary People of America who are not aligned with a Party. Provided below, along with a Declaration of our reasons for this action is a list of suggested common sense goals for our Citizens' Rights effort, called the *"Twenty-Two Intentions."* Although some will view this as controversial, most will likely agree that they are well based and seem reasonable regarding our position versus the Ruling Elite of the Parties.

Also using common sense, as did our Founders, we will *not* direct this effort at the government. We prefer to view our government, based on its Founding Documents and most of its laws, as a proven, inspired entity that these Parties are misusing. Instead, *our demands will be directed to those political Parties who control our government and have functionally debased its common sense in favor of Party sense.*

If we are successful in our discussions, we will follow with a series of online presentations and local "live" gatherings to discuss our intentions, including participation by both the "umbrella" group and each of the various associated groups. We will request that every ordinary American consider these intentions, and if they identify commonality in some or most of them, to join us.

We will all have to network—personally and on the web— to gain the momentum that will motivate people to join with one of the many local groups of center-right origin. These are the groups where the silent majority is coming alive. We must show ourselves and the Parties that we can get the voices of the many to be with us. There will likely be a member cost, in order to allow the groups to function and to communicate. That cost will be minimal, but its value will be priceless.

Additionally, I plan to be broadcasting about our movement and being a clearinghouse for your ideas and thoughts. Get current details at NonPartisanAmericans.com.

I hope that you will find groups associated with the NPA approach your means of exchanging the power of the Party for the power of The People. By adopting the center-right thinking of the NPA, *we will seek to infuse our government with the common sense of The People*, and to stop the uncommon nonsense of the Parties.

Our first plan of attack is *not* to become a political Party, but rather to work to limit the existing Parties just as the Founders sought to limit power over The People. But, if the preferred "Alliance Plan" fails, we must not rule out becoming a Party, if necessary, in a "Plan B."

We recognize that the political elites are tied in with the financial elites (Domhoff, William) and with interest groups of foundations, lobbyist and law firms (Dye, Thomas R.) The existing major Parties control the media and connect with the flow of business and organizational money sources to such a degree, that to oppose them both head-on is not likely to be successful. We also recognize that there's so much damage being done so quickly that time is of the essence.

Instead of direct opposition, we will choose to battle as the first Americans did, in a series of skirmishes instead of in big battles, where we are certain to be outgunned and misreported. We intend to become the *ally* of the Party that agrees to follow as many of our NPA goals as possible. We will organize and aggregate, and we will deliver our personal votes only to the candidates who agree to our intentions and to put them into place or into law. In this way, we can potentially become one of the larger special interest groups in the country.

Our special interest, in fact, is that of the country itself.

We are lobbying for the character and principles of the American nation—the nation that will not accept mediocrity, a wildly expensive but poor educational system, or excuses for not following or enforcing its laws.

We are lobbying to end apology and encourage appreciation. We are lobbying for the requirement of personal responsibility and reward for hard work. It is not about us individually; it is about putting the power with The People where it *belongs*.

It is about returning America to the path of prosperity and to its place as the beacon of what is right for all of the millions who came to help build it and the many thousands who have helped defend it. If we grow large enough and stay that course, we can change the future of our nation.

One of the Parties will see that without us it may be more difficult to win. The obvious likely Party to ally with us is the Republican's, since we seem to have more Values in common. Both NonPartisans and Republicans generally believe in the proven Values of Freedom and a Free Market as set out by our Founders and have proven their validity in making America great. Our significant presence would force both Parties to consider changing from seeking what *they* want to doing what the ordinary People want, and that is our mission. The Parties must change the way they do business or they will lose our support to those who will.

Through our influence, our government will then be restructured according to the goals we set, something like the *Twenty-Two Intentions* presented below. If we ordinary American citizens can unify in this manner, we will become a political force that must be reckoned with. Our power will come from our numbers, not through trading votes for cash, pleading or through physical force. Through unity, we ordinary People can eclipse the power of any lobbyist, any moneyed group, and any union or other special interest that exists. We stand for something greater than any Party; we stand for our *Nation*. We are driven by our passion for something wider and deeper than any of the Party Elite; the desire to represent the interests of our nation, rather than ourselves.

In America today there is no structure that is in place to represent the interests of the America established in its Founding Documents, found in its traditions, and documented by its history of success. There are a few disparate groups, each supposedly doing a part, but that is obviously not enough.

* * *

There are those in the Washington leadership who have stated that our Founding Documents are not important and have little bearing on our lives today. Yet these are the documents that define our Rights. Along with our traditions and history, they define our culture and, most importantly, the status of the ordinary People.

If we allow others to proclaim these writings to be of little value or worthless, then we are agreeing that our Rights may be of little value; those Rights are the only thing that separates us from Tyranny and dictatorship.

If we don't reinforce our demand for government adherence to these Rights, our Documents and our laws, then they will feel free to *decide* what those Rights are and what America is to be. We don't want any group of Ruling Elites deciding what the definition of America should be. We already have a definition. It is found in our Constitution, it contains our Rights and the process by which our definition is permitted to change. That process does not accommodate proclamation, intentional misleading, or policy making that is contrary to the Constitution, whether such behavior is exhibited by bureaucrats, by executive orders, or by the personal views or Party loyalty of appointed judges. In fact, our Documents encourage us to *refuse* such control.

The NonPartisan Americans reject the Ruling Elite and its Parties, political Party usurpers, controllers, dictators, royalty, or any form of pretenders who seek to govern us. We will govern ourselves, and we intend to dismantle any process or structure that minimizes our ability to do so.

About sixty five years ago, in World War II (WWII), our nation successfully defended itself from an external group of countries who sought to take away our Freedom. An exquisite commemoration to the men and women who achieved that success is constructed on the Mall between the Lincoln Memorial and the Capitol Building in Washington D.C. Every one of us needs to visit the WWII Memorial and then see the others, including the Viet Nam Memorial. On September 11, 2001, we were attacked by yet another group that hates our Freedom and wants us to live according to *their* rules.

We have always had to fight to keep our external enemies at bay, and we are continuing that effort. Now we must *also* fight to keep our *internal* enemies at bay, as well. We are facing an enormous internal threat to our Freedom from the political Parties that control our government, particularly the Democrats. Their huge power grab has shown what most of us thought *im*possible to actually *be* possible. We must recognize this threat and we must use the power of our concentrated votes to change the direction of our nation and to put the power into The People's hands instead of the Party coffers.

Consolidation is our First Step

We need every American who agrees with our thrust to join in this effort. We need each to realize that their personal vote in the coming elections may be among the most important votes ever cast in history; that these elections will decide not only our leaders, but also the course of America.

Will the most prosperous and powerful nation ever, driven by the personally responsible, the industrious believers of Freedom stay its course of prosperity, or will it be turned to a new course by wealth and power transfer to those of collective responsibility and a right to what others have earned? In part, the answer to that will be decided by what you do in reaction to this book. If you do not join us as an individual or in a group that is committed to the thinking of the NPA, it not only doesn't help us, it actually helps *them*.

Every vote is going to count, and the opposition leaders will work hard to have every "Taker" out to the polls. If you don't feel quite ready to join, please consider the following section.

Declaring the Problem

As we consolidate around our similarities and organize to move forward, we must begin our most critical effort, that of establishing our collective and concise demands. These demands will be referred to as "intentions," a terminology that better reflects the flexibility that may be required in order to succeed in such a large effort, one that could possibly impact millions of Americans and even influence the direction of the ordinary People of other democracies.

The following list is a self-explanatory composite of the major issues that are of prime concern to us ordinary People. We can say them unfettered by the support for any Party. It captures most, but not all, of the complaints that have come about from the years of Party domination of our government. This is a "Declaration" of the primary issues before us. In the spirit of our Founder's Declaration, it is articulated by ordinary People who seek to affirm and secure their Freedom before Tyrants.

The Declaration of the NonPartisan Americans

The non-aligned, independent and other NonPartisan citizens of the United States of America lodge these grievances against the major political Parties of our nation.

Whereas, the major political Parties of the United States of America have sought to control the governance of our nation for the benefit of themselves and in opposition to our Rights as guaranteed in our founding documents.

Whereas, these Parties have acted in ways detrimental to the American people, namely:

To intentionally foster economic class, race, gender and generational conflict, harming national unity;

To manipulate the free press upon which The People depend;

To diminish Rights that they are sworn to defend, namely: the Right to equal treatment by the government; the Right to control our own lives and property; the Rights to privacy, to free speech and to bear arms;

To build and hold a wedge position between The People and their government;

To ignore the founding of this nation as being based on Rights from our Creator, rather than granted from the Parties or any person;

To establish control of education and then fail to teach our children to become responsible contributing citizens of our nation;

To corrupt the educational system to foster adherence to doctrine that is contrary to the intentions of our Founding Documents;

To encourage American citizens to depend upon political Parties and government for their well being;

To use the tools of our government to act in favor of special interest groups who support their Parties and to hurt or disparage those who do not;

To redefine "Freedom" to include "Freeloading";

To prepare costly legislation in secret and force passage without adequate review by opposition or The People;

To fail in providing security of our persons and properties;

To collude in avoiding accountability of Party officers, elected officials and government employees;

To fail in keeping the nation's economics in good order;

To badly manage offices of government as instruments of their Party rather than as servants to The People;

To poorly execute the tasks of government, harming the environment and destroying the savings and jobs of The People;

To represent their personal and Party interests above the interests of The People;

To mislead and lie to The People for personal or Party gain and to the detriment of The People;

To scorn and belittle the ordinary People;

To trade off the Rights and privileges of Americans and the offices of The People for personal or Party gain;

To appoint judges who judge on personal views or in favor of their Party rather than blindly for fairness to all the nation's People;

To enforce laws unequally or not at all, for the benefit of those who support their Parties;

To fail to secure our nation's borders while disparaging, and encouraging foreigners to disparage, the very citizens who are being damaged and killed by that failure;

To attack business and block the use of natural resources knowing that prosperity only comes from successful business and from wise use of natural resources;

To execute the national budget in a deceptive manner filled with hidden and unaccountable expenses;

To tax The People in a difficult, deceptive and unequal manner, with some paying virtually nothing at all;

To fail to acknowledge and reinforce in The People, that all American government is *inferior* to The People.

Be It Resolved: that these citizens, pledged in allegiance to the United States of America, will right the wrongs cast on this nation by the Parties and move from languishing as a government by and for the Party to flourishing as a government by and for The People.

It is our intent, it is our national duty, to affirm and secure our rights which includes ordinary People ruling this free market nation. We join in a *Citizens' Rights Movement* in order to peacefully achieve this goal.

Given this Declaration of the glaring problems presented above, we need to express specific goals to repair them. The following list of "Intentions" is meant to affirm our rights as citizens and to establish a representative government by The People rather than by political Parties.

The Twenty-Two Intentions of the Citizen's Rights Movement

1. **Replace influence on government by the special interests groups with influence by The People.** The Parties are really super interest groups using our government for the benefit of themselves and their supporters. It is no wonder that they seem so separate from the People's interests; they are.

2. **Eliminate political corruption of economics, including having an unbalanced budget and no national plan.** Party goals had an influence, at minimum, in collapsing our housing market and our economy. This capability needs to be eliminated. The unbelievable debt being accumulated now threatens to do more damage than war and must be stopped and rolled back.

3. **Establish, at every government level, the responsibility to make certain that all adult citizens have equal Rights, equal responsibilities, and equal treatment under every law.** Much of the disunity and many of the current problems we have now are because the Parties find excuses for not following the intent of the Constitution, are not equally applying the law, and are ignoring common sense; we must reverse that immediately.

4. **Enforce and enhance all laws, including those against illegal alien entry, presence, employment and voting.** Qualify all immigrants for health, and not being a

burden but rather a contributor to society before entry; score each as to likelihood of immersing into the American culture and reject the unlikely. This is exactly what every responsible nation on earth does and what America has long done as well; this was the primary activity at Ellis Island. We are a nation of laws and it is common sense that they are all executed equally and to their full extent.

5. **Improve healthcare access and reduce cost without a government takeover.** Polls show that the plan passed unilaterally in 2010 by the Democratic Party is unpopular. As more accurate information becomes available, the more the taxpayers do not like it and the more economically threatening it becomes. Few know that in 2013 it mandates a 3.8% tax on the sale of some residences *and* on some unearned income. This needs to be stopped, reviewed, revised or replaced. It is far more important that such a huge, permanent plan be affordable and desired by the People than considered as a "victory" by temporary government officials.

6. **All citizens will receive accurate training regarding this nation's history, values and personal responsibilities, including the formation of prosperity through capitalism.** So that we can all work together, it is important that our citizens have shared knowledge of our nation's heritage and purpose, and how its economy functions. All citizens should know what has worked in our economy and others of the world, so that they can make informed decisions when voting and for succeeding in their own lives.

7. **Establish term limits at all levels of government.** Personal bureaucracies and stale ideas are far more likely than efficiency to be the outcome of allowing representatives to stay in office without limit.

8. **Eliminate partisan and lifetime appointments of judges and the ability of judges to do anything unless it is free from prejudice, personal feelings, and law external to the United States.** Justice in our diverse society can only be fair if it is blind to the characteristics of the people involved; judgments must be made according to the American law, its Constitution, and by judicial standards, not by biased Party ideology or personal thoughts. Any judge doing otherwise is to be removed immediately and the case re-judged fairly.

9. **All government officials and other employees will participate in similar benefit packages and at similar pay levels or less than the people in the private sector.** By all accounts, many, but certainly not all, government employees produce nothing, are the least efficient workers in our society, and the least qualified; yet, job for job, they are paid more and have far better pensions and benefits than in private enterprise. Since a large government reduces the importance of the individual, it must be radically reduced at all levels. We need fewer government employees, not more. The Parties, spending our money, not theirs, have created this situation.

10. **No person paid by public funds should be permitted to teach, promote or act in any way advocating against the American Constitution or the interests of**

our democratic republic while at work. Only a currently serving elected official and direct-report staff are permitted to be partisan while being paid from public funds; no other persons or groups supported or paid by the public's funds can be partisan. There is no wisdom in having The People pay for those who would destroy the nation they are paid to serve. As in private enterprise, dissent from those who pay is fine, but not during their work hours.

11. **Those government employees who do not perform well will be removed, and the workforce will staff at levels similar to the private sector.** The low level of work productivity and quality of government employees is a national joke that most taxpayers see as a national disgrace. This will require deep concessions by, or disallowance of, unions among government employees.

12. **Make English the only official language of the nation with required use at all government levels.** Personal ethnic interest is understandable. Ethnic centrism is not. If you are permanently in this nation, you are either on your way to becoming an American or you are an American, with allegiance to *this* nation. A vital part of what makes our multicultural nation viable is allegiance and continuity of communication, despite our desirable diversity.

13. **Increase domestic production of energy from all sources, to be 85% either domestic or supplied by allies in five years.** This will assist in reducing the deficit, will enhance security, and will help pay for developing new pro-environment domestic energy

sources. America has some of the greatest reserves of energy in the world, and invented nuclear power, but these Parties have forced us for decades to transfer our wealth and treasure to our enemies to buy theirs. That stupidity will end.

14. **Create an intelligent transition plan to full domestic environmentally conscious energy production and use, while minimally disrupting American business and American living standards.** We need to gradually move to sources of energy other than fossil fuels, both because fossil fuel resources will ultimately be depleted and because such use pollutes the environment. However, we know that energy is the basic building block of human comfort and success, so all efforts to achieve this transition need to prudently respect its importance in our economics, our security and in our standard of living.

15. **All normal legislation must include a "Citizen Impact Statement" which will identify its "winners" and "losers," along with their demographics and location.** Legislation must also have automatic performance review and termination dates, be certified as read by considering officials, contain no "earmarks," bear no misleading title, and have at least twenty days for review by the opposition and The People prior to being voted upon in Congress. The arrogance of our legislators in following a permitted but flatly undemocratic legislative process that rewards Party supporters rather than protecting the entire citizenry, that is approved in stealth, and that uses bad information is wrong. The government will no longer

make law *over* us without appropriate safeguards and input *from* us.

16. **The Federal government must establish standards to protect the person and property of the disabled, infirmed and aged citizens, protecting them from predatory caretakers, consultants and others who may prey upon them.** It is inexcusable that our most vulnerable citizens must live in fear of abuse because such harm often goes unpunished.

17. **All citizens who earn income should pay at least some income tax; otherwise, non-payors are totally free to support tax increases.** Everyone needs "skin in the game." Taxes are burdensome to anyone, and those who pay the most generally benefit the least. A different taxation, perhaps a form of flat or fair tax should be considered.

18. **No money from any foreign entities will be allowed in support of any election in America.** Only proven citizens will be allowed to vote, and no tampering with elections will be tolerated. Severe penalties for attempted or actual violations will be mandatory. No free nation can remain free when it allows debasing of the elections of The People.

19. **Public education must be results-oriented.** Its end result must not just be people who can read and write our common language, but also people who are personally responsible citizens who can contribute to furthering the nation whose responsibility will become theirs. Special rules, unions and uncooperative students can no

longer be permitted to block the success of The People's enormous investment in our future. If standards of achievement cannot be met by public leadership, then schools perhaps should be run by private enterprises that have demonstrated the ability to achieve results. Public schools do not exist for the good of personnel or unions; their primary purpose is to help students learn to help themselves for the good of the nation.

20. **All citizens and any business or institution will be free to take a stand on any topic without fear of reprisal from any source.** Because a group might have any particular point of view is no reason to silence them in the public arena. Our Free society cannot allow atheists and the anti-religious a voice but threaten the tax status of spiritual organizations that speak politically. Nor can it permit only one point of view to be spoken at any institution, including colleges and universities that receive public funding of any type.

21. **Reduce all crimes against The People by 50% in seven years and revise the law enforcement and Court systems so as to consistently demonstrate protection and service to the innocent rather than to the guilty.** The People are tired of their victimization and the harm to themselves and their children when criminals are released to hurt other innocents. Those organizations that release violent felons before their full sentence is served must be held financially liable to those that are victims during the time that criminal should have been still incarcerated, and the responsible people should be removed from their position for incompetence.

22. **The government will develop and promote a national set of goals protecting our constitutional rights, designating an end to poverty, proven basic education, and demonstrated levels of security—economically; militarily; and in *every* neighborhood.** Because recent administrations have shown that Parties can attempt to change so many rules, the businesses and People of our nation are untrusting and are frozen in place, afraid to take risk and spend money. Many live in fear for their futures. Most of this originates with elected officials trying to achieve the goals of their Party at the great expense of The People. This must be stopped, reversed, and a structure put in place to discourage this from happening again.

We hold these goals as critical in nature. We are a nation of more than 300 million mostly ordinary People. We will not be held back by a paltry few Party elitists who take the position that they just know what is right because they went to the right schools or have contacts with a few powerful people; we are The People who pay most of the taxes demanded on everything we do, earn or consume, and we refuse to be crowded outside while handfuls, in fancy rooms with closed doors, decide our futures; we are the parents who don't want our children to be taught how to not offend but rather how to succeed for themselves and our unified nation; we are those you treat like inanimate assets to be lied to and about and used as needed; we are the descendents of the hopeful and self responsible that King George knew and that generations of royals in Europe and the tyrants of the world have faced; we are ordinary Americans awake and together, numerous, and focused; we are the proven worst enemy of any external or internal threat to our nation, and we intend to take back the power that you *think* is yours.

We propose to define the commonality we share as the many discreet groups and individuals referred to as *NonPartisan Americans:* our common interest is in our Founding Documents and the Rights that they guarantee us. The political Parties have, at best, failed to protect them and, at worst, seek to diminish them. We wish to consider our nation in front of the Parties and The People at the front of the nation. As our Founders refused to recognize the authority of English Royalty between them and their governance, we now refuse to accept the political Parties between us and our governance. We are terming our efforts to rectify political Party actions and inactions as the *Citizens' Rights Movement.*

I am just an ordinary Joe American, like you. The thinking and plans here are unprecedented and not backed by some elite support group with millions or a big organization like a union or lobbyist. Most would term mine a "grassroots" effort, but I confess that I think it is even more basic than that; it is like having one small plant with tiny roots. But this effort will find its strength because it comes from the *soil* that holds that single blade of grass. It comes from the *same soil* that our colonists walked on. It is the *land* in the "land of opportunity" that millions came to. It is the very *dirt* that that our Founders held in their hands as they spoke the words that changed the possibilities of all ordinary People for all time. And it is the *ground* that our nation grew from and that thousands and thousands of Americans have died for. What more magnificent a base could we have?

Proposing a Remedy: The Citizens' Rights Movement®

- Increase Strength in Congress

- Build a powerful Citizens' Agency into the Federal Structure

- **Pass a Citizens' Rights Amendment**

✳ ✳ ✳

Citizens' Rights: Threatened but Fixable

Out of what we know comes what we must do. We know that our Rights have been reduced and threatened. We must move to affirm our rights and secure them; a Citizens' Rights Movement.

The world is *not* a steady state in which things do not change. Rather, the world is always changing and always demanding us to be changed with it. So it is in weather, health, nature, economics, relationships—and so it is in government.

". . . power would extinguish liberty; . . . so that she has, as it were, the enemy always at her gate"[61]

The world is not a safe place where good always wins and the story is complete. The story never ends. Good is always under attack by the bad that despises it. Our free government, based on the natural desires of ordinary People, is a gift of good, crafted by Founders who were inspired to create a place where ordinary People could happily achieve the extraordinary. As our Founding Documents show, we ordinary People own this group of *Citizens' Rights*, and government exists to guarantee them. Now our government is under attack by the same natural forces that, throughout history, have sought to subjugate the common people, to take power and wealth and use it for control. Those forces are on the march in America, and their objective is to increasingly control us. Our government is, in a sense, in captivity, and it is our duty to free it.

---

[61] Asmus, B., & Billings, D. *It's Tea Time Again* (1995). Phoenix, AZ: AmeriPress. Quoting Trenchard and Gordon, p.44.

This is a time of realization, a time to allow ordinary People to see clearly the threats against them. There are forces present without, in the form of our nation's enemies, and they are present within, in the form of the nation's political Parties. Today, the main threat to our Liberty is the Democratic Party, but tomorrow it could be *any* other Party or group that wishes to take advantage of any weakness they can find in our structure.

Any attacker seeks to find a way through existing defenses, which means that our defenses require constant improvement. The faults in our defenses for our Liberty were used to allow these Parties to gain power over us. This dangerous condition has been exposed now by the aggression of the current Democratic Party leaderhip, showing the flaws like leaking cracks in a dam. People who seek to reduce our Liberty and limit our pursuit of Happiness have been placed into positions of power. They have proven their disdain for property rights by openly seeking to transfer the property of some to others who support them. They have shown their willingness to threaten the well being of all of us by unbridled spending for causes of their own rather than for the causes of the citizens who must pay for it. They are the Ruling Elite, once again rising against the ordinary People and, as always, claiming their efforts are for The People's own good. They are the *enemy at the gate,* and they represent the immediate threat we must vanquish.

We must defeat them as quickly as possible by using our voting process. As they grow in strength and boldness, surely they will seek to destroy this ability of ours to hurt them by changing rules, corrupting the base of voters, allowing illegitimate voters, opening avenues for cheating, miscounting, and raising the numbers required to reduce their power. We must question, we must inquire, we must demand, we must confront and we must not accept the lies and deceit that are surely forthcoming. We must tolerate nothing less than the Rights and responsibilities accorded us in the Founding Documents.

Ours is a noble effort to defeat the enemies of Liberty within and to reestablish the direction of our nation's government. It must focus on the rights and responsibilities of unified citizens rather than on what is best for the Parties. We must convert our government and the media from trying to create the will of The People and acting to control them to responding to the desires and needs of citizens who control themselves. The citizens seek protection and leadership, *not* control.

> "Ours is a noble effort to defeat the enemies of Liberty within."

Once we secure ourselves from these more immediate internal dangers, we will seek to re-secure ourselves from the other enemies of our nation. The People must refuse to permit its government to be used by power seekers who put our children and fortune in harm's way as a means of projecting their personal power. But it also cannot encourage, assist or tolerate those who threaten or in any way do harm to The People of this nation, from *any* quarter.

Our first and primary effort must be to defeat the Party most threatening to the traditions, Documents and promise of this nation. We can succeed, by joining with the other major Party under strict agreement and expectations.

The over-all plan is to remove power from the most threatening Party and then reduce the power of *any* Party by increasing the power of The People. Simply put, we will seek to join with Republicans to completely overwhelm the Democrats, *if* the Republicans will agree in advance to changes in the structure of our government that will forever reduce the power of *any* political Party.

This is the crux of the plan: to join in a temporary alliance with the Republicans in order to defeat the Democrats *and* to change the structure so that the Parties have less power, and the People have more power; the government will be smaller and the individual will become larger. By combining the NPA and the Republicans into an alliance for Citizen's Rights, we intend to defeat our common enemy and also to make it so that no Party can threaten our freedom like this again. We will soon know if the Republicans really have the vestiges of being the defenders of Freedom that they claim; common sense tells us that both Parties have been at least somewhat complicit against us.

If Republicans are more responsibly oriented to the Constitution, they will ally with us and help map out the way to the greatest prosperity and the most secure Liberty we have yet known.

If not, we intend to form a new kind of Party, whose goal will be to defeat all Parties and then dismantle after establishing a system of digital democracy based on direct voting.

The latter choice is not the desired end, and it may have many unknown pitfalls; but if the true issue lies between the Liberty of digital democracy and the proven Tyranny of Socialism, then "Give me Liberty."

The Plans are explained below. It is all about the numbers. We must have enough thinking people committed to the NonPartisanship cause that the Republicans will agree to some limits on their Party that will accommodate the changes we seek.

It will take a commitment and perhaps a "show of force" to make them see the wisdom of such an alliance. The commitment is the action of joining with other NonPartisan Americans, through any local affiliated group or by simply signing up at NonPartisanAmericans.com. After that, we all need to support the effort by reading, communicating, rallying, offering what financial support we can, and most importantly, by voting together in an impactful way to achieve three specific goals or "benchmarks" detailed below.

The "show of force" will be to join in a block to fund and elect sympathetic Tea Party, Independent, and other NonPartisan candidates in the coming elections. We must be certain not to split votes and give Democrats seats by default.

My fellow ordinary Americans, we are in deep trouble. There is no time for making wasted "statements" with your vote now; this is a time to act decisively. We absolutely *must* vote and do so in a *strong* block; no vote can be wasted at any level. We must focus our votes as if free democracy depends upon it, because it really does. We must stop them here. And if we do, we can be an example for the possibilities for all democracies, existing or hoped for.

Strength in Congress Will Secure Citizens' Rights

First Benchmark: Take control of both Houses of Congress.

Purpose: To reduce the power of Democratic Party control, blocking their ability to act unilaterally, doing whatever it wants to us. They used their majority in both the House and the Senate—along with the Presidency—to force a rapid expansion of Liberty-reducing control over business, finance and healthcare, denying input by the opposing Republicans, and not listening to input from The People. Taking control of part or all of Congress will stop additional abuses, and it will hurt the Democrats' control at state and city levels, too. We must be mindful of the ideology and backgrounds of many of the leaders of this Administration. Unprecedented abuse of a lame duck session occurred and future abuse of presidential Executive Orders is possible. Their leadership has shown a willingness to push the limits of undemocratic behavior.

In the States we have seen how, without exception, Democratic Attorneys General attempted to stop their States from opposing efforts such as nationalized healthcare, even though all polling indicates that The People do not want it. In the cities, we have seen how the Rights of Americans have been diminished and elections possibly tampered with. There are "sanctuary cities," controlled by Democratic Party supported officials, allowing immigration violators to live without punishment. They are expected to support the Democrats in return. As Americans, we cannot allow *any* Party to engage in selective enforcement of the law for any reason, especially for doing so on behalf of a group that favors the Party in control of law enforcement! Removing one of the Federal Houses from Democrats helped stop their abuse of America, but we will need them both.

Second Benchmark: Propose laws to put the nation's power back into the hands of ordinary People.

Purpose: By reducing the Democrats to a minority in both Houses, we will be able to propose laws needed to stop our government from being an enemy to our prosperity and progress. With only a simple majority, the Democratic President would be under pressure to compromise but could still veto. But the majority in Congress allows the proposal and public discussion that will allow public involment and increase pressure on the President. New laws can eliminate the misdirection and failure of our educational system, eliminate activist judges, get control of our borders, wisely expand the use of our own abundant natural resources, and use that wealth to balance our budget and eliminate our deficit. Once we secure enough seats in elections, *and* the Presidency, we can begin *rolling back* the

> *"...stop our government from being an enemy to our prosperity and Freedom."*

efforts to dismantle the Founder's America. Simultaneously, we will begin to install the agreed to structural changes, such as the establishment of a **Citizens' Rights Board** (detailed below) that will raise The People above the Parties, and re-establish the importance of our unifying traditions, our successful history, and our Founding Documents. We will help secure for us and our posterity the Freedom and Prosperity that is the proven promise for *all* The People of this nation.

Third Benchmark: Gain two-thirds control of both Houses in Congress.

Purpose: Pushing the Democrats this low through the Citizen's Rights Alliance plan, we can, if necessary, override any Presidential veto of proposed Party power gutting laws and have the ability to propose a version of the **"Citizens' Rights Amendment" (CRA),** as explained below. The **Citizens' Rights Amendment** seeks to affirm the rights of the States and to more permanently move power from the Parties to The People. The passage of this Amendment XXVIII will require approval of three quarters of the States for ratification, in order to become law. The very thing that makes it difficult to accomplish is what secures it from future tampering. Once in place as the proposed details show, the Rights and Liberty of the ordinary People will be improved and more secured against the kind of internal enemy that confronts us now.

* * *

For the sake of our nation, we can see that in order to stop the enemy at our gate, which is the leadership of the current Democratic Party, we must avoid "making a statement" with our vote or by not voting at all. We cannot afford to vote for a candidate who clearly cannot win or waste a vote by not casting it. The numbers of people in support of the Democrats is large, and they want us to be divided and our votes to be disbursed or nonexistent so that they can keep us from stopping them. Any delay allows them more time to recruit others to support them by using our money through: establishing more government jobs that do little; by brainwashing our children to follow them over a cliff; by placing more people on welfare or on some dependency on them; and by establishing more programs of favor in exchange for votes.

In addition, the "anchor babies" are signing up to vote for the Democrats especially since the Democrats at Federal, State and city levels are united in not enforcing immigration and border law.[62] This is a perfect example of the way in which the Parties function to overcome the separation of powers that the Founders intended to protect individual citizens.

Stop and think about this situation. The government is refusing to enforce border and immigration controls, even though it is clearly the law and they are sworn to uphold it, and even though the polls show clearly that The People want them to. They are supposed to act for The People and follow the established laws, and they instead are acting in a way that *harms* The People directly and threatens the accuracy of elections which are held to protect us all from those like them.

I have written this book so ordinary Americans like me will have a resource that can help them to better understand both the special nature of America and the situation that we are now in. I have pointed out that the basis for our Freedom and nation is found in our very readable Founding Documents, and I provided a copy for every reader's home to read and share with family and friends. I have offered up some history to help with understanding the Founders who wrote them and the intent that they had

______

[62] "Arizona Immigration Law—SB 1070 backlash spurs Hispanics to join Dems" The Arizona Republic, page 1, June 8, 2010.

in doing so. I have made the case that Ruling Elites have always sought to control common people and are presenting themselves in the form of our political Parties now. The Parties have come between us and our government, and the overt aggressiveness of the Party in power today is making that clear for folks who seldom think about such things. This is causing an uncomfortable confrontation but it is also presenting an unprecedented opportunity to move our democratic republic to the next level.

The Democratic Party is using its power as a tool to foster disunity by selectively enforcing or creating laws, making legislation in secret, taking our assets, and even confiscating businesses. They are giving breaks to their supporters, all the while attacking and vilifying those who speak against them. They are overspending, not supporting our traditions, expanding government and seem to support our enemies and ignore our allies. They are converting our nation into someplace in their imagination—or into something we do not want. The detail may be doubted and argued, but not the power-grabbing moves. The American People are not a part of these actions, which are an attempt to substantially modify our country by reducing Liberty.

Those in office are sworn to uphold the Constitution, but they are ignoring it and proceeding to make huge changes. They are purposefully keeping The People out of a process that rightfully requires their direct involvement and perhaps Constitutional amendment. They are taking the actions historically similar to those a king or dictator imposes upon conquered countries. The current Democratic Party leadership, sadly, has become—and it must be said—an internal enemy of our nation. A time may come when their punishment will be considered, but today we must concentrate on stopping them. It is fair to separate the leaders from the major supporters at a second level, and also to isolate a third level of ordinary People who might mistakenly and blindly support them and need to understand and stop. This internal enemy is up to radical things that require a radical response.

*   *   *

The Citizens' Rights Board: An Agency for The People's Interests

The response we are proposing is new and radical. We will seek to change the structure of government to be more nonpartisan so as to make it less responsible to special interest groups like the Parties and their supporters.

We will seek to establish a new Agency in, but independent of, the Federal government and any Party—similar to the Federal Reserve System. "Independent within the government" is the phrase The "Fed" used to describe its ability to make decisions without approval by the Executive branch and having just oversight by Congress. We are calling it the **Citizens' Rights Board (CRB)**.

As the name implies, its primary role will be to represent the intent of the Constitution and the Rights of The People within our functioning government. It will include nonpartisan people who are activists, political scientists, economists, researchers, Constitutional lawyers, scholars and historians, statisticians and technology specialists, and reformed lobbyists and journalists. It would exclude any former appointed or elected bureaucrat or government official and any demonstrably partisan persons. We want a cadre of knowledgeable people not beholden to anyone or to any Party, to be a watchdog over Washington, D.C.—a unique group that will be rewarded for exposing activity counter to the interests of the ordinary People instead of being rewarded for hiding it.

While there are many Departments and Agencies through-out the Federal government, none exists that comprehensively represents what the entire Federal entity was originally designed to protect and assure; i.e., the Constitutional and traditional rights and the interests of the ordinary People. There is no group setting standards and monitoring and reporting on all aspects of operation, making certain that the government is used to further The People's Rights, not hinder them; that activities are fair and done appropriately and efficiently for The People; that regulations and laws made are fair and equal and equally enforced. With no such protective arm within our government, it is no surprise that the Liberty of ordinary People has been gradually diminished for more than two centuries.

If such an agency had been in existence ten years ago, Enron might not have happened. The collapse of the hous-ing market, accommodated by the actions of the Legislative branch and the inaction of the Federal Reserve System, would likely not have occurred. We would not have let the Parties force us to buy energy from our enemies instead of using our own energy resources, which are among the world's largest. Those debacles would have been anticipated and called out to The People by means of this internally funded group. There would have been no Party power able to keep the truth from The People. In fact, the non-existence of the CRB right now is the biggest threat to it getting established. Both of the Parties will likely attack a proposal to create it, and we will not be able to obstruct them, because the CRB is not there to block them and expose them. Much like in the film "It's a Wonderful Life," where the world was a different place when the person of good intent was there to fend off bad things for the people of his town, so the CRB must be the group of good intent to protect us and prosperity.

The existing departments, bureaus, agencies, offices, and committees represent functional areas and special interests of the Federal government and groups in support. In the Executive branch there are fifteen Executive Departments, including the Departments of Education, Defense, and Homeland Security, all of which report to the President. There are also independent Agencies, including the Central Intelligence agency (CIA) and the Federal Reserve System; that is where the CRB will be established.

Our proposal is to establish the CRB as a constant, objective monitor and reporter to The People on the activities of the Federal government. The CRB will serve as do the Congressional Budget Office (CBO) and Government Accounting Office (GAO) in the sense that it will provide independent, nonpartisan information about the government. However, it will make reports primarily to The People directly, not to those inside the government, where it would likely be stifled or modified.

It will also report to other related parties within the government and the to the press and other media. This will put pressure to be accurate and honest on Presidential and other press briefings and reports, which tend to say what the politicians want to be heard. The current information from our government comes without oversight, is most often taken as truth and has proven not to work for The People. With the CRB in place, they will provide follow-up commentary on all such briefings. Imagine a State of the Union address with a usual response from the Republicans and Democrats followed by a response from the CRB.

We ordinary folks need to operate and plan our lives and businesses based on what is *really* happening, and since the government has so much influence on us, we must know accurately, and in a timely fashion, what they are *actually* doing and planning. The CRB is aimed at putting the Parties in a more exposed position, bringing and keeping The People and their government more directly together.

Without replacing them, the CRB will be doing a better and more thorough job than the press does, and will not be compromised by the Parties. Through the Citizens' Rights Board, those who currently think of themselves as kings, queens and other royalty over The People will be reduced to being ordinary People themselves, and this will help the power and freedom they have taken from us be restored to us, and remain with us.

We have all heard the politicians of both Parties urging "Comprehensive Immigration Reform." Most believe that is politician-speak that really means easy citizenship and voting rights for between 12 and 20 million illegals—or more. We need to know that number accurately before any action is taken other than border closure. Most want the border completely controlled prior to further action. Had CRB already been in place, we would have been provided with an accurate number constantly for decades which would likely have forced action before the kind of crisis it is today. "Knowledge is Power" and the CRB is about timely knowledge for The People instead of permitting untimely untruths as it is now.

Consider that we more urgently need "Comprehensive *Representation* Reform" to bring the government more in line with truth and the existing citizens than to legalize the presence of millions of some of the least educated people on the North American continent by "Comprehensive Immigration Reform."

The Citizens' Rights Board is to become a new structure placed in the government as a means of *reducing the power of the Parties and improving our representation.*

The six key areas where this could be accomplished are in:
- planning
- accountability
- the judiciary

- elections
- legislature
- energy procurement

Each of these areas would be covered by a separate Division. The NPA, as a lobbyist for The People, would support such efforts and the Party that agrees to put these in place.

Partisan groups like ACORN, which functioned like an Agency of the Democratic Party, have been allowed to receive public funding to support their very partisan work. That is shameful, and *all* funding for partisan groups must be stopped (our Attorney General should perhaps be prosecuting, demanding repayment and confiscating the public property they possess). Such money would be more fairly used by CRB, a nonpartisan Agency in the government that represents *all* citizens and *no* Party.

There are currently regulators, agencies, monitors and Czars who have oversight on all critical aspects of private businesses and citizens on behalf of the government and the Parties. But there is little monitoring by the citizens over the business of government and the people who operate it. Incredibly, the government even exempts itself from sexual harassment rules and from drug testing rules that are commonly required in private enterprise. The Government Accountability Office (GAO) handles audits, legal opinions and policy reviews. Its mission, since 2004, has been to measure performance and accountability by the government. Perhaps it could be renamed, re-missioned and expanded for the more broad efforts *under* the Citizens' Rights Board.

Again, the CRB would be independent, like the Federal Reserve System, meaning that it would function within the government but removed from partisanship. It, too, would be an Agency of the Executive branch, with oversight by Congress. Like the Federal Reserve Board, its leadership would be appointed by the President and approved by the Senate using established guidelines that prohibit partisanship.

Along with seeking to stop earmarks, stopping deficit spending and requiring a balanced budget, which would all be helpful to the citizens but not to Parties, we need a sustained watchdog like the CRB that will demand a higher level of positive and helpful activity from those assigned to represent The People. The CRB would consist of six divisions that would be active in different areas, but all would focus on *making the government more responsible to The People*. This Agency and the work of these Divisions should be able, for the most part, to be established by legislation or by Executive Order. Again, there is no Constitutional scholar here; it may be that as much as a Constitutional amendment may be required to get some of the Twenty-Two Intentions achieved. If that is needed, then the sooner the effort begins, the sooner it will be achieved.

The bottom line is what most of us common sense, ordinary People already realize: Our nation is being operated by Party hacks who operate with mostly *their* best interests in mind. As a result, they expand control over us by taking our money and power. They operate our nation like an amusement park that charges too much for tickets, does not keep the rides moving, and seems not to care about the security or concerns of the people there. We must take this moment of clarity, provided by the recklessness and arrogance of the current Administration, to reclaim our park.

Citizens' Rights Board Divisions:

Division of National Planning
1. Produce key national goals and roadmaps to achieve them
2. Provide a National Energy Plan

3. Provide stability of stated national direction for public, business and politicians
4. Provide performance plans for all government departments
5. Oversee the substantial but gradual reduction in the size of government in a non-disruptive manner
6. Investigate and terminate all financial support of partisan discriminating or ineffective efforts

We all know that in order to take a trip, get into a college, or start a successful business, you need to have a plan. We are a nation of more than 300 million people without a long-range plan that maps out our national government's goals and how to get there. Because we have no plan, we are moving inefficiently from crisis to crisis, and politicians are free to act on a whim and without accountability. This is the reason it seems as though we never learn anything as a nation and that problems are always blamed on those who are no longer involved. Following are some tangible examples.

In the 1970s, we had a low point in the supply of energy, mostly oil. As a result, we had the famous "gas lines," in which people often had to wait in miles-long single lines to get fuel. But you may not know that the crisis also closed many parks, as well as many businesses and schools, and some people died. It was a huge crisis, but there was no energy plan to prevent it, nor was such a plan developed after it was over. Today, more than *30 years* later, we still have no plan, and ordinary People are not even certain why the original shortfall occurred. Instead, even though many pundits at that time stated the need to produce our own fuels for security and economic reasons, our government, controlled by the Parties, has done little to secure and increase our domestic energy supply.

Trillions of our dollars have been shipped to our enemies to purchase from their sources, while our gas, coal and oil reserves are virtually untouched. Nuclear technology, invented by the United States and which is the cleanest and safest energy source the world has ever known, is rarely permitted here. Meanwhile, the Middle East cities with man-made islands, huge skyscrapers and indoor ski facilities have mostly been built with our money, needlessly. And *they* are also underway to develop their own substantial nuclear powerplants.[63] We have no plan to compare any politician's actions against, and we are not sure why such things, which defy common sense, even occur. We must send all of us to Washington, and the CRB with a Division of National Planning is a way to do that.

This Division could prepare a set of documents that would be a performance plan for our national government not for free enterprise. It would set 5-, 10- and 15-year goals for specific results-based performance for every Federal department, including the key areas of importance: energy production and consumption, Gross Domestic Product, Economic Freedom Index rating, median household income, median household spendable income, savings rate, employment, formation of new businesses, internal and external security measures, crime rates by region, election validity, military capability by threat, results of education, and budget needs for entitlements. A reasonable goal might include the establishment of English as the only official language and include a plan to achieve and maintain that standard.

Such information and assured intentions will engender stability and help our businesses and institutions make better

---

[63] (2010, September, 25). Middle East Countries Race for Nuclear Power, Professional Reactor Operator Society. http:// www.nucpros.com/content/ middle-east-countries-race-nuclear-power

plans on how to achieve their own success, just as it will assist our government going forward. It will help The People and businesses see ahead and prepare while making those in government accountable for achieving these national government goals rather than those of their Parties or themselves. It will help take the politics out of the vital directional issues of our country. During campaigns, comparative information showing politicians' individual efforts versus these plans might actually replace the lies and backstabbing normally seen.

Government has grown to be nearly half of all the nation's economy. We need to reduce its size and the expense of government; this will lessen its control and increase our Liberty as well as help balance the public budget. It needs to be smaller so as to reduce dependency and encourage personal responsibility and to minimize the barriers of starting and expanding business and thus creating new wealth and jobs. More successful business creates increased streams of taxes which can help minimize taxes needed from the citizens.

The Division of National Planning will establish a comprehensive plan to reduce the size of our federal government throughout the nation and the world. It is imperative that the planned reduction be accomplished in a gradual and orderly manner so as to minimally impact the daily life of people and businesses. The first focus must be on waste and corruption. It is well known that approximately 25% of the billions spent on Medicare and Medicaid is spent on waste and corruption while only a few percentages are lost in the private sector. This means that by simple introduction of similar private sector safeguards might allow, for example, a 15% increase to our seniors *and* still have a 10% savings, but it is not done. The People are robbed and go without while its

> "...government is too big to function well and too powerful to care."

Party controlled and overpaid government is too big to function well and too powerful to care. The size and reduction might be measured by the percentage of GDP represented by the entire government sector. Targets might be to have a staged reduction from its 2010 level of 44% of GDP to 38% by 2020, 30% by 2025 and to 25% by 2030.

Such substantial modification will require major changes such as the closing of entire departments, closing entire lines of service, substantially improving government employee and facility productivity, selling off little used assets and moving government efforts to the private sector. For example, all Federal Departments and programs should be reviewed by the CRB for efficacy and actual service to the public. If, say, the goals of the Department of Education would be better performed by local governments or private enterprise, eliminate it and send all or part of its approximately $75 billion annual budget ($204 million 365 days a year) to those local entities.

After the initial establishment of the nonpartisan National Plans, every five years, the best and brightest thinkers and teachers of America and the world (instead of politicians and their friends in the Ruling Elite) in all related fields could be invited to participate in a carefully nonpartisan review update of the National Plans culminated by a report to The People.

Division of Accountability
1. Make officeholders and officials accountable for statements, communications, and failure
2. End *anyone* being "above the law"
3. Prosecute *all* wrong doing
4. Review and revise all government employee pay and benefits in relation to the private sector
5. Find and remove any entity on American soil that supports terrorism

A primary purpose of this Division would be to monitor and report on all oral or written statements by every major Federal office holder and appointee. It would compare current and past statements and actions and then report directly to the constituents and to government leadership regarding consistency and accuracy. The goal is accountability. The Division will factually compare the past and present positions of key Federal employees or candidates. The Division would keep and report a quarterly "consistency profile" on all office and position holders, including administrative appointees and upper level bureaucrats.

These same politicos often seem to make unsubstantiated claims and assertions. The People making personal and business plans have no easy way of knowing the accuracy or truth of their remarks and writings and cannot afford errors from public misdirection or poor performances.

The media are nearly useless in policing this problem for The People; in fact, today they are like partisan politicians themselves—or worse—since they frequently claim objectivity. Under this Division, all Federal officeholders including all Federal judges, administrative appointees and upper level bureaucrats would also be subject to an "accuracy scoring" on every comment, writing and speech they present. This scoring will be prepared based on objective, nonpartisan facts by the Division of Accountability and reported to both The People and to government and Party leadership.

The People should be able to expect good behavior from those in all positions of governance at all levels. We repeatedly see evidence of bad behavior, which mostly goes unpunished because the Parties protect their own and there is an air of being "above the law." This is unacceptable.

We intend that this Division will also monitor the behavior of these politicos, and that penalties equal to the non-government penalties for similar infractions *will* be imposed. There will be no fixing of tickets, no sexual harassment without penalty, no abuse of fiduciary responsibility without repayment and incarceration. In short, there is to be no special treatment of any government official or group of officials.

We ordinary Americans want answers to things that just do not make sense about our government. For example, why is the Federal Reserve System not part of an independent investigation to establish its accountability in the 2008 financial meltdown? Since 1978 its objectives have included keeping, "economic growth in line with the economy's potential to expand; a high level of employment; stable prices (that is stability in the purchasing power of the dollar); and moderate long term interest rates."[64] Had it met these objectives, that meltdown might have been averted or lessened. Why didn't it? This Division will seek to assess failure, assign accountability and fix the problem anywhere The People are harmed.

It is a travesty that government employees and others receiving money from the public are not subject to the very drug testing that was devised and promoted by the Federal government and interjected into private enterprise. We should have random drug testing and mandatory penalties for all those who get a public paycheck or a welfare check from The People. If it is good that every truck driver is subject to these programs, it must be good that every representative and staff and every judge be subject to the same requirement.

The People have lost their trust in those running our government because they have been so often mislead or lied to. We have seen Party leaders claim that there is more than one truth. That is not possible. It is so important, let us restate it here: Truth has been understood for thousands of years to be

---

[64] The Federal Reserve System, Purposes and Functions. (2005, June). Page 2, Washington, D.C.

this definition: "1. Conformity to fact or actuality. 2. Fidelity to an original or standard."[65] There can be different points of view, and there are different opinions on how things should be, but there is only one non-spiritual truth, and that is based on facts. The People can form their own opinions, but we need facts and truth to do it, not untruths; otherwise our power is taken from us.

We will not debate "what the meaning of is, is." We will no longer tolerate those who lie by inventing new definitions for words. If our representatives lie or mislead us, we intend to know it and we intend to punish them for it, and not wait until the next election. We intend to take the "consistency profiles" and the "accuracy scoring" and set standards for activity in these areas. We want rules in place in Congress so that failure to meet these standards will be known by The People, and those failing will pay mandatory fines and be subject to imprisonment when leaving office, whether by expulsion from that office or by expiration of their elected terms. All government employees will have the same retirement and benefits as the majority of the private sector; the same mony, the same value, and the same age to receive benefits. All separate government pensions will be phased out and the public sector will be made to match the private sector that pays them.

This Division would also be in charge of prosecuting any non-traffic legal and ethics violations by office holders in the applicable criminal jurisdiction, including lobbyist-related activities. The Division would also set the pay grades of all officeholders and government employees, as well as their benefit scales. No government jobs would pay more than any corresponding non-governmental jobs, and no federal employees will have a more generous benefit plan than a similar level non-governmental

---

[65] American Heritage Dictionary (2nd College ed.). 1985.

employee. Pay and pension levels will be based on the performance of the economy. If non-government pensions lose or gain payout, then government pensions will mirror that change, just as in the private sector. In short, there will be no special treatment of any government employee including those elected.

Ordinary Americans are horrified by the unaccountability of the government in not following the rule of law or of common sense. We cannot fathom how illegals live and work with impunity, how criminals are freed to attack innocents again, how polling places go without enforcement on intimidators or campaigners. We are sickened by having foreign countries permitted to show legal support for Federal action against one of our States, Arizona, but a renegade court prohibits that State from legally answering. This Division needs to assure accountability for those that harm or intend to harm citizens and that means no entity that supports terrorism or is supported by terrorists will be permitted to be free on American soil.

Division of the Judiciary
1. Performance rate judges to the Public, recommend sanction or dismissal to the president
2. Limit presidential directives, proclamations and war powers
3. Establish Federal initiative capabilities

The Judicial Division of the CRB Agency would monitor and report on the actions and judgments of all members of the Federal judiciary. For new Federal judges, it would prepare a "Nominated Judge Profile," with a critique and scoring on bias, that would be distributed to all those involved in nominating, reviewing, approving or appointing any Federal judge, and such reports would be available to all media and the public as well. The Division would monitor sitting judges for both impartial and nonpartisan behavior (Constitution Article III, Section 1). This Division would prepare and report quarterly a "clean judgment profile," which would be a report card on the performance of judges. Federal judges serve at the district, appellate or Supreme Court levels and are appointed "for good behaviour" (Constitution, Article III). The term of appointment is generally for life. That protection from The People may induce Federal judges to create legislative policy from their protected sinecure on the bench. It allows bias and favoritism—and even experiments like considering the laws of other nations before our own, without fear of repercussion. The notion of Federal judicial royalty engenders Tyranny, especially in regard to individual Federal judges. Justice requires blindness, not bias, in our courts; partisanship is ruinous and judgement must seek always to be about the law.

There are nine justices at the Supreme Court level, judging together, and the appellate Courts also judge as a group. But there are 685 individual District Court judges who judge individually. Among them are "activist" judges who attempt to make policy/law to apply to all America. There are also rulings by judges ruling alone and with thin legal evidence that have broad effect. As an example, in August of 2010, California District Chief Judge Walker decided *against* a referendum, previously approved by seven million California voters, which had defined marriage as between a man and a woman. Regardless of the issue, a judicial structure that allows unelected people to wield such power marginalizes the power of the vote and causes concern about fairness among ordinary People.

Law is intended to be developed in the Legislative branch, where Americans are more broadly represented, and by the Executive branch, where the President is constantly subject to re-election. To end judicial policy making, a set of redefining laws may require enactment so that all Federal judges could be monitored for "poor behavior" meaning partial, partisan or personal judicial standards, and that review would be tied either to term limits for all judiciary or removal for cause. Such judicial improvement may require a proposal to amend the Constitution's Article III. This Division will review the issue of the Federal courts and the assurance of fairness, and seek the best means of improvement.

There is also a concern with overreach of power in the Executive branch. At this time, any person occupying the position of President can legally issue an "Executive Order" that becomes "policy" without legislative action. These orders may define or detail the manner in which a law is carried out such that no outside party must review these orders before they become "law." They are, in effect, "decrees" by the President, as if that was a position of dictatorship or monarchy. They mostly fall into two categories—"directives" and "proclamations." Directives are likely to be orders directing the Executive branch to operate in a certain manner. Proclamations are usually used in honor or relating to something narrow, but sometimes they are more expansive in their effect, as was the case with emergencies and use of the Land Antiquities Act of 1906.[66] This act allowed individual U.S. presidents to set aside millions of acres of the nation as national monuments, thus influencing mining, forestry, energy and other business and policy decisions, often negatively—and without any oversight from either the Legislative or the Judicial branches of govenment. Such orders have sometimes caused great issues among the States and between the States and the Federal government.

---

[66] Nielson, J. & Malakoff, D. (2008, May 23). Bush Eyes Unprecedented Conservation Program. NPR.org. http://www.npr.org/templates/story/story.php?storyid=90766237

All Presidents have used these powers—and most with care and deference to the separation of powers—until the last Democrat before President Obama, Bill Clinton, occupied the Oval Office.

A particular incident exposes that the existence of such powers leaves openings for abuse. It deals with President Clinton's effort to act on behalf of his labor union supporters. In 1993, President Clinton had sought to push a law through Congress that would make it illegal for a company to hire permanent replacements for striking workers. Rebuffed by Congress, he issued Executive Order 12954, which would just *make* it so. The Republican-held Congress saw that this order was reversed and all subsequent Labor Department efforts were backed out. The court described the President's act as a "breathtakingly broad claim of the non-reviewability of presidential actions." Clinton had tried to simply make law by himself, because the hundreds of elected people in Congress—which holds the Constitutional power to make all laws—would not. He overreached, but in this case, the doctrine of separation of powers worked.[67]

This Division would seek to use law to lessen the power of any single president, reserving the power entrusted to the groups of elected representatives. It will make that limitation part of a Citizen's Rights Amendment, if needed.

Today, we have President Obama, who has shown a desire to overreach authority granted to his office and perhaps granted to the Federal government at all. His Party's majority in both Houses of Congress for two years blocked action from opposition. His Democratic Party leaders appear to put their goals and their control above the words and intent of our Constitution

---

[67] Gaziano, T. (2001, February 21). The Use and Abuse of Executive Orders and Other Presidential Directives. The Heritage Foundation. http://.www .heritage.org/reaserch/reports/2001/02/ The-Use-and-Abuse

and the traditions of our nation and showed The People that any aggressive party could do that.

This situation was demonstrated in the action taken over the bond holders for Chrysler in 2009. There were even apparent Administration threats used against an attorney engaged by the bondholders.

The same attitude was evident in 2010 regarding the Deep Water Horizon oil spill, as well. It involves an Executive Order imposing a moratorium on drilling affecting more than 30 deep water drilling operations in progress.

First, there is a question about the basis of that order: The Administration cited a report of scientists recommending this moratorium, but the scientists who authored the report then countered it. The scientists disclosed the Administration had *added* that false recommendation to their report. They stated they would have advised against a moratorium. (Note that no one was incarcerated for this fraudulent behavior.)

Second there is a question of the Executive Order being an overreach, but the Democratic Congress will not act to confront a member of their own Party. Also there was the bold "informing" of BP by the Administration that they must pay those affected by the moratorium, but there is no law that makes them liable for the government's regulatory plan.

Finally, the Administration had BP set up, under threat, a $20 billion escrow account to pay claims against BP, ignoring BP's right to defend itself against claims. This is the making of law without the Congress or the oversight of the People and is exactly what our Constitution was written *not* to allow.

Congress can take action to limit Executive Orders or modify them, but as a practical matter, that is ineffective. First, Congress is always busy, with many laws and budget items constantly demanding attention, so it may be overlooked or postponed. Secondly, once again we see Party structure undermining the separation of powers; if even one of the Houses of Congress is controlled by the sitting President's Party, it is not likely even to be reviewed—and normally that means often. The House of the same Party will be in lock-step allegiance to the Party line and the Party leader, who is the President. These proclamations are used often, and they frequently touch on issues of substance to the People. We, The People, need review ability and a channel to push The People's problems to the front of Congress's line of considerations. And this President has established that we need something even greater to block the President and his staff from acting without legal authority and precedent to achieve some other Party-driven ideological victory like increasing control over healthcare. Unchecked actions like these are inappropriate and could lead to other actions that might be of similar substance but would promise a worse outcome.

We, like all democratic nations, must be a nation of laws, fairly and equally applied. We do not have or want a dictator or a royal leading us. Therefore, this Judicial Division would also automatically and immediately review all presidential orders for judicial and constitutional compliance issues and report a summary to both the President and the Supreme Court, as well as Congress and The People. It will seek to establish a consistent tool to block overreaching by any President and lack of action on behalf of The People by modifying law or by its inclusion in the Citizens' Rights Amendment.

While the issue of limiting what individuals in our government can do without involvement of The People is important, it is only one side of the power equation. On the other side is the idea of increasing what the citizenry can do without the lawmakers.

One means of accomplishing this is the "Initiative and Referendum" tools that are already used in many States. An "Initiative" permits voters in a given political subdivision to propose new laws directly for inclusion on a ballot in a public election and without using the State legislature. A "Referendum" allows the voters who object to a piece of legislation (Acts) that their State legislature has in place by petitioning to have the issue put on the public ballot and being voted upon by The People. Together, they allow a means of combating the inaction or poor action of legislative bodies that are ignoring the will of The People, usually in order to act in concert with the Party's line on a topic. These tools, often thought of as one, exist mostly with both the "Initiative" and "Referendum" capabilities in place. In 2010, twenty-four States had some form of these tools, most also applying to their State Constitutions.[68]

This idea, used at the State level, seems to indicate that allowing Americans to vote on topics is a good thing; it is the mass of ordinary People deciding about an issue that they would be subject to and pay for. Some recent examples of the use of these tools include:

2010: California Referendum 1454. (09-0104) — meant to respond to the high unemployment rate by suspending Air Pollution control laws related to Global Warming until the unemployment rate is reduced to a certain point and remains there for one year.

2010: California Initiative 1414. (09-0063 Amend #-1NS); — an initiative for a Constitutional amendment to prohibit that State from re-allocating budget dollars away from where they are *supposed* to be spent by law.

---

[68] State-by-State List of Initiative and Referendum Provisions. (2010, June 18). Initiative & Referendum Institute at the University of Southern California. http://www.iandrinstitite.otg/ststewide_i%26r.htm

> *2010 Washington State: Referendum 71;* — a voter driven attempt to roll back a State Bill that was passed and treats partners at the same level as marital spouses. The supporters of R 71 believe that the law they want rolled back provides an avenue to legally remove blocks that keep homosexuality from existing on the same level as heterosexuality throughout American culture.

Note that the issue here is not whether you approve or disapprove of these efforts, but rather the principle of permitting you to.

This recognized tool has about a century of history in the States. If our proposed Division were successful in establishing it at the Federal level, it would be possible to initiate new national legislation originating from The People, as well as to block or turn back unwanted federal legislation.

Note that if this "Initiative and Referendum Process" were already available at the Federal level now, a referendum on the unpopular 2010 healthcare legislation would likely already be underway. Without it, as it is now, we would have to depend on the Democratic Party dominated Senate, which passed it mostly without reading it and is in Party unity with the Democratic President who proposed it. In other words, barring a decision on unconstitutionality, The People have little recourse from unpopular Party centric legislation unless we can remove the offending Party from office and replace them with a majority of representation that would side with The People.

As the States have discovered, just having the next election to act against those who passed unpopular legislation is not enough. Party members consider the Party goals to be more important than The People's desire, so the Party trumps the democratic intent of our Constitution. A structural change to allow nationwide, Federal "Initiative and Referendum" procedures will simultaneously reduce Party power and increase the power of The People. In our presentation of our proposed Constitutional amendment, the "Citizens' Rights Amendment", we explain "nullification" as another approach for a voter referendum on Federal legislation. Increasing the opportunities for The People to vote is a way to minimize the few controlling the many. It seems like a way to answer many of the questions that harm our unity; instead, some issues just go on existing and remain troubling and divisive.

Division of Elections

- Protect the American voting process
- Investigate having Parties pay most or all of Party Primary Election costs
- Consider changing the primary process to a pre-election where the top two vote getters stand for the general election
- Certify candidate eligibility
- Monitor, fine and ban inappropriate campaign materials
- Eliminate Party use of gerrymandering voting districts
- Assure nonpartisan validity and accuracy of the election process, including voter identification and imposing heavy penalties for voter fraud

The objective of the **Division of Elections** is to make elections less partisan and to assure that elections are fair and deserving of their status as the trusted foundation of democracy.

The "primary election" is a recognized process active in every State, the voting mechanism by which final candidates for each elective office are decided. Usually this works like a pre-election, where the registered voters in major Parties select their candidates for the next "general election" by a balloting specifically tied to Party registration.

The later general election includes the winners of the "primaries," plus any additional candidates running as independents or representing any of the minor Parties.

The People should not have to pay for the process by which Parties decide who their candidates should be. In reality, The People are paying to reduce their choices! This Division needs to study and then recommend a solution that would have Parties each paying for their own primaries. As an alternative to depending upon public funding of their candidate selection process, the Parties could instead decide internally, or with inexpensive digital voting, who their candidate will be. Another option could be to eliminate primaries and allow whomever wants to run to do so. Whoever garners the most votes in the single general election is the winner.

Interestingly, in June 2010, California voters approved Proposition 14, an amendment to the State constitution that changes the nature of the State's primary election process, which was similar to the traditional process. Beginning in January of 2011, this "Open Primary" scheme went into effect, which results in the top two vote-getters for each office becoming candidates in the general election.

This format is generally viewed as less partisan, but it allows candidates to choose whether or not to disclose their Party affiliation on the printed ballot. Given the wide overlapping of Party controls, this may be considered as "stealth partisanship." At minimum, this initiative in our largest state indicates a willingness by The People to modify existing election practices dominated by the Parties.

The CRB Division of Elections will also have the power to fine a campaign for misleading or false campaigning. Many candidates use questionable statements or outright lies against their opposition and thus cheat voters out of making good decisions. The People are abused by Parties and individuals who make a mockery of their democratic system and will no longer tolerate it. The Division of Elections would create standards and guidelines for ethical campaigning and would possess a monitoring capability with authority to take immediate action against violators. A hypothetical "penalty" might be: 200% of the amount they paid for each advertisement containing the lie being paid to its opponent/s, plus a requirement that the offender spend 100% of the original advertising cost to produce and distribute statements of public admission and correction.

The Division would also monitor all elections and certify that candidates are in compliance with eligibility requirements and election laws, including term limits. Those who become or attempt to become candidates falsely will face mandatory fines and incarceration periods. This Division would be tasked with assuring that voting is accomplished according to the law, and work directly with the FBI to send cheaters of any type to prison. Once established, this Division would seek to monitor and review the eligibility of all candidates nationwide, retaining notarized copies of all documents.

The Division of Elections would have the further responsibility of establishing "Fair Voting Districts" (FVDs) for every state. The FVD approach would digitally devise the voting districts based on using the geographic center of the state as the center of the first state district, proportional population, contiguous presence, and compactness, which also supports neighborhood interest. The final plan may include a different methodology to reach the intent, but the intent is to eliminate the continuous debasement of the Liberty of the ordinary People by the manipulation of self-serving Party politicians who traditionally change district boundaries to assure their desired outcome in an election. Called "gerrymandering," this traditional Party manipulation of Democracy assures election of the maximum number of the controlling Party's candidates by re-defining the boundaries of voting districts in its favor. This is a taking of power by the Parties from The People, and denies the intent of our Contitution. Its toleration by our elected and appointed representatives, officers and judges is a clear indicator of the domination of the Parties and the widespread disregard for both our Constitution and common sense that has infected the good government that was gifted to us by our Founders. It is unconscionable that any group be allowed to subvert the election process, upon which

> "It is unconscionable that any group be allowed to subvert the election process."

democracy depends, by literally altering the "playing field" where votes are cast so as to alter the counts. The Fair Voting District concept will eliminate this unfair partisan control over our elections and our lives.

The Division of Elections would also be responsible for overseeing all Federal elections to assure validity and accuracy. Its primary responsibilities would be maintaining the quality of the voting base and eliminating voter fraud.

The base of voters must be protected and must include all those people—and *only* those people—who have a legitimate Right to vote. If an accurate voter group cannot be identified and maintained, no election by The People could be fair and accurate, and democracy fails.

We have experienced groups *purposely* registering unqualified or nonexistent voters in order to get an advantage for their Party or issue. This is an unacceptable affront to every American; it is the theft of democracy from law abiding citizens and a disgrace to all who have served this nation. The current state penalties for voter fraud are as if it is a traffic ticket or, at worst, a drunk driving charge. It is as if we are encouraging and condoning such acts. Federal standards for monitoring and for levying mandatory penalties will be established by this Division for Federal elections and encouraged at all State levels.

Voter fraud is known to include voting multiple times, using another's identity by those not entitled to vote, sometimes with collusion by poll officials or workers. While these types of voter fraud should be handled under the same standards as above, we need to help secure the voting booth directly. A consideration would be to maintain a voter database that contains a fingerprint file that could be electronically read at any polling location, thus providing an instant eligibility check. Anyone attempting to vote but not passing this check would cast a provisional ballot to be checked and then would be subject to later mandatory arrest and prosecution in the event the identity presented is fraudulent. Such debasing activities as instant registration, clearly allowing for fraud, would be reviewed and found to be either operated without harm to the voter base or, if impossible, recommended for termination. Those attempting to tamper with an accurate election, including intimidation and campaigning rule violations, at any level, must be subject to harsh mandatory criminal and civil penalties, whether they be groups (including Parties) or individuals. The lack of these obviously needed penalties is another indictment of our current Party controlled government.

Division of Legislature

- Establish and enforce legislative process requirements including eliminating misleading titles and hidden or inappropriate parts of bills
- Limit bill size, prohibit earmarks, impose and monitor automatic "sunset" provisions, issue certifications confirming a reading by the voting members

- Review for certification that legislation is neutral with regard to race, color, sex, religion and national origin ("RCSRO neutral")
- Develop the initial national budget based on professional rather than political considerations

A **Division of the Legislature,** focusing on structure and content, would establish new rules regarding the legislative process in order to eliminate the consistent Party efforts to mislead, hide wasteful spending, treat citizens unequally, and accomplish deals by including inappropriate provisions.

This Division would begin by developing a standard naming convention system to be used at the Federal level and as a model for the States and lower legislative bodies regarding the naming of all bills in the Senate and House. This system is needed in order to eliminate the present use of misleading titles and confusing references to purposely affect The People and influence the outcome of voting.

"Political language is meant to make lies sound truthful and murder respectable," wrote author George Orwell in *Politics and the English Language*, a 1946 essay.[69]

This Division would intend to remedy written deception in the preparation of legislation. As a nonpartisan entity within the Federal government, the Division of the Legislature would seek to make all legislative efforts absent of misleading words. It would also seek to make all legislation readable and understandable by ordinary People.

It further would intend to limit the length of most legislation to 35 pages, but the limit would vary by type. If it cannot be done in 35 pages, it will require breaking it into understandable parts. This would discourage the catchall legislation they

---

[69] Orwell, G. (1946). *A Collection of Essays*. New York: Harcourt. P. 156.

want and instead require working through the issues for those they represent.

Legislation currently gets put into big packages for multiple reasons, none of them definitely good for The People. First, in hundreds of pages, it is obviously easier to hide items that the authors or others do not want to be seen. Months after the passage of the 2,400-page healthcare bill, both companies and individuals were discovering how they were to be affected. A bill, in either House of Congress, may also become voluminous in order to include incentives for those who might be opposed to the legislation to vote in favor of it. Our elected officials will add provisions that have no relation to a bill's title or summary—but that some other legislator does want. So without discussing and deciding what is best for The People, they do what is best for them by including that desire in some unrelated legislation. While hiding in plain sight, it does not get the attention or vetting by those that might have interest because those that share an opposite interest don't even know it is there. The end result may be two or more bad things for The People—where there should have been none. As an example, this seems to be the strategy the current administration is using on the southern border issue. They are holding out for "comprehensive immigration reform" so they can put a bill together that will act on closing the border but also have some provision to get the illegals here on a pathway to voting for their Democratic Party. There is also some speculation that the Democrats may use this "reform" to include special efforts to bring in people from Muslim countries to help form yet another publicly supported "victim" group that will in turn support their Party.

It should be noted here that the President could issue an Executive Order tomorrow to close the border to all but legal traffic. The reason he does not do that is likely his intention to benefit himself or his Party. While he and the past presidents all have proceeded in a way to benefit their person or Party, hundreds of ordinary Americans have been robbed, raped, kidnapped and murdered. This is just another indication of how our "representatives" are commonly focused on and committed to their Parties, and demonstrates exactly why we must remove them from their position over us.

There are some who think that voting out "bad" politicians will make it all better. It won't, and there is not enough time to try it again anyway. Personnel change does not work. It did not with the Gingrich "Republican Revolution" in 1994, nor will it now. The current structure needs to be changed to allow new life like the water needs to be changed in an aquarium full of dead fish.

The Division of Legislature would also review each piece of legislation to make certain that there were no earmarks or other provisions not directly applicable to the Bill's title and intent.

The Division would set the date and prepare performance summaries on programs to be reviewed for continuation so as to avoid becoming ineffective due to automatic sunset provisions.

The Division would require written certification from all voting representatives and from the President, confirming their actual personal reading of any legislation upon which that official will vote or sign. If they have to miss a few dinners or parties, so be it. Legislation is their primary job, and we expect their personal involvement and responsibility. If they do not like it, they can serve us best by finding a different job. The Division will monitor and report on these activities to the President and directly to The People.

Since the beginning, our nation has rightly demanded that its People work hard to allow equal opportunity for all by not giving in to our human propensity to treat unequally those not like us. This is a noble endeavor, unprecedented in history. Equal treatment of our diverse citizens from many lands is a primary value of our nation and a necessity for harmony and unity. But as we have pointed out earlier, the Parties use our government to reward and punish using unequal treatment as a primary means of extending power over the citizens. Along with legal Justice, Equality demands blindness by the government of what any particular citizen is, physically, or believes in, spiritually. Neither a court's judgment nor any legislation can play favorites and be true to the intent of the Constitution and the expectations of a free People.

Through this Division, no governmental activity would be permitted that would be for or against any citizens based on "race, color, sex, religion or national origin." Every Bill or Executive Order would need to be certified by this Division as being "RCSRO (Race, Color, Sex, Religion, National Origin) neutral." Failure to receive that certification will be immediately reported to the Supreme Court, the CRB, The President and The People.

This Division would also be an unbiased, nonpartisan source of information for the lawmakers in both Houses of Congress as well as Executive and Legislative branches, and The People themselves. This would not be an American government think-tank, but rather a global resource consisting of the best available nonpartisan sources to contribute in their areas of expertise and research. These sources would provide research and data related to legislation, position paper and policy preparation. In this capacity, they would cultivate relationships with experts around the planet and act as a contact center and clearinghouse to incorporate the best facts and thinking into the actions of the Federal government.

The existing Congressional Budget Office (CBO) is a politically compromised agency, as was evident it the handling and yielding to complement the Democratic plans for healthcare in 2009–10. Three months after reporting that the healthcare plan would "pay for itself," in July 2010, they reported that the county was headed for bankruptcy and the burdensome new health plan was a substantial contributor. The CBO is at best ineffectual in presenting key data to The People, and at worst, part of the problem that has helped build the current deficit to repeated record levels. It probably should be disbanded or incorporated into this Division.

Revenue, the job assigned the U.S. House by the Constitution's Article I, should be also be addressed by this Division.

The second part of planned actions would present a proposed Citizens' Rights *Amendment* to detail this issue. The problem is the political nature of revenue because the House is the source of all revenue bills. They create vast expenditures by stuffing the budget with projects of little value other than to specific campaign or Party supporters, including lobbyists and their interest groups. Congress takes money from whatever can be made available to cover at least some of these payback expenses. That is why there is no money in the Social Security account—Congress has been spending it all along, yet consistently telling those paying into it with every paycheck that it is there for them. Congress continually submits last minute high deficit budgets and then browbeats the current president into signing it. The president is not provided a means to eliminate any single part of it via a "line item veto" and so must accept or reject it all. The House then blames the overspending and deficit on the president whose tenure ends after no more than two four-year terms in office. The House, of course remains (having no term limits) and repeats the process, complete with blame, president after president.

The budget development process should begin in the hands of nonpartisan professionals and then pass to the Party-dominated chamber of officials.

Under this Division, such budget makers would include the best economists, accountants and experienced business people, looking out for America rather than being led primarily by those looking out for their Party. The idea of keeping the national budget focused upon nonpartisan requirements versus political goals and schemes seems much more appropriate than the present system and will respond much better to our need to balance the budget and increase our control, instead of the Parties, over our government. Indeed, if we are to get out of the Party-based economic mess we are in, now is the time, and it would probably be best established by the inclusion in the Citizens' Rights Amendment described below.

Division of Energy Procurement

- Create a plan to secure a stream of energy to the U.S.; wisely utilize domestic U.S. energy resources, put nuclear on line
- Protect business, economy and prosperity

The **Division of Energy Procurement** is a logical necessity. The existing Department of Energy seems focused on regulation not on domestic production of low cost energy to fuel our economy and defenses.

It can only be considered an unacceptable abomination that the United States, the world's largest energy user, does not have a solid long-term plan to provide itself with energy. It should have a specific strategy to provide itself with all the energy it needs at the cheapest price possible, maximizing our own resources and minimizing environmental impact.

In 2008, World Energy Magazine and TV quoted me as saying that "energy is the basic building block of human comfort and success".[70] It was and will remain so as far as we can see into the future. With that fact firmly in front of them, this Division would act decisively and quickly. We must get our own resources on line not only to secure us and to be a key to helping balance our trade deficit and budget, but also to fuel our businesses cheaply and assure their success and our national prosperity.

America created the oil business, but our government, dominated by the Democrats and not stopped by Republicans, has strangled our production and drastically limits production from sources on our own Federal lands and most of our continental shelf. This oil that we already own is one of the greatest financial assets in the world. Wealth primarily comes from business or from natural resources, and this is natural resource wealth. This is the source of wealth that the Middle East demonstrates well how it should be utilized. They are using it to support their lifestyle, and they are building up businesses and infrastructure that will continue to build wealth even after the oil is depleted.

The U.S. is having financial issues and our oil, coal and gas are pure money in the bank. Incredibly, our Administration's plan is to somehow develop a miraculous new technology that would replace oil. They do this by increasing taxes, which hurts us and business. *If* their miracle effort did work, it would make one of our most valuable national assets basically worthless. We are told to have the government, king of all that is inefficient, take our money to make a replacement for oil, which will reduce the value of our asset; all this while using less oil, which will hurt business, and with higher taxes,

---

[70] (2010, October, 13). World Energy Interviews "Joe American." http://www.worldenergysource.com/wetv/american/

which devalues our lifestyle. Only the blindest Party ideologue could agree to this.

As far as the hoped for miracle energy source? The U.S. already *found* such a miracle; a means to make a pile of rocks power a city, a carbon clean *nuclear* energy. But for more than fifty years, primarily the Democratic Party has continually blocked its use, as well as the use of coal, and has made us dependent on oil. Since they block our own oil, too, we must source it abroad, shipping our wealth to those who do not like us—and financing terrorists. Rejecting all energy sources, their wisdom is to use less and pay more, pass on nuclear even as the Middle East is building that source and look for something else!

> "Yes, we have an 'energy problem' — it is the Democratic Party."

Yes, we have an "energy problem"—it is the Democratic Party. Their leaders seem to despise the security and prosperity of ordinary People. The Democratic Party seems to constantly seek ways to *control* us, not to *empower* us.

Energy is the substitute for labor via technology, allowing us to do more for less. To reduce our use is to harm productivity, business and lifestyle. We must produce more of our own and use it wisely to develop new, more environmentally friendly, means of energy production. It is a fantasy to think of reducing our consumption to impact the environment unless our major world competitors do the same; they would just replace our consumption with theirs and the planet would suffer the same pollution, differing only in that it originates in a different place. The people of the world want to emulate the energy-based western lifestyle, and they intend to do it. Industrial success, for now, requires cheap labor and/or cheap energy to compete successfully. We cannot just radically cut consumption with the reality of the situation as it is. We must be efficient, but we must make a plan and execute it carefully to minimize the impact on American business, economic security and the quality of life.

This Division would focus on common sense solutions to our energy needs. This, by definition, would exclude Party interests and their supporting interest groups. It would be about wisely fueling the nation that seeks to be the most productive and prosperous place on the planet for the next 150 years.

Imagine the impact on the Middle East if the powers there would not let them use their natural resources. We would have no money problems either, if America was not blocked by the Party system from using our natural energy resources. American energy resources are among the greatest in the world, and whoever says different is a misleading liar. View my video about energy on YouTube. Nearly two *million* people have passed it around; it is one of the most viewed videos of its type in the world. Go to YouTube.com and type in *Joe American Challenges the Candidates*. I am the "Joe American" seen on this video and in many other ways. It was the response to this video by so many ordinary Americans like me that prompted the writing of this book. This video, this book, these ideas really *are* from us ordinary Americans. There is no sham Party affiliation, no money from anybody, just ordinary People who really believe. This is the real deal and I hope that you will join with us, to reclaim the country that the Founders made for us. Tell your friends this truth, and talk about this opportunity. Refer them to the NonPartisanAmericans.com website, and tell friends and every family member to become a proud part of history by joining an NPA group. Let this book be what it is, the ordinary Americans' "Guide for an Extraordinary Nation."

* * *

Citizens' Rights Amendment (CRA)

Many of the suggestions we have made would not seem to require Constitutional amendments, but some will—or would—be better achieved in that manner. The actual course of action will be determined as we acquire the skill sets needed to decide.

There are some things that will very likely require an amendment, and should be pursued under the appropriate title, the **"Citizens' Rights Amendment"** (CRA). According to the Constitution, Article V, the process for an amendment is to have two-thirds of both Houses or two-thirds of the States propose it and three-quarters of the States ratify it. It is purposely difficult, and achieving this effort will help to make certain that the Parties and Ruling Elite will take a position of power subservient to The People and will not be easily able to return to threaten the People's Rights nor any State's Rights.

There are some things that we cannot allow administrative efforts, judicial findings, or actions of Congress to affect. The basics of Equality, Life, Liberty and the Pursuit of Happiness, Freedom and a free-market economy must not be easily threatened by these temporary positions, especially those done by individuals without public oversight.

The Ruling Elite, using the Parties, has shown that it can and will use our elected and appointed positions to diminish our Freedoms, to reduce the possibilities for prosperity for ordinary People and to re-establish Tyranny. *Their* purpose today is the same as throughout history; have the few control the many. *Our* purpose, our dream, our gift and duty to humankind, is FREEDOM.

The following Sections of the CRA are proposed to secure us by revising our Constitution to include: better control of the preparation of our budget; allow the rapid removal of a sitting Federal Administration for anti-Constitution performance;

permit The People to originate and vote on legislation directly; and to mandate that government enforce all laws and execute all programs with equal benefit to all citizens.

Section 1.
The Right to a Free Market Economy

"The right of citizens of the United States to pursue Life, Liberty and Happiness with a Free Market economy shall not be abridged by the United States or by any State."

The success of ordinary People living in free control of their person and property has been well demonstrated over the past two centuries. Free Market Capitalism has remarkably and consistently improved the length of life, the quality of life, and the security in life for generation after generation of ordinary People. Unfortunately, the Ruling Elite who would rather possess control than allow Freedom, continues the age old quest to rule over those ordinary men and women. This Section of the Citizens' Rights Amendment is intended to be a protection to make that more difficult to happen. It will make it necessary to have broad involvement of The People in any decision to move away from Capitalism. Like all of these proposed Sections of the Citizens' Rights Amendment, the details and precise wording will be decided on by those with substantial education and abilities in the details, just as in the Founders' process. But we must begin with the ideas, so here they are in written form, ready for discussion and improvement.

Section 2.
Budget Preparation

"All Bills for Revenue shall originate in the Citizens' Rights Board and then be submitted to the House of Representatives."

According to the Constitution, Article I, Section 7. "All Bills for Revenue shall originate in the House of Representatives," pass through the Senate and then, with review by the President, become law. The President can only review and accept or reject the entire budget being submitted, and it frequently is delivered at the last minute. The Democratic controlled House did not submit a budget nor even establish the spending cap for the 2011 fiscal year before the end of the 2010 fiscal year on September 30, 2010. It is assumed that the reason was to hide the figures from the public to block any negativity about the Democrats that would affect the coming midterm election in November 2010. The budget preparation method is completely politicized and has run amuck, especially in the last six years. Both Parties traditionally blame the bloated and wasteful budget on the president—who term limits out while the Congress remains without term limits to do it all again. Because of this sort of continued irresponibilty and Party centric activity, the financial stability of our nation and the value of the dollar are now at risk. The Citizens' Rights Amendment seeks to remove the budget from the politics, lobbying and special interest groups and instead prepare the budget based on being balanced between revenue and expense, on needs rather than wants, to budget with respect to planned goals, and to minimize inappropriate expenses. Its origination would begin with nonpartisan professionals preparing a budget by the numbers and without politics that includes favoring supporters and disfavoring others, and paying back or paying off. Under the CRA and the Division of Legislature, once the professional budget preparation is complete it would then begin its usual journey starting with the House. They would of course interject politics into the budget, but perhaps less so than in the past (because a full separate report disclosing just the proposed changes would be made available) since the original "professional" budget would be delivered to the media, the

Citizens' Rights Board Divisions and The People. This would clearly discern the added political parts and require explanation and justification by those who proposed political changes. The same would be done at the Senate as the budget moves through, accumulating political interjections openly for review.

The new budget process will limit deficit spending and not allow earmark ("pork barrel") projects. Spending must be no greater than the revenues received, unless an emergency is declared by the president and approved by a majority in Congress, likely for war or natural disaster and likely needed to get us safely back to a balanced budget now. The limit of the deficit would be 10%. If a greater deficit is required, the issue must be taken before the voters of the entire general public with a full explanation, including the anticipated means of borrowing and repaying that debt, and a majority approval. No earmarks will be permitted.

"Earmark" is an American term for the designation by Congressional representatives of specific recipients in appropriation legislation. This permits public money to flow to specific entities, usually within the designating member's district. The designees are usually friends and supporters, and likely financial or political contributors of the member. It circumvents competitive bidding requirements and Executive branch management of that item in the bill. It is a way of paying off supporters with the public's money and getting money to your district to encourage support. This tactic is used to make inserts into all appropriations bills and fills the "pork barrel" that angers ordinary taxpayers. Just the 2009 Omnibus Spending Bill included 8,750 "earmarks" totaling $7.7 billion[71] and was approved by President Obama, who had vowed to not sign a bill with *any* earmarks.

---

[71] Martinez Monsuvais, P. (2009, March, 3). Pesky Earmarks still in the eye of budget storm, *Christian Science Monitor*. http://www.csmonitor/ USA/Politics/2009/0303/pesky-earmarks-still-in-eye-of-budget-storm

The new budget would always be delivered to the sitting president a month before the end of the fiscal year, August 31. It would be prepared with reference to achieving the National Plans (see pg 237). It would prohibit some expenses: those that support nations that oppose the United States in the United Nations in more than 25% of the votes taken; for any program that is not neutral regarding "race, color, sex, religion, or national origin" (RCSRO neutral); that supports any individual, institution or group that is an actively partisan supporter of any political Party; and others, to be determined. The President will be granted line item veto power, allowing the removal of individual parts of the budget. (See the **Division of Legislature**, above.)

Section 3.
Federal Term Limits

"All Federal elected and appointed offices shall have limitations restricting their term of service."

The Constitution sets term limits on the office of President by means of Amendment XXII. This was put in place because of the Founder's unanticipated four terms achieved by President Franklin Roosevelt. The unanticipated rise of the Parties that overshadows the separation of powers and of a Party that is anti-business and anti-democracy help us see the danger to democracy inherent in long term and life term occupation of our important offices. The House of Representatives will be limited to three of their two year terms. The Senate will be limited to one of their six year terms. All Federal Judges, including the Supreme Court will have a single eight year appointment. At its end, they shall stand for a majority vote of confidence before the voters of their respective districts or their appointment process, and every four years after that. If they fail any confidence vote, the existing appointment process will be used to replace them.

257

Section 4.
Vote of Confidence in Administrative Leadership

"If The People lose faith in the Federal Administration they may vote out that administration by a vote affirming "no faith" by the general population in each of two-thirds of the States."

The ordinary People should not have to wait and suffer years of damage by an inept or corrupt administration. Neither should they be required to depend upon any Party to eventually rollback the laws and damage imposed by an administration in which they have little or no trust or confidence. Some may argue that "you get what you voted for." In reality, with the currently permitted well presented lies, media bias and historical and personal information control, it is conceivable that the voters may well *not* know the *true* persons or the positions of those they voted for. Blaming the voters seems a convenient distraction from the real culprits. In addition, the key staff appointments of an Administartion are not made until after election, and these are important in defining and discerning an incoming administration's capabilities and what it is truly about. Requiring suffering for years, or even permanent damage because of The People having believed campaign deception defies common sense. The CRA will offer a common sense means of securing the ordinary People. The need for this protection has arisen because of changes since the writing of the original Constitution.

We currently have a deficiency in our ability to govern ourselves that resulted from the changing technology that has evolved since the original writing of our Founding Documents. The Citizens' Rights Amendment will remedy this problem. In the time of our Founding Fathers, in the mid-1700s, communication was slow. Primarily because of that, it took a long time to make things happen. Today, in the twenty-first century, communication is instant. The Democratic Party leadership is showing us now what a problem this can be for The People. They have moved more quickly than any previous administration with forcing controversial legislation, forcing votes without opposition input, increasing business regulation and taxes at all levels, raising the deficit by hundreds of percent in a matter of 18 months, and by forcing through healthcare legislation that the CBO reported later may bankrupt the country. The rapid movement includes modifying scientists' reports on the Gulf oil spill to support their desire to stop drilling, not enforcing the border laws without getting concessions from Republicans to allow illegal residents citizenship so as to influence the outcome of elections in their favor, filing a lawsuit against the State of Arizona for passing a law to enforce immigration laws, withholding budget approval for our fighting troops in the field until they can get social program concessions in the budget, and much more. They seem to be engaged in a multi-front shock attack against America to put in a Socialist agenda. That was echoed by Wall Street insider Charlie Gasparino on August 10, 2010, when he reported on Fox News that there are key economists now openly discussing that specific matter in boardrooms. The Administration is taking many actions, and many—if not most—American taxpayers view them as negative moves that threaten the nation. This is accomplished through Party control of our Representatives, not through us. Today, the Parties use these blocs to seek what they want in power, money, or political agenda; in current control, it appears the Democrats' bloc is acting intentionally, stupidly, or both, to reduce Freedom and harm Capitalism.

Actions are being made without deference to the Constitution, to the opposition Party, or to The People. They are imposing new regulations on business and threatening people who question or resist. The traditional process of governing has been to inform, consider opposition input, convince, and then to move forward as unified as possible. This Administration does not include opposition, and simply does what it wants to do, putting all of The People in the position of having to stop them. Two times in the current primaries, the Administration oversaw trying to offer Federal jobs to certain politicians if they would not run against the candidate they preferred. The recourse for negative action in the past has been to await the "next election" and then vote the negative administration out. This Presidency has demonstrated that in today's *high-velocity* communication world a poor administration can do so much damage so quickly that waiting until the next election is not practical.

The Citizens' Rights Amendment proposes a provision that will allow The People an avenue to remove a negative Federal Administration from power at any time through a "vote of confidence" process. Any State could initiate a vote of confidence, and, if two-thirds of the States agree within six months after initiation, then the existing administration would be removed from power. They would be replaced by a group identified by the immediate past Presidential election candidate that received the second most electoral votes.

This suggestion immediately brings to mind the issue of need, in that we do have impeachment capability in the Constitution. True enough, and it was a well intended tool provided by our Founders. However, as we have stated earlier, the Founders did not anticipate the presence of political gangs known as the "Parties" today. Impeachment begins in the House Judiciary Committee which investigates it. The chairperson of the committee and a majority of it members may be members of the President's Party and not likely to find serious fault with their leader. *If* they find reason, then it is voted on by the entire House, where a simple majority can approve the "Impeachment," which leads to appearance before the Senate for trial. If two-thirds of the Senators vote for impeachment, the Senate then removes the President from office, and the replacement is the Vice President.

The majority of the House may also be of the President's Party. When fellow Party members are in charge of the Judiciary Committee and have the House majority, these two hurdles are not likely to be overcome, despite the severity of the charges against the President. It would be like asking a group of street gang members to send their leader to a trial on weapons charges, knowing that if they simply refuse, nothing can happen to their leader. It is not going to happen because of "loyalty to Party over law." At the time the Founders designed this impeachment process, our public offices were generally filled by people who had something called "honor." This means "Personal integrity maintained without legal or other obligation."[72] Honor would cause the President to follow his Constitutional oath to "preserve, protect and defend the Constitution" as The People's first level of protection. Honor would also compel the House members to follow their oath to "defend the Constitution against all enemies, foreign and domestic." Honor is lost. Today, loyalty to the Party line trumps doing what is right for personal principle or for the Constitution and The People it protects. In this manner, a primary defense of The People and the States to fend off Tyranny has been overcome. The CRA is a way to get it back, and a way to restructure so no group can act as dictators in the future.

---

[72] American Heritage Dictionary (2nd College ed.). 1985.

Section 5.
Nullification of Federal Law

"If The People oppose a Federal law they may vote to eliminate that law by a vote affirming that opposition by the general population in each of two-thirds of the States."

The idea behind this Section of the Citizens' Rights Amendment is similar to the "no faith" Section above. It offers a means for the People to eliminate a Federal law without having to wait for years and depend on Parties. The Parties use the Federal government to control ordinary People; this Section of the CRA will provide The People a reasonable means of diminishing that control. To make clear its intent, the vote of The People will be further defined to "be in no way reviewable, appealable or subject to veto in any manner, and will become as law immediately and require that the nullified law be rolled back so that it is as if it had never existed, except in its historical documentation."

Section 6.
Federal Initiative Legislation

"American citizens may originate legislation to be placed on the general election ballot for direct voting. If the voters approve of the proposed measure in each of twenty-five percent of the States, it will be placed on the ballot of the following Federal general election and passed if a majority of those voting are in favor and it is constitutional."

This is a tool that needs to be added to the People's arsenal against Tyranny. There is currently no means for the People to initiate legislation at the Federal level. All legislation must originate from the Congress. When the Founders conceived of this policy, our Representatives were not anticipated to be full-time professionals in Washington D.C., nor aggregated by the Parties as voting blocs under their control. Instead, the Representatives were supposed to spend much of their time at their homes, being part of their communities and thus in touch with the desires of their constituents, which they would seek to match. But in contemporary America they are controlled by Parties, representing those organizations, not us. They vote on issues their Parties want and generally will not even consider allowing voting on issues their Party does not want. It is for this reason that The People do not get to decide issues like abortion implementation, decriminalization of marijuana, gun ownership details, having unions in government and mandatory equal treatment by our government.

Twenty-four States have laws that allow initiatives, meaning that their citizens may propose their own laws and vote on them. Interestingly, most of the States that do not allow The People this much authority are the States dominated by the Democratic Party. Understand that these States could easily extend that privilege, but the Democratic Party chooses to not let them have it. "But wait," some of you might say, "they are all about The People!" Wake up. If you do not get that the Democrats have become our primary Party of Tyranny, consider that even in their primary elections, the Democratic Party, not the Republican, reserves the right to have their insider operatives cast the deciding votes on who will run; the State primaries do not matter if the Party controllers want someone else, they just override the vote of the ordinary Democratic people, as they did in Chicago in 2010.[73]

---

[73] Quinn has no Right to Override Democracy. (2010, March 2). Chicago Tribune. article collection. http://articles.chicagotribune.com/2010-03-02/news/chi-100302zaha_briefs_1_override-ballot-integrity-Illinois-democratic-party

Section 7.
Equal Treatment Requirement

"No government entity at any level is permitted to establish or enforce legislation or programs which favor or disfavor any American citizens based on race, color, sex, religion or national origin nor to enforce any legislation unequally or not at all."

Our government was ingeniously designed by our Founders, fully conceived as both a means of empowering ordinary citizens to flourish and of protecting them from Tyranny. Part of that design has been circumvented by the manner in which political Parties use the government's power to enforce laws and execute programs. The Constitution and its amendments establish that all laws are to be applied equally to all States and all people. It is an old story, well covered herein, that rulers would routinely target or functionally apply laws to favor supporters or to penalize non-supporters. That is exactly why it is not permitted in America. But the reality is that the Parties are the primary abusers of the intention of equality that is guaranteed to all Americans. They always have been. The slavery of Blacks, the Jim Crow South, no voting for women, segregation and affirmative action programs are all situations in which Parties made excuses for "having" to run the government as a machine of institutionalized discrimination. Their targets of disfavor have been Blacks, Native Americans, women and Whites; and all would be again, if the Parties could make an advantage of it. Not surprisingly, those who *benefit* from government discrimination always support it. Both the discrimination against the Christians in Russia by Stalin and the Jews in Germany under National Socialism were applauded by non-Christians in Russia and by non-Jews in Germany. Under Party direction, the government creates the excuse as to why it is "right" and "correct," the beneficiaries love it, and those who are disfavored by it term it "unfair." Regardless of any justification, people knew in the past and know today that government efforts and programs that do not treat all people equally are wrong. They can lead to terrible outcomes.

The human tendency to dislike anyone who is not like them, along with the human willingness to get something for nothing, makes institutionalized discrimination by government an effective Party tool. In establishing the Union of Soviet Socialist Republics (USSR), Stalin transferred the property and money of Russia's wealthy and educated to his government and his supporters. Hitler made the Jews the scapegoat of Germany's problems and transferred their wealth to those whose favor he courted. Today, the Federal Administration seems to be expanding inequality in America. It is transferring wealth from those most likely to be opponents to beneficiaries who are their known supporters. But in America we have Liberty guaranteeing control of our property, and our leaders are sworn to uphold our Rights. That was true in pre-Hitler Germany, too. There seems to come a time when we must realize that the status of citizens' rights is tenuous and that *active defense* is required. If enough nonpartisans realize that the time is now, this Section will remove the teeth from this devastating tool of abuse.

This Section will require all laws to be applied and applied equally by any government entity, without exception. If a law is created, it is to be enforced, and if it is not to be enforced, then the same process that created it needs to dismantle it. The laws that remain are the laws that must be followed. And they must be applied equally and without regard to race, color, sex, religion or national origin (RCSRO Neutral). The People expect of our government the same that it expects from us. For example, if you pick and choose for your benefit which rules of the IRS code to follow, you know how the government would react. If you are building a building and decide that the building code does not apply to you, the government will force you to comply with building codes and safety standards. How about if you run a business but decide you will pay some people more based on their gender?

This Section of the CRA will make the Federal government adhere to Contitutional Amendment XIV and allow all citizens an equal footing before the law, standing for their capabilities and merit not upon race, sex, color, religion or national origin. It has been the promise of our Founders and the hope of ordinary People for centuries that our nation would treat us all the same, not on what we are, but by what we do. It will require that all laws be enforced equally among all States and all People.

While there is Federal law that establishes that there can be no discrimination based on "race, color, religion sex or national origin," the government routinely does the opposite by favoring some in those categories and not others. There are "sanctuary cities" where Federal immigration laws are not enforced against Mexicans. There are programs that provide special benefits for Blacks to protect their jobs. Some Americans get educational or other assistance based on their gender. For decades, some government contracts have excluded vendors based on their color or sex. Through such practices, our government enforces laws and programs in a way that discriminates for some and thus against others.

The way this appears to be accomplished denies the logic of those being discriminated against, as it likely did in earlier times when the excuse was "Negroes are considered 'property' not humans" when "separate but equal" somehow made sense and "women were better suited for the home" was common thinking. In each case, the government seemed to develop a scheme by which they could avoid the Constitution's intent of equal treatment; it actually is the Parties using our government to achieve their goals, not ours. Once again the Parties used the trust and commitment to country of ordinary People to get or hold power by favoring some over others.

Today the court's scheme is a "classification" scheme that considers cases based on different groups (determined by them) and the effect legislation has upon them. Once again these Party-appointed officials use their ideology to slice the citizens into groups. Time and again they ultimately justify the Party intent of Party devised legislation to legitimize providing favor and deny the intent of the Constitution that there be no favor. Added to this slicing into groups scheme are three levels of scrutiny: Third tier (or least scrutiny); intermediate (or "heightened"); and strict scrutiny. So, "divide the people into groups and apply attention based on these arbitrary groups"; that seems like a twenty-first century version of the eighteenth century approach that allowed slavery to exist. Doesn't our guarantee of *equal* treatment seem like it requires *no* grouping and the *same* level of analysis for all? If equal treatment were the rule, it would help The People to begin to trust their government again.

The government's job is to establish equality, and it could and would, except that political Parties would rather gain benefit by using *our* government as *their* tool. No Party can be permitted to have "friends" based on its willingness to deny equal treatment under the law. Denial of voting rights, separate seating areas and restrooms, affirmative action and prejudiced juries all seem like great ideas to those who benefit, but the intent of our Constitution and our laws, our history, as well as common sense, tells us that the government must apply all laws and do so equally. There can never be equality in a nation in which the government acts as if "some are more equal than others."[74] And it seems that there can be no equality as long as Parties of the Ruling Elite control our government rather than ordinary People. We may believe in Equality and Liberty, but the biggest "inconvenient truth" of our time is that if these beliefs were reflected in our government, it would remove one of the greatest tools by which the Parties keep us divided and under their control.

Section 8.
Citizenship

"Every person born of at least one American citizen parent within the border of an American territory is granted Rights and responsibilities as a natural American citizen."

Citizenship is *not* simply a legal term for being in a particular place.

Citizenship is *not* a bill for others to pay for you with benefits they have earned.

Citizenship is a shared commitment to the Law and historical Values of a nation, and to the Rights and responsibilities they confer and require. Citizenship is something to contribute to, not to take from. It puts you on a path with others who share in enhancing and improving the pathway while enjoying passage along it. It commands the American to respect and treat as equal all People on that path, and it requires not only that you be personally responsible, but also that you help protect that path, even to your death. As a citizen, your reward is free determination of your place and pace in the progression, and your duty is to earn your passage and to embrace the pathway, until your journey's end; delivering it well to those that continue on. That is citizenship.

---

[74] Orwell, G. (1946). *Animal Farm*. London: Penguin Books.

And that is the message that each school must teach our future citizens.

There are some who trivialize citizenship as just a political instrument to increase Party power. They point to the Fourteenth Amendment and claim that "all persons born here are citizens." They completely miss the mark in what these words were written about. They would tell you that these words make it just fine to break the laws of immigration, give birth here so that the new child becomes not just a citizen, but our burden. That makes no sense at all, unless it is you who is breaking in or supporting someone who is. It is amazing how those that benefit unfairly always happily defend their "right" to take advantage.

First, the fact of being a lawbreaker disqualifies a person from legal entry, which is the first requirement to become a citizen. This is long true in the United States, including all the entrants from Ellis Island, and it is true throughout the world. So the very act of coming in illegally disqualifies a person for citizenship. Some would still pronounce that the child of illegal parents is entitled to the right of citizenship by the parent's presence on American soil. And that is an insult to all those that Amendment XIV was written for. The "fourteenth" was written for the children of American slaves. It was provided for people who really did earn the citizenship for their children by enduring whips and chains and hatred. It clarified that those people, newly free citizens, would have their future children born free.

It is a direct insult to every slave descendent that this Amendment, created in the spirit of atonement and in recognition of the infliction of wrong, be used as an excuse for undeserving pretenders and those who support them. If it cannot be accomplished by law, the CRA will seek to clarify that a citizenship birth must be to at least one DNA-certified American parent.

Section 9.
States' Rights

"The Federal Government will, by whatever means necessary, secure the nation's borders from any movement of people, goods and services not authorized by law; the States have the right to monitor and verify this effort and to assist and augment the Federal effort if for any reason the States deem the Federal government is not fully achieving this Constitutional duty."

The balance between the Federal government and the States has always been an issue. Most would argue that the growth and aggressiveness of more recent Federal administrations has placed the States on defense. The Federal Government sued Arizona in 2010 over its State Senate Bill "SB1070". The Federal intention is to block Arizona's ability to enforce Federal immigration law because the Federal government either doesn't or does so unequally or partially. These sorts of action portend a futher reduction in States' Rights. With the realization of such a possibility at the forefront, now would be the time to firm up States' Rights by means of the CRA. Much discussion will be required, but three early considerations would be the inclusion in the CRA of solutions related to enforcing immigration law—or any law—when the Federal government cannot or will not do so. The others relate to the 2010 healthcare plan, which includes forcing a State's citizens to buy a product, as well as the issue that some States were provided special financial deals to vote in favor of the plan. This seems like the "special treatment issue" raised to the level of an entire State's population.

We want to confirm and secure America as a free country with a free market. That can be achieved by joining many together and using law to seal the cracks where the enemies of Liberty have planted weeds. We can also make a Constitutional amendment like the "Citizens' Rights Amendment" proposed here to further clarify and solidify the power of the ordinary People. Whether regarding States' Rights or any of these issues, there will be a great deal more careful input needed to fulfill the purposes intended. There will be time to do that. For the present, it is the idea that it *can* be done that is important. We ordinary People can get what we need to allow us to upgrade the defenses to protect our Liberty from its newest recognized enemy, The Democratic Party leadership, and from future similar threats as yet unknown.

SIX

Executing Plans

The Citizens' Rights Movement intends to alter the structure of American democracy so as to reduce the power of any Parties and increase the power of The People. It will affirm and secure the Rights shared equally by all ordinary People. There are *two* plans, because we are committed to succeed in this historic effort to affect an *Evolutionary* Point of Change in America; a change that will result in placing most control of government into the hands of the ordinary People, the very People who bear much of the cost of government decisions originated by the political Parties. The favored "Alliance" plan recognizes the current strength of the American political Parties. To fight them head on would require raising huge sums of money and the conversion of all media to nonpartisanship. If it came at all, it would take many years, while damage by the Parties to America would continue. It would be similar to two well armed big city burglars robbing a small town bank while the single local cop tries to recruit a posse of nearby town officers with enough guns to mount a successful attack. Meanwhile, the burglars are shoving money out the back door.

There are potent forces working daily to rob us of our Freedom and treasure. We must act decisively and quickly. Our

273

first step is to successfully meld the various independent and anti-Party groups and individuals into a large nonpartisan group that finds commonality in shared goals and vision for America's future. In the "Declaration" and the "Twenty-Two Intentions" we have proposed a beginning set of goals with a vision, and label those who agree with some or most as NonPartisan Americans or NPA. Sub-groups notwithstanding, we will coalesce into something akin to the NPA "Declaration". The "Twenty-Two Intentions" described on other pages of this book map out the framework of goals of the "Citizens' Rights Movement" to affirm and secure the Rights of America's ordinary People. As we come together, gaining strength from numbers, we will attempt to alter America's political landscape by utilizing the very system that currently supports the Parties so well. The structure of our system has allowed the emergence of an enemy within; that is our *actual* situation. That system, controlled by Parties and not by The People, plus having a Press that supports a Party line rather than a commitment to our nation, has combined selfish special interest groups together to out-vote our opposition.

If we coordinate the scattered millions of us who are now recognizing our national reality, the Parties will want (and likely be forced to need) us to support them in order to win the coming elections. The polls show that overall there are about as many of us identifying ourselves as "voters without a Party" as either Party has voters in their groups. If we organize well around the key points upon which we agree, the numbers supporting the Citizens' Rights Movement could grow to be very large. The driving notion is to have the diverse array of center right groups outside the Parties agree upon the "common denominator" represented in the Citizens' Rights Movement presented here. Of course it can be improved, but the point is to seek *commonality,* rather than to mirror any contributing group's own image. Each group or individual may have its primary topic, like taxation or nullification, or a special geographic area or even an identifier like some part of the Tea Party. These particular interests are great and need to continue. They will serve to fill the need of activism at all level of government because the Parties are active at all levels. The Citizens' Rights Movement will not supersede the structures or hard working people already in place, but rather will function as a complement to our diverse groups. It will provide an overall banner for all of us that is comprehensible and appealing to the undecided and the not yet active and as an difficult identifier to those who oppose us; it is simpler for opposition to attack a tax system or a moniker, but difficult to attack diverse ordinary People seeking to secure their written Rights. The simple front banner that presents our common thread as securing the Rights of all ordinary Americans is both true and appealing. This message should also serve as a driver to encourage new members into the existing groups that are part of this coalition. *Our strength is to be found in those numbers.*

The many ongoing individual gatherings are the right thing to do and must continue, but we need to *demonstrate unity* in a big and politically powerful way. We must come together in order to have maximum effect, to have the power of a voting bloc. The Parties have shown that they will listen to nothing else. Our objective is to essentially become the largest lobbying group in the nation. Our power to deliver more votes and active support than the AARP, big business, or the labor unions will command the acquiescence of at least one of the Parties to our intentions. Let's look at the details of this first plan, and then at a second plan. The back-up plan ("Plan B") will be the next step if we cannot, for any reason, be successful in the first.

The Alliance Plan

We will organize along the lines of a coalition group. Rather than organizing around an age group, like AARP, or supporters of organized labor, like the unions, the Citizens' Rights Movement will organize around our support of the Rights and core Values that have made America a success. I believe that a major cause for these ideals getting pushed aside over the years has been the absence of a significant group actively pressing for them; that is, no one protecting the basics of America. In the reality of today's democracy, we need to provide a lobbyist for America; a "Lobbyist for Liberty" and all she represents.

We trusted our elected officials to do that. We believed that they were sworn to do that—and would. But we were wrong. When the flags came down in classrooms and a new curriculum disparaged our nation, there was no one there to fight it. We thought that was not a good idea, but we trusted those who made the decision. When stopping governmental discrimination against minorities became governmental discrimination against others, we knew that all Americans were supposed to be equal, but we trusted our officials. We have since witnessed a forty-year institutionalization of yet another pattern of governmental discrimination. When we saw the recent financial crisis, we trusted those who said our politicians were not involved, but that was not accurate. Time after time, we have silently trusted and have been silently betrayed. We were told that people had no healthcare because of insurance companies, and the government could change that without new taxes on ordinary citizens. This was false. Now we are told to believe that our officials will not spend us into oblivion and are expected to believe that.

Since the heyday of the indisputable American victory in 1945 and the American nationalism that followed, many anti-nationalist causes have been organized or expanded their work. The ACLU and ACORN represent well-known examples of what most of us term "leftist" groups that are always attacking what we consider to be America. It is fine to seek to refine the promise of our nation, but such groups have gone far beyond that. With teachers' unions and left thinking in public schools, many of America's youth enter the adult world with negative mindsets about their nation and about personal responsibilities. The history of the world, the activities of our nation's enemies, and the present internal state of our country are indicators of the danger of unopposed negative activity within our nation. In 2009, it became evident that the Democrats, to whom we have currently entrusted the administration of our country, had been channeling our tax dollars to support ACORN. This group, with offices across the entire country, was found to be not only partisan to the Democrats, but it was also involved in subverting our democracy by destroying its valid voting base through submitting many thousands of false voter registrations; and they used *our* money to do it! Now we learn that labor unions have grown among the Party employees who inhabit our government, and today they see themselves as more important than ordinary People and private enterprise. They do not realize that all money comes from private enterprise and all power resides in ordinary People. Astonishingly, government workers are now paid on average twice what their private sector peers are paid.[75]

Sadly, many of our government workers and their unions attack capitalism and America. They are an openly Socialist group that is attacking our nation, and getting the money from the public who pays their salaries. These groups are major supporters of the Democratic Party. Instead of seeking to defend our national culture and laws, Party politicians seem more prepared to advance their agendas and those of such groups as these, but

---

[75] Cauchon, D. (2010, August 10). Big Gains for Federal Pay. *The Arizona Republic,* pp. A1, A4.

they do have a weakness. The Parties always have listened to the "squeaky wheel" and sought to support those who support them. It is this character trait that we must mine. If we organize and get the numbers, *we* will be the 800-pound gorilla in the Congressional meeting rooms. We will also be doing our nation and future Americans a service by acting on our duty as citizens. The Preamble of the Declaration of Independence: says, ". . . it is their right, it is their Duty, to throw off such Government." This is our "First Right" the one first mentioned in the Founding Documents and the Right from which all others flow; the Right to control our government so that it serves *us*. We can do this by peacefully utilizing the democracy we are guaranteed.

So the plan is to use the very structure that vexes us now and diverts our power to the Parties to turn it back to us. And who is *"us?"* We know from meetings and polls that most Americans are neither far right nor far left, but rather in the center and a bit to the right. In practical terms, that may mean that although most of us ordinary Americans believe in God, we do not wish to condemn or discriminate against homosexuals. Our Centrist position may mean that although most of us are conservatives with respect to business and economics, we may be likely to favor things like the controlled medical use of marijuana. The center is wide, and its commitment to the country is deep. Being in the center certainly means that we are not enamored with the extremes of *either* Party. Until now, we were the "silent majority" that simply assumed that those we put into office and public service would, in some way, reflect us and our interests. Despite Party wrangling, we assumed that the strengths of Freedom and Capitalism were safe, at least from internal enemies. Now we see that was not true. The strengths of our government have been slowly eroding under political Party control for some time, and those now in control care little for the rules or traditions of our land, which they openly defy. For all the reasons mentioned in this book, our standard of Freedom and Prosperity are, for the first time, in doubt. We can see it and we *can* do something about it. We can use our democracy, without chaos or violence, to replace those who hold our offices and to alter the structure, just as the Founders intended. Experience has shown us that changing personnel alone is not enough. *Personnel and structure* is the way. We must act now or we will lose the opportunity to use it. Our nation is wounded by those who did not and do not deserve our trust. We must be the first responders for our nation, because the Parties that we have trusted will not or cannot. *We* can and we must; hence, the Citizens' Rights Movement.

For those of us who are attracted to this nonpartisan effort, neither Party matches what we want in a political organization. But most of us would agree that the Republican Party is much closer to our center, and, I believe, we can "train 'em" and do it quickly. Of necessity, **The Alliance Plan** calls for a *probationary* alliance with the Republicans *if they adopt the key elements of the Citizens' Rights Movement*. Evidence will be seen as we establish a dialogue between the Citizens' Rights Movement and the mainstream of Republicanism and as they adopt our key positions in their literature, candidate talking points, and candidate selection for the coming elections. In 2012, we should see solid planks in their platform that reflect ideas matching or similar to many of the ideas in this book. If we bring the numbers, the volunteers, the money, and the votes and align them with the Republican efforts (but always identifying ourselves as NonPartisan Americans in support of the Citizens' Rights Movement) we will defeat the current Democratic Party leadership activities that many of us view as the greatest threat our nation has ever seen.

I know that many of us feel that the Republican Party is a problem, too, and we are right. Like the Democrats, they are part of the Ruling Elite that seeks the control of the many. While they shone brightly in some ways when Ronald Reagan was President and with Representative Gingrich in the House, they have since gone off track, overspent our dollars, and not only did not stop the housing and financial debacle from occurring, but even contributed to it. **The Alliance Plan** is a *plan of necessity* that calls for us to join them in order to win against a far worse enemy. This is similar to the USA joining with the Soviets to defeat Germany in the Second World War. The objective of defeating the common enemy required immediate attention, and then we sorted out the rest later. That strategy worked then, and it will now.

The Republicans, too, have lost track of what has made America exceptional, perhaps another victim of our national structure that has no lobby for the ordinary People and for the American self. We must take the Republicans to the woodshed and get their minds right. We must make them see the error of earmarks and the necessity of controlling the borders. They must commit to eliminating deficits and establishing accountability. In order to assure their Party *reform*, we will require concessions that will lessen the power of all Parties and strengthen the power of The People.

We will establish Citizen monitoring and national character preservation entities within the structure of our government. It simply cannot be left to chance or to the Parties. That we know, does not work.

These actions will help assure that our nation can resist any future attempt to return us to the frightful position we are in today, a time in which government is on a rapid march of expansion and control, business is afraid to hire, and wealth transfer from those who pay taxes to those who pay little or nothing is being forced on an economically threatening scale. The ordinary People, who arguably do the most and pay proportionately the most, are afraid for their country and for their own well being. This should never be so in any democracy not under armed attack.

At minimum, we would expect to have the Republicans work with the NPA to:

- Reduce the control of the political Parties in the governance of America so as to assure transparency, accountability, and the conveyance of all benefits of the nation to The American People and *not* to the organizations that seek to control them.
- Minimize the disunity fostered by political Party partisanship. It separates The People from their government at the cost of Freedom, Fairness, Equality and treasure.
- Eliminate public support for anything related to political Parties—money, space, time, recognition, and security. Use of public funds to support particular political Parties is similar, or perhaps the same, as supporting particular religions.

Let me explain the PROBATIONARY point mentioned a few paragraphs ago. It is so important to our country that we succeed, that we must prepare for a "Plan B" if it fails.

Both Parties may fight us at first, and they have the media to use as attack dogs to discredit us and mislead others. We will use the Internet and social networking, of course. But these Parties are in control and could push back hard. The Democratic Party leaders have already shown that they will likely use the control of government to intimidate and threaten, accuse and attack. It is clear that most of the media is their lapdog. Our alliance with the Republicans, if it can be made for the next several years, must not encourage permanency. While *our hope is that the GOP can be reformed* to be the correct choice for a majority of most taxpaying voters of America, there is power and there are egos to be dealt with, and these can override both logic and reason.

There are no guarantees in politics. That is why we want to encourage separate identification even while we would operate as an ally. Not only are we likely to get more generous concessions by retaining our own identity, but also we will be prepared to move to Plan B, which is outlined below, if we must.

This **Alliance Plan** is not the whole answer; I am just an ordinary American delivering ideas to be considered. But this is a place to start. We will be collecting and vetting ideas from everywhere in the international forum at NonPartisanAmericans.com. I am certain that more and better things will come out as we move ahead, for that is the way things work. But we *must* get started now.

Growing the Numbers

If you have not yet done it, go out on the Internet, then to youtube.com and type in "Joe American challenges"; you will see a talk that I prepared during the past election cycle. That talk, showing concern about both of the Parties and about common sense thinking, struck a chord. Astonishingly, this simple and serious message that I did with a snapshot camera at my dining table was passed around to nearly 2,000,000 American viewers. Nearly two *million!* Compare that to the views of other serious political talks you see listed on YouTube. It will become clear to you that we are not alone. It wasn't propelled by any TV coverage or by celebrity content; it was not entertainment; rather it was the *message* that moved it based on the common sense thinking that so many of us share. Knowing that there are so many ordinary, concerned citizens in our land has been my encouragement and it should be yours. That is precisely what we must have. And that is precisely what our Founders knew we would someday need. It will take many of us to do this work; but there really are *many* of us.

So we must get going, and it starts with simply letting us know that you are up for it, into it, or otherwise interested. Go to the website at NonPartisanAmericans.com and check in, if you have not done so yet. Tell your friends, too. The only way they will likely know about this is if *you* tell them. Send the link to the website to everyone who may be even slightly curious. Become a Member and start doing the "Member Things" that you see there. If we get significant numbers, say above 100,000, we will call for the Citizens' Rights Movement Leadership Conference requesting representatives of all Independents, Tea Party groups, 9/12 groups, Town Hall and other like-minded nonpartisan groups and individuals to a web meeting. We will identify and improve upon our common themes and begin an agreement delineating and describing our intentions and roles in the coming elections. I want to clarify that the NPA is not intended to take over any groups, but rather it will be like a lobbying entity and consultant for *all* the groups and individuals who share a common interest in our Rights and want The People to control our government, not the Parties. The Citizens' Rights Movement intends to be the Big Umbrella and perhaps the Big Voice that we are missing.

Plan B: Digital Democracy

This secondary/backup plan would begin a direct but difficult effort to marginalize—or even eliminate—political Parties. Essentially the NPA would become a new political Party with the objective of diminishing Party power and raising this power of the People using modern technology. This would be a bold move. This effort would seek to modify the way representation occurs in our democratic republic. The current form has shown to not represent the voters well. For years, D.C.

has been disconnected from The People, and is dramatically worse today. Now we see legislation passed without reading, no opposition permitted, and sudden, immediate voting.

We need look no further for the mockery of our representation than the healthcare bill. It was developed by one Party behind closed doors, totally excluding nearly one-half of all Americans from representation in the matter. It was supported by stunningly misleading statements, forced through against the accepted procedures of the Senate, and passed despite a majority of The People being against it. Similar to our Founders, we now seem to have taxation and governance without representation. If we do not succeed in reducing the power of the Parties in a probationary alliance with the Republicans, then we must pursue the more bold remedy of "Plan B".

An option we must seriously consider is to restructure our democracy to reflect the capabilities available today. We would consider changing the structure of democracy in a manner that appears not to rely on Constitutional amendment, which would circumvent much of the resisting capability of the Parties.

It is true that nothing like we are suggesting here, as a last resort, has been done before; but it has never been technically possible until now. We would seek to apply a high-tech approach to our governance, permitting an enhanced and highly direct democracy to transfer power from the Parties to The People. It would seek to influence significantly all levels of governance in America. It would be based on the Founding Documents that led to our national success, yet it will be revised to eliminate the failures created by institutionalized partisanship.

The NonPartisan Americans/NPA "Digital Democracy" Plan

Consider the establishment of a system of direct voting in which every vote has an actual bearing on every candidate and issue for which it is cast. This would be set up as "Digital Democracy," where all issues at all levels will be voted on directly by qualified voters and then each elected representative *must* cast his/her vote *according to their constituents' vote*. If established, the NPA would certify candidates that meet its standards for nonpartisanship, adhere to its Intentions, and sign a written agreement to follow its program for Digital Democracy.

Digital Democracy Goals

- Take away the power of Political Parties by which the few control the many. They have long served as a tool to gain and maintain controlling power for the few from certain families, schools, and social strata, race, or religion. If we are executing this "Plan B," it is because the Republican Party would not help The People transfer the power of the Parties to The People.
- Remove the ability of those in the political Parties to control information sources and its distribution. The People require accurate information to make good decisions regarding their governance and their personal lives and need unquestionable sources not allied to any political Party.
- Deny public financial support for any political Party— no support for elections put on for political Parties, no support for any entity that is in any way partisan. These Parties are private, partisan organizations and should not be paid for by the public.
- Eliminate the disunity fostered by political Party partisanship. It separates The People from their government at the cost of Freedom, Fairness, Equality and Treasure.
- Expunge any partisan bureaus, individuals, structure and traditions in the government. The legacy of gang rule over The People must be dismantled.

- Prohibit partisan appointees other than the cabinet, including all judges; fair service and justice for The People demand it be so.
- Encourage citizens to withdraw financial support to any political Party and to any corporations, organizations or media that are biased toward any Party.
- Uncover, point out and protest any effort by the Parties to keep their unauthorized stranglehold on the American government.
- Put financial or other support only behind nonpartisan candidates who have never been any Party's candidate and are sworn to be nonpartisan through NonPartisan American Certification.
- Achieve the goals and objectives of the NPA Declaration and the Intentions at all political levels.
- Modify the national government's funding structure to better serve the interests of the nation and The People. It needs to be reformed on both the revenue side and on the expense side. First, these two must be aligned so that The People are protected from unaccountability, waste, and currency debasement. Consideration must be given to permitting deficit spending only in temporary, emergency situations or perhaps even restricted by a new Constitutional Amendment that would require approval by the States. On the revenue side, there are the possibilities of "flat tax" and "fair tax" (as well as other models) to consider, but recognize that we must have everyone paying into the national tax stream. There is an element of fairness but there is also a real world reason; i.e., any democracy must be protected against those who would selfishly vote themselves money without regard for fellow citizen or nation. Everyone needs to feel the pain of necessary taxation.

Unlike mainstream Party candidates, NPA Certified candidates would not be brokers of their constituents' power on behalf of Parties, lobbyists or themselves. Certified candidates would be sworn to adhere to Digital Democracy guidelines and primarily serve as conduits of information for their constituents. When it is time to cast any vote related to their elected position, they would commit to casting official votes that match the results they receive from the internet gathered sub-votes of their constituents. Information out, digital sub-votes collected and recorded, matching official vote cast. That is it. The People would have spoken. No smoke filled rooms, no lobbyists, no secrets, no celebrity politicians; just the power of The People at work.

Basics: The NPA will seek to identify and certify candidates for offices at all levels of government who will commit to using Digital Democracy as a basis for casting whatever official vote(s) they are responsible for. As elected officials certified by the NPA, they must poll all of their constituents via computers and then *must* cast their official vote to match the majority from the poll. There is inexpensive software already available to do this, which could be easily utilized by every representative in every elective district. NPA would customize one of these or could create its own software.

Why?

If the choice is to seek a new structure for our democratic republic or to separate from Liberty and accept greater loss of Freedom and perhaps Socialism, this effort would be a better choice. The methodology would make the representatives actually *be* representative of their constituents. The lack of computer technology in the past forced us to accept that we ordinary People could not vote directly on the issues and laws. It was not functionally a possibility because of the time to communicate and to make and count votes. That is no longer true. Just the New York Stock Exchange alone handles all transactions and settles all accounts to the penny for about one billion transactions *every* weekday. It is monitored simultaneously, and a complete record of every single transaction and all summary reports is made with virtually no fraud. Indeed, additional billions of transactions are handled throughout the world each day by banks and retail outlets. Securely handling hundreds or thousands of votes in a city council election/issue vote or even some millions in a Federal Senate district can be done today with relative ease.

By using Digital Democracy, the NPA elected officials will truly represent their constituents, not simply be *said* to represent them because they have a home address in their district. We will still maintain the democratic republic that is the basis for our nation, but by the Digital Democracy method, those elected will be truly representative of us. Currently, we elect people to represent us in the official voting but then they really vote for what they think, or more likely what *their Party or other special interest wants*. The last thing they represent is *us,* but that is exactly who they *should* represent. This Plan will make them do it.

With NPA-elected officials, the power of the Party is eliminated. Our candidates would be committed to vote only to match their own voting district majority or they are contractually required to pay a substantial fine, be rebuked and perhaps forced contractually to resign. They will be accountable to The People who put them there to represent their interests, not those of any Party.

With NPA-elected officials, lobbyist and special interest influence *disappears*. Since relationship, bribery and collusion could not determine the official vote to be cast, as it can currently be and often is, these factors are moved to the background and The People's desires are moved to the foreground. Instead of having celebrity status, politicians who can now be controlled by the Party or bought by special interests (those interests often likely different than those the ordinary People), will transcend such control. NPA officials will have the primary job of conveying the issues at hand directly to their constituents, based on facts, offering an explained recommendation, monitoring their district polling on the issue or legislation, and casting their official vote accordingly. This activity will require them to read and know, just as a teacher must know academic subject matter in order to convey it to students. These representatives are reduced to a clerical function with trust instead of having a celebrity function with power.

The Plan includes establishing a presence in each State and from there setting up a network of ordinary People NonPartisan American committed candidates at the county and city levels, as well as in elected district offices, including school administrations.

The NPA effort in this alternative Plan B is truly "grassroots," which is both a blessing and a curse.

The blessing is that once there is an understanding of the goals and that it is truly generated from the ordinary People up, not just some scam of the Ruling Elite, many People will find it appealing and want to join in and support it.

The curse is that there will be no money available as in the political Parties that we oppose. No companies will offer money because they plan to get that (and more) back through a government contract payback. There will be no union sending cash to assure they gain a concession or some huge pension plan at the expense of the taxpayers or the competitiveness of an American business. We will not be a political Party using public money and votes to pay supporters as the Democratic Party and ACORN have done. And we will not receive public money from a generous Federal grant in exchange for supporting a political Party as the National Endowment for the Arts (NEA) apparently did in the late summer of 2009. Rather, those are precisely the sorts of corrupt, abusive and illegal activities of the major political Parties, to which our "lost" American media consents by its silence, and that we seek to eliminate. We must attract all those people and organizations that value Truth, Fairness, our Founding Documents and the Rule of Law to help support our efforts in turning back the tide of lies and deception that the current political Parties embrace. We will have to make it on the purity of our actions, on the correctness of our intent and on our passion for our nation. We talk here of attempting to make a major change in the way government is done without using any weapons, as in a revolution. Instead, we seek to create an NPA Evolution, using common sense and common people.

Why Not?

This would be a hard fought battle, waged both against political Parties and other antithetical interests at the same time. Most of us can recognize the validity and the potential for good government that is offered by the NPA "Digital Democracy" approach. On the other hand, many will not like it because they now reap rewards from the system as it is, and these rewards will be lost to them with the advent of a new system.

Happily (for you), you will be reassured of the efficacy of the Citizens' Rights Movement itself by the vigorous attack that will be forthcoming against it from the political Parties and those who support them and realize great gains from them. They will hate it.

Once fully established, it would eliminate the Tyranny of the American Ruling Elite class that is currently in place.

The Elite will likely fight very hard to stop any group from destroying the "amusement park." They will seek to destroy those who stand against them.

It will take true vision and dedication to see it through, but the notion of Liberty of ordinary People is at stake. They will assert that we ordinary People do not know enough or are not smart enough and that we should not be allowed to directly determine the course of government.

This condescending attitude fits the Ruling Elite, but here is what we know: thousands of years of human history show that people will naturally act in their own self interest. So it is with both the Elites and with the ordinary People. That knowledge finds evidence in decades of the exploitation of ordinary Americans. We have witnessed the actions of the Ruling Elite class and the political Party gangs that they have created. They act constantly in their interest to secure and expand their power and their wealth by using our government as a means. If we ultimately come to the point at which we must seek to implement this "Plan B" seeking more direct control in our government using the technology of today, it will be because *they* caused it.

It is the Parties that have mocked the meaning of our Founding Documents, boldly discounting their meanings. It is these Parties who would have us believe that the ordinary People are better served by reducing their Liberty and their Freedom to control themselves and their property.

> "...the Parties ... have mocked the meaning of our Founding Documents, boldly discounting their meanings."

"Just allow us to have this power over you." "It will be better for you and your nation." They lie. Theirs is the boldest lie in human history. It is the one best known. It is the lie that has oppressed the ordinary People since human life began. It is the lie that has caused the drudgery of centuries and the chaos of rebellion. It is the lie that persisted until America was born and created modern democracy. It is the exact lie of dictators that have killed millions and subjugated millions more as they convinced free people to believe it. They, too, said that "the constitution is tired," that "law should be based not on limiting the state but on achieving the goals that the Party knows are right for the state."

They, too, said that judges should not be impartial or follow the law but rather consider the current goals stated to be more important by the Party. They convinced some and used them as a bridge to force others. Even the worst of our "diseducated" today know of the disastrous fate of Germany and the Soviets—a fate that we do not wish to share.

SEVEN

Concluding Remarks

For ordinary People who give up their Freedom to others, the results can be as dire as destruction or it may be only the loss of opportunity and potential success traded off for a more equal outcome.

Where Freedom is reduced, the ordinary men and women can succeed only within defined boundaries, and the "state" controls the choices.

Perhaps that is what Americans want. But millions and millions of people came to America for the opportunity to *succeed*. That is strong evidence of their true desires. And if there is a possibility of departing from what America has been since its beginning, shouldn't we, as a Free People, *decide* that issue?

Shouldn't we have an open debate with in-depth discussion of the subject prior to moving away from what has been the central value of Freedom in America?

If those who promote the notion of giving up freedoms and increasing control by the Party truly *believed* that theirs was such a good and acceptable idea, why not put it to a vote?

Instead, what we see is the opposite. We see the loss of transparency, we see forced legislation, we see twisted rules, the appointing of partial judges, we see the transfer of wealth, and we see rules, regulations and laws not enforced.

In short, we see the increasing isolation of our government from The People and its acting without our consent. Consequently, we are forced to act, because the Parties have caused our government to go away from us.

America, because of its position of leadership among the democracies of the world, now stands at a crossroad for all humanity. We, the ordinary People, are standing at the intersection. We don't represent ourselves alone, we represent the ordinary People from all of history. The decisions we make and the efforts we take in the short months and years ahead will determine the future for all the ordinary men and women that follow.

We have the power to determine that direction. If we don't, the direction will be determined for us. There is going to be change. The Democratic Party leaders are taking aggressive action and putting us on the defensive. We are clearly being challenged to resist. The attack on our Liberty and economic system today is as clear as the attack on Pearl Harbor. We must either accept the changes imposed by those who want greater rule over us, or we must fight back and impose *our* will on *them*.

They are leaving us no choice, and they are thinking that we are too weak or too stupid to turn back their aggression. For the first time, we can see how far a Party can go in the current structure. It can be a dictatorship, an enemy at the gate. Now is the time to turn them back and block their return. This is the day. No matter what the Democratic Party says now, they showed that they, and any Party, can become an enemy to a free People. We have seen that our current structure allows it. We must act in a way that blocks *any* Party from becoming an enemy to our Freedom in the future.

The ordinary People can never again trust the Parties to act on their behalf. For true and positive change for the benefit of ordinary Americans, we must stop supporting the Parties with time and money and votes. Instead, we must firmly lead them, as in **"The Alliance Plan,"** or we must reduce or eliminate their power over us, as in the backup **"Digital Democracy"** plan; either way, we must trust ourselves, and we must act. Now.

* * *

And so it comes down to three questions:

Do we have a structural problem in our government that has allowed the power to rule to flow away from The People?

If so, who holds that power today?

And finally, *can* we and *will* we do something about it?

As to the first question, the power to rule has been eroded as the political Parties and the government they control have grown. Our governmental structure, as brilliant, unique and wonderful a gift that it is, has some flaws; it was only a brief time before the spirit of domination that naturally inhabits some few began to find its way in. The resulting political Parties have since established a blanket of control under which their leaders have reduced our Freedom and wealth and increased their own.

As to the last question of can we and will we put the power back where our Founders planned it? The answer begins now and with you. This book puts a concept and plan on the table for discussion and refinement. Will enough of us seize the duty our Founders assigned us to watch over our government and keep it serving The People?

Will *you* act?

Will *you* commit?

Will *you* talk to your friends and family about it?

Will *you* tell them to get this book, go to our website and prepare to be counted and to vote?

Will *you* stand for your Freedom, your Prosperity, your future and your family?

Will *you* step up to affirm and secure the Rights granted by the Creator as the Founders did?

Go to the NonPartisanAmericans.com right now; not later, at this very moment!

Become part of the NonPartisan Americans that will win by using the best weapons ordinary People can have; our *unity* and our *vote*.

Please make a commitment, right now, to join us in combining our strengths so that we roll back this attack and improve our defenses. Do this for yourself and those you care for. Do this for your nation. Do this for **Freedom**.

As I have said before, "*It will take many of us. But there are many of us.*"

NonPartisanAmericans.com

Tim Horn,
Founder, Ordinary American, NonPartisan

APPENDIX A

The Declaration Of Independence

IN CONGRESS, JULY 4, 1776.
THE UNANIMOUS
DECLARATION
OF THE
THIRTEEN UNITED STATES OF AMERICA.

WHEN, in the Course of human Events, it becomes necessary for one People to dissolve the Political Bands which have connected them with another, and to assume, among the Powers of the Earth, the separate and equal Station to which the Laws of Nature and of Nature's GOD entitle them, a decent Respect to the Opinions of Mankind requires that they should declare the Causes which impel them to the Separation.

We hold these Truths to be self-evident, that all Men are created equal, that they are endowed, by their CREATOR, with certain unalienable Rights, that among these are Life, Liberty, and the Pursuit of Happiness.—That to secure these Rights, Governments are instituted among Men, deriving their just Powers from the Consent of the Governed, that whenever any Form of Government becomes destructive of these Ends, it is the Right of the People to alter or to abolish it, and to institute new Government, laying its Foundation on such Principles, and organizing its Powers in such Form, as to them shall seem most likely to effect their Safety and Happiness. Prudence, indeed, will dictate, that Governments long established, should not be changed for light and transient Causes; and accordingly all Experience hath shewn, that Mankind are more disposed to suffer, while Evils are sufferable, than to right themselves by abolishing the Forms to which they are accustomed. But when a long Train of Abuses and Usurpations, pursuing invariably the same Object, evinces a Design to reduce them under absolute Despotism, it is their Right, it is their Duty, to throw off such Government, and to provide new Guards for their future Security. Such has been the patient Sufferance of these Colonies; and such is now the Necessity which constrains them to alter their former Systems of Government. The History of the present King of Great-Britain is a History of repeated Injuries and Usurpations, all having in direct Object the Establishment of an absolute Tyranny over these States. To prove this, let Facts be submitted to a candid World.

HE has refused his Assent to Laws, the most wholesome and necessary for the public Good.

HE has forbidden his Governors to pass Laws of immediate and pressing Importance, unless suspended in their Operation till his Assent should be obtained; and when so suspended, he has utterly neglected to attend to them.

HE has refused to pass other Laws for the Accommodation of large Districts of People, unless those People would relinquish the Right of Representation in the Legislature, a Right inestimable to them, and formidable to Tyrants only.

HE has called together Legislative Bodies at Places unusual, uncomfortable, and distant from the Depository of their public Records, for the sole Purpose of fatiguing them into Compliance with his Measures.

HE has dissolved Representative Houses repeatedly, for opposing with manly Firmness his Invasions on the Rights of the People.

HE has refused for a long Time, after such Dissolutions, to cause others to be elected; whereby the Legislative Powers, incapable of Annihilation, have returned to the People at large for their exercise; the State remaining, in the mean Time, exposed to all the Dangers of Invasion from without, and Convulsions within.

HE has endeavoured to prevent the Population of these States; for that Purpose obstructing the Laws for Naturalization of Foreigners; refusing to pass others to encourage their Migrations hither, and raising the Conditions of new Appropriations of Lands.

HE has obstructed the Administration of Justice, by refusing his Assent to Laws for establishing Judiciary Powers.

HE has made Judges dependent on his Will alone, for the Tenure of their Offices, and the Amount and Payment of their Salaries.

HE has erected a Multitude of new Offices, and sent hither Swarms of Officers to harrass our People, and eat out their Substance.

HE has kept among us, in Times of Peace, Standing Armies, without the Consent of our Legislatures.

HE has affected to render the Military independent of and superior to the Civil Power.

HE has combined with others to subject us to a Jurisdiction foreign to our Constitution, and unacknowledged by our Laws; giving his Assent to their Acts of pretended Legislation:

FOR quartering large Bodies of Armed Troops among us:

FOR protecting them, by a mock Trial, from Punishment for any Murders which they should commit on the Inhabitants of these States:

FOR cutting off our Trade with all Parts of the World:

FOR imposing Taxes on us without our Consent:

FOR depriving us, in many Cases, of the Benefits of Trial by Jury: FOR transporting us beyond Seas to be tried for pretended Offences:

FOR abolishing the free System of English Laws in a neighbouring Province, establishing therein an arbitrary Government, and enlarging its Boundaries, so as to render it at once an Example and fit Instrument for introducing the same absolute Rule into these Colonies:

FOR taking away our Charters, abolishing our most valuable Laws, and altering fundamentally the Forms of our Governments:

FOR suspending our own Legislatures, and declaring themselves invested with Power to legislate for us in all Cases whatsoever.

HE has abdicated Government here, by declaring us out of his Protection, and waging War against US.

HE has plundered our Seas, ravaged our Coasts, burnt our Towns, and destroyed the Lives of our People.

HE is, at this Time, transporting large Armies of foreign Mercenaries to complete the Works of Death, Desolation, and Tyranny, already begun with Circumstances of Cruelty and Perfidy, scarcely paralleled in the most barbarous Ages, and totally unworthy the Head of a civilized Nation.

HE has constrained our Fellow-Citizens, taken Captive on the high Seas, to bear Arms against their Country, to become the Executioners of their Friends and Brethren, or to fall themselves by their Hands.

HE has excited domestic Insurrections amongst us, and has endeavoured to bring on the Inhabitants of our Frontiers, the merciless Indian Savages, whose known Rule of Warfare, is an undistinguished Destruction, of all Ages, Sexes, and Conditions.

IN every Stage of these Oppressions we have Petitioned for Redress in the most humble Terms: Our repeated Petitions have been answered only by repeated Injury. A Prince, whose Character is thus marked by every Act which may define a Tyrant, is unfit to be the Ruler of a free People.

NOR have we been wanting in Attentions to our British Brethren. We have warned them, from Time to Time, of Attempts by their Legislature to extend an unwarrantable Jurisdiction over us. We have reminded them of the Circumstances of our Emigration and Settlement here. We have appealed to their native Justice and Magnanimity, and we have conjured them by the Ties of our common Kindred to disavow these Usurpations, which would inevitably interrupt our Connexions and Correspondence. They too have been deaf to the Voice of Justice and of Consanguinity. We must, therefore, acquiesce in the Necessity, which denounces our Separation, and hold them, as we hold the Rest of Mankind, Enemies in War, in Peace Friends.

WE, therefore, the Representatives of the UNITED STATES OF AMERICA, in GENERAL CONGRESS Assembled, appealing to the Supreme Judge of the World for the Rectitude of our Intentions, do, in the Name, and by Authority of the good People of these Colonies, solemnly Publish and Declare,

That these United Colonies are, and of Right ought to be, FREE AND INDEPENDENT STATES; that they are absolved from all Allegiance to the British Crown, and that all political Connexion between them and the State of Great-Britain, is, and ought to be, totally dissolved; and that as FREE AND INDEPENDENT STATES, they have full Power to levy War, conclude Peace, contract Alliances, establish Commerce, and to do all other Acts and Things which INDEPENDENT STATES may of Right do. And for the Support of this Declaration, with a firm Reliance on the Protection of DIVINE PROVIDENCE, we mutually pledge to each other our *Lives*, our *Fortunes*, and our *sacred Honour*.

John Hancock.

GEORGIA, *Button Gwinnett, Lyman Hall, Geo. Walton.*
NORTH-CAROLINA, *Wm. Hooper, Joseph Hewes, John Penn.*
SOUTH-CAROLINA, *Edward Rutledge, Thos Heyward, junr. Thomas Lynch, junr. Arthur Middleton.*
MARYLAND, *Samuel Chase, Wm. Paca, Thos. Stone, Charles Carroll, of Carrollton.*
VIRGINIA, *George Wythe, Richard Henry Lee, Ths. Jefferson, Benja. Harrison, Thos. Nelson, jr. Francis Lightfoot Lee, Carter Braxton.*
PENNSYLVANIA, *Robt. Morris, Benjamin Rush, Benja. Franklin, John Morton, Geo. Clymer, Jas. Smith, Geo. Taylor, James Wilson, Geo. Ross.*
DELAWARE, *Caesar Rodney, Geo. Read.*
NEW-YORK, *Wm. Floyd, Phil. Livingston, Frank Lewis, Lewis Morris.*
NEW-JERSEY, *Richd. Stockton, Jno. Witherspoon, Fras. Hopkinson, John Hart, Abra. Clark.*

NEW-HAMPSHIRE, *Josiah Bartlett, Wm. Whipple, Matthew Thornton.*
MASSACHUSETTS-BAY, *Saml. Adams, John Adams, Robt. Treat Paine, Elbridge Gerry.*
RHODE-ISLAND AND PROVIDENCE, &c. *Step. Hopkins, William Ellery.*
CONNECTICUT, *Roger Sherman, Saml. Huntington, Wm. Williams, Oliver Wolcott.*

APPENDIX B

The United States Consitution

We the People of the United States, in Order to form a more perfect Union, establish Justice, insure domestic Tranquility, provide for the common defence, promote the general Welfare, and secure the Blessings of Liberty to ourselves and our Posterity, do ordain and establish this Constitution for the United States of America.

Article I.

Section 1
All legislative Powers herein granted shall be vested in a Congress of the United States, which shall consist of a Senate and House of Representatives.

Section 2
The House of Representatives shall be composed of Members chosen every second Year by the People of the several States, and the Electors in each State shall have the Qualifications requisite for Electors of the most numerous Branch of the State Legislature.

No Person shall be a Representative who shall not have attained to the Age of twenty five Years, and been seven Years a Citizen of the United States, and who shall not, when elected, be an Inhabitant of that State in which he shall be chosen.

Representatives and direct Taxes shall be apportioned among the several States which may be included within this Union, according to their respective Numbers, which shall be determined by adding to the whole Number of free Persons, including those bound to Service for a Term of Years, and excluding Indians not taxed, three fifths of all other Persons.

The actual Enumeration shall be made within three Years after the first Meeting of the Congress of the United States, and within every subsequent Term of ten Years, in such Manner as they shall by Law direct. The Number of Representatives shall not exceed one for every thirty Thousand, but each State shall have at Least one Representative; and until such enumeration shall be made, the State of New Hampshire shall be entitled to choose three, Massachusetts eight, Rhode Island and Providence Plantations one, Connecticut five, New York six, New Jersey four, Pennsylvania eight, Delaware one, Maryland six, Virginia ten, North Carolina five, South Carolina five and Georgia three.

When vacancies happen in the Representation from any State, the Executive Authority thereof shall issue Writs of Election to fill such Vacancies.

The House of Representatives shall choose their Speaker and other Officers; and shall have the sole Power of Impeachment.

Section 3
The Senate of the United States shall be composed of two Senators from each State, chosen by the Legislature thereof, for six Years; and each Senator shall have one Vote.

Immediately after they shall be assembled in Consequence of the first Election, they shall be divided as equally as may be into three Classes. The Seats of the Senators of the first Class shall be vacated at the Expiration of the second Year, of the second Class at the Expiration of the fourth Year, and of the third Class at the Expiration of the sixth Year, so that one third may be chosen every second Year; and if Vacancies happen by Resignation, or otherwise, during the Recess of the Legislature of any State, the Executive thereof may make temporary Appointments until the next Meeting of the Legislature, which shall then fill such Vacancies.

No person shall be a Senator who shall not have attained to the Age of thirty Years, and been nine Years a Citizen of the United States, and who shall not, when elected, be an Inhabitant of that State for which he shall be chosen.

The Vice President of the United States shall be President of the Senate, but shall have no Vote, unless they be equally divided.

The Senate shall choose their other Officers, and also a President pro tempore, in the absence of the Vice President, or when he shall exercise the Office of President of the United States.

The Senate shall have the sole Power to try all Impeachments. When sitting for that Purpose, they shall be on Oath or Affirmation. When the President of the United States is tried, the Chief Justice shall preside: And no Person shall be convicted without the Concurrence of two thirds of the Members present.

Judgment in Cases of Impeachment shall not extend further than to removal from Office, and disqualification to hold and enjoy any Office of honor, Trust or Profit under the United States: but the Party convicted shall nevertheless be liable and subject to Indictment, Trial, Judgment and Punishment, according to Law.

Section 4

The Times, Places and Manner of holding Elections for Senators and Representatives, shall be prescribed in each State by the Legislature thereof; but the Congress may at any time by Law make or alter such Regulations, except as to the Place of Choosing Senators.

The Congress shall assemble at least once in every Year, and such Meeting shall be on the first Monday in December, unless they shall by Law appoint a different Day.

Section 5

Each House shall be the Judge of the Elections, Returns and Qualifications of its own Members, and a Majority of each shall constitute a Quorum to do Business; but a smaller number may adjourn from day to day, and may be authorized to compel the Attendance of absent Members, in such Manner, and under such Penalties as each House may provide.

Each House may determine the Rules of its Proceedings, punish its Members for disorderly Behavior, and, with the Concurrence of two-thirds, expel a Member.

Each House shall keep a Journal of its Proceedings, and from time to time publish the same, excepting such Parts as may in their Judgment require Secrecy; and the Yeas and Nays of the Members of either House on any question shall, at the Desire of one fifth of those Present, be entered on the Journal.

Neither House, during the Session of Congress, shall, without the Consent of the other, adjourn for more than three days, nor to any other Place than that in which the two Houses shall be sitting.

Section 6

The Senators and Representatives shall receive a Compensation for their Services, to be ascertained by Law, and paid out of the Treasury of the United States. They shall in all Cases, except Treason, Felony and Breach of the Peace, be privileged from Arrest during their Attendance at the Session of their respective Houses, and in going to and returning from the same; and for any Speech or Debate in either House, they shall not be questioned in any other Place.

No Senator or Representative shall, during the Time for which he was elected, be appointed to any civil Office under the Authority of the United States which shall have been created, or the Emoluments whereof shall have been increased during such time; and no Person holding any Office under the United States, shall be a Member of either House during his Continuance in Office.

Section 7

All bills for raising Revenue shall originate in the House of Representatives; but the Senate may propose or concur with Amendments as on other Bills.

Every Bill which shall have passed the House of Representatives and the Senate, shall, before it become a Law, be presented to the President of the United States; If he approve he shall sign it, but if not he shall return it, with his Objections to that House in which it shall have originated, who shall enter the Objections at large on their Journal, and proceed to reconsider it. If after such Reconsideration two thirds of that House shall agree to pass the Bill, it shall be sent, together with the Objections, to the other House, by which it shall likewise be reconsidered, and if approved by two thirds of that House, it shall become a Law. But in all such Cases the Votes of both Houses shall be determined by Yeas and Nays, and the Names of the Persons voting for and against the Bill shall be entered on the Journal of each House respectively. If any Bill shall not be returned by the President within ten Days (Sundays excepted) after it shall have been presented to him, the Same shall be a Law, in like Manner as if he had signed it, unless the Congress by their Adjournment prevent its Return, in which Case it shall not be a Law.

Every Order, Resolution, or Vote to which the Concurrence of the Senate and House of Representatives may be necessary (except on a question of Adjournment) shall be presented to the President of the United States; and before the Same shall take Effect, shall be approved by him, or being disapproved by him, shall be repassed by two thirds of the Senate and House of Representatives, according to the Rules and Limitations prescribed in the Case of a Bill.

Section 8
The Congress shall have Power To lay and collect Taxes, Duties, Imposts and Excises, to pay the Debts and provide for the common Defence and general Welfare of the United States; but all Duties, Imposts and Excises shall be uniform throughout the United States;

To borrow money on the credit of the United States;

To regulate Commerce with foreign Nations, and among the several States, and with the Indian Tribes;

To establish an uniform Rule of Naturalization, and uniform Laws on the subject of Bankruptcies throughout the United States;

To coin Money, regulate the Value thereof, and of foreign Coin, and fix the Standard of Weights and Measures;

To provide for the Punishment of counterfeiting the Securities and current Coin of the United States;

To establish Post Offices and Post Roads;

To promote the Progress of Science and useful Arts, by securing for limited Times to Authors and Inventors the exclusive Right to their respective Writings and Discoveries;

To constitute Tribunals inferior to the supreme Court;

To define and punish Piracies and Felonies committed on the high Seas, and Offenses against the Law of Nations;

To declare War, grant Letters of Marque and Reprisal, and make Rules concerning Captures on Land and Water;

To raise and support Armies, but no Appropriation of Money to that Use shall be for a longer Term than two Years;

To provide and maintain a Navy;

To make Rules for the Government and Regulation of the land and naval Forces;

To provide for calling forth the Militia to execute the Laws of the Union, suppress Insurrections and repel Invasions;

To provide for organizing, arming, and disciplining, the Militia, and for governing such Part of them as may be employed in the Service of the United States, reserving to the States respectively, the Appointment of the Officers, and the Authority of training the Militia according to the discipline prescribed by Congress;

To exercise exclusive Legislation in all Cases whatsoever, over such District (not exceeding ten Miles square) as may, by Cession of particular States, and the acceptance of Congress, become the Seat of the Government of the United States, and to exercise like Authority over all Places purchased by the Consent of the Legislature of the State in which the Same shall be, for the Erection of Forts, Magazines, Arsenals, dock-Yards, and other needful Buildings; And

To make all Laws which shall be necessary and proper for carrying into Execution the foregoing Powers, and all other Powers vested by this Constitution in the Government of the United States, or in any Department or Officer thereof.

Section 9

The Migration or Importation of such Persons as any of the States now existing shall think proper to admit, shall not be prohibited by the Congress prior to the Year one thousand eight hundred and eight, but a tax or duty may be imposed on such Importation, not exceeding ten dollars for each Person.

The privilege of the Writ of Habeas Corpus shall not be suspended, unless when in Cases of Rebellion or Invasion the public Safety may require it.

No Bill of Attainder or ex post facto Law shall be passed.

No capitation, or other direct, Tax shall be laid, unless in Proportion to the Census or Enumeration herein before directed to be taken.

No Tax or Duty shall be laid on Articles exported from any State.

No Preference shall be given by any Regulation of Commerce or Revenue to the Ports of one State over those of another: nor shall Vessels bound to, or from, one State, be obliged to enter, clear, or pay Duties in another.

No Money shall be drawn from the Treasury, but in Consequence of Appropriations made by Law; and a regular

Statement and Account of the Receipts and Expenditures of all public Money shall be published from time to time.

No Title of Nobility shall be granted by the United States: And no Person holding any Office of Profit or Trust under them, shall, without the Consent of the Congress, accept of any present, Emolument, Office, or Title, of any kind whatever, from any King, Prince or foreign State.

Section 10
No State shall enter into any Treaty, Alliance, or Confederation; grant Letters of Marque and Reprisal; coin Money; emit Bills of Credit; make any Thing but gold and silver Coin a Tender in Payment of Debts; pass any Bill of Attainder, ex post facto Law, or Law impairing the Obligation of Contracts, or grant any Title of Nobility.

No State shall, without the Consent of the Congress, lay any Imposts or Duties on Imports or Exports, except what may be absolutely necessary for executing its inspection Laws: and the net Produce of all Duties and Imposts, laid by any State on Imports or Exports, shall be for the Use of the Treasury of the United States; and all such Laws shall be subject to the Revision and Control of the Congress.

No State shall, without the Consent of Congress, lay any duty of Tonnage, keep Troops, or Ships of War in time of Peace, enter into any Agreement or Compact with another State, or with a foreign Power, or engage in War, unless actually invaded, or in such imminent Danger as will not admit of delay.

Article II.

Section 1

The executive Power shall be vested in a President of the United States of America. He shall hold his Office during the Term of four Years, and, together with the Vice-President chosen for the same Term, be elected, as follows:

Each State shall appoint, in such Manner as the Legislature thereof may direct, a Number of Electors, equal to the whole Number of Senators and Representatives to which the State may be entitled in the Congress: but no Senator or Representative, or Person holding an Office of Trust or Profit under the United States, shall be appointed an Elector.

The Electors shall meet in their respective States, and vote by Ballot for two persons, of whom one at least shall not lie an Inhabitant of the same State with themselves. And they shall make a List of all the Persons voted for, and of the Number of Votes for each; which List they shall sign and certify, and transmit sealed to the Seat of the Government of the United States, directed to the President of the Senate. The President of the Senate shall, in the Presence of the Senate and House of Representatives, open all the Certificates, and the Votes shall then be counted. The Person having the greatest Number of Votes shall be the President, if such Number be a Majority of the whole Number of Electors appointed; and if there be more than one who have such Majority, and have an equal Number of Votes, then the House of Representatives shall immediately choose by Ballot one of them for President; and if no Person have a Majority, then from the five highest on the List the said House shall in like Manner choose the President. But in choosing the President, the Votes shall be taken by States, the Representation from each State having one Vote; a quorum for this Purpose shall consist of a Member or Members from two-thirds of the States, and a Majority of all the States shall be necessary to a Choice. In every Case, after the Choice of the President, the Person having the greatest Number of Votes of the Electors shall be the Vice President. But if there should remain two or more who have equal Votes, the Senate shall choose from them by Ballot the Vice-President.

The Congress may determine the Time of choosing the Electors, and the Day on which they shall give their Votes; which Day shall be the same throughout the United States.

No person except a natural born Citizen, or a Citizen of the United States, at the time of the Adoption of this Constitution, shall be eligible to the Office of President; neither shall any Person be eligible to that Office who shall not have attained to the Age of thirty-five Years, and been fourteen Years a Resident within the United States.

In Case of the Removal of the President from Office, or of his Death, Resignation, or Inability to discharge the Powers and Duties of the said Office, the same shall devolve on the Vice President, and the Congress may by Law provide for the Case of Removal, Death, Resignation or Inability, both of the President and Vice President, declaring what Officer shall then act as President, and such Officer shall act accordingly, until the Disability be removed, or a President shall be elected.

The President shall, at stated Times, receive for his Services, a Compensation, which shall neither be increased nor diminished during the Period for which he shall have been elected, and he shall not receive within that Period any other Emolument from the United States, or any of them.

Before he enter on the Execution of his Office, he shall take the following Oath or Affirmation:

"I do solemnly swear (or affirm) that I will faithfully execute the Office of President of the United States, and will to the best of my Ability, preserve, protect and defend the Constitution of the United States."

Section 2

The President shall be Commander in Chief of the Army and Navy of the United States, and of the Militia of the several States, when called into the actual Service of the United States; he may require the Opinion, in writing, of the principal Officer in each of the executive Departments, upon any subject relating to the Duties of their respective Offices, and he shall have Power to Grant Reprieves and Pardons for Offenses against the United States, except in Cases of Impeachment.

He shall have Power, by and with the Advice and Consent of the Senate, to make Treaties, provided two thirds of the Senators present concur; and he shall nominate, and by and with the Advice and Consent of the Senate, shall appoint Ambassadors, other public Ministers and Consuls, Judges of the supreme Court, and all other Officers of the United States, whose Appointments are not herein otherwise provided for, and which shall be established by Law: but the Congress may by Law vest the Appointment of such inferior Officers, as they think proper, in the President alone, in the Courts of Law, or in the Heads of Departments.

The President shall have Power to fill up all Vacancies that may happen during the Recess of the Senate, by granting Commissions which shall expire at the End of their next Session.

Section 3

He shall from time to time give to the Congress Information of the State of the Union, and recommend to their Consideration such Measures as he shall judge necessary and expedient; he may, on extraordinary Occasions, convene both Houses, or either of them, and in Case of Disagreement between them, with Respect to the Time of Adjournment, he may adjourn them to such Time as he shall think proper; he shall receive Ambassadors and other public Ministers; he shall take Care that the Laws be faithfully executed, and shall Commission all the Officers of the United States.

Section 4

The President, Vice President and all civil Officers of the United States, shall be removed from Office on Impeachment for, and Conviction of, Treason, Bribery, or other high Crimes and Misdemeanors.

Article III.

Section 1

The judicial Power of the United States, shall be vested in one supreme Court, and in such inferior Courts as the Congress may from time to time ordain and establish. The Judges, both of the supreme and inferior Courts, shall hold their Offices during good Behavior, and shall, at stated Times, receive for their Services a Compensation which shall not be diminished during their Continuance in Office.

Section 2

The judicial Power shall extend to all Cases, in Law and Equity, arising under this Constitution, the Laws of the United States, and Treaties made, or which shall be made, under their Authority; to all Cases affecting Ambassadors, other public Ministers and Consuls; to all Cases of admiralty and maritime Jurisdiction; to Controversies to which the United States shall be a Party; to Controversies between two or more States; between a State and Citizens of another State; between Citizens of different States; between Citizens of the same State claiming Lands under Grants of different States, and between a State, or the Citizens thereof, and foreign States, Citizens or Subjects.

In all Cases affecting Ambassadors, other public Ministers and Consuls, and those in which a State shall be Party, the supreme Court shall have original Jurisdiction. In all the other Cases before mentioned, the supreme Court shall have appellate Jurisdiction, both as to Law and Fact, with such Exceptions, and under such Regulations as the Congress shall make.

The Trial of all Crimes, except in Cases of Impeachment, shall be by Jury; and such Trial shall be held in the State where the said Crimes shall have been committed; but when not committed within any State, the Trial shall be at such Place or Places as the Congress may by Law have directed.

Section 3

Treason against the United States, shall consist only in levying War against them, or in adhering to their Enemies, giving them Aid and Comfort. No Person shall be convicted of Treason unless on the Testimony of two Witnesses to the same overt Act, or on Confession in open Court.

The Congress shall have power to declare the Punishment of Treason, but no Attainder of Treason shall work Corruption of Blood, or Forfeiture except during the Life of the Person attainted.

Article IV.

Section 1

Full Faith and Credit shall be given in each State to the public Acts, Records, and judicial Proceedings of every other State. And the Congress may by general Laws prescribe the Manner in which such Acts, Records and Proceedings shall be proved, and the Effect thereof.

Section 2

The Citizens of each State shall be entitled to all Privileges and Immunities of Citizens in the several States.

A Person charged in any State with Treason, Felony, or other Crime, who shall flee from Justice, and be found in another State, shall on demand of the executive Authority of the State from which he fled, be delivered up, to be removed to the State having Jurisdiction of the Crime.

No Person held to Service or Labour in one State, under the Laws thereof, escaping into another, shall, in Consequence of any Law or Regulation therein, be discharged from such Service or Labour, But shall be delivered up on Claim of the Party to whom such Service or Labour may be due.

Section 3

New States may be admitted by the Congress into this Union; but no new States shall be formed or erected within the Jurisdiction of any other State; nor any State be formed by the Junction of two or more States, or parts of States, without the Consent of the Legislatures of the States concerned as well as of the Congress.

The Congress shall have Power to dispose of and make all needful Rules and Regulations respecting the Territory or other Property belonging to the United States; and nothing in this

Constitution shall be so construed as to Prejudice any Claims of the United States, or of any particular State.

Section 4

The United States shall guarantee to every State in this Union a Republican Form of Government, and shall protect each of them against Invasion; and on Application of the Legislature, or of the Executive (when the Legislature cannot be convened) against domestic Violence.

Article V.

The Congress, whenever two thirds of both Houses shall deem it necessary, shall propose Amendments to this Constitution, or, on the Application of the Legislatures of two thirds of the several States, shall call a Convention for proposing Amendments, which, in either Case, shall be valid to all Intents and Purposes, as part of this Constitution, when ratified by the Legislatures of three fourths of the several States, or by Conventions in three fourths thereof, as the one or the other Mode of Ratification may be proposed by the Congress; Provided that no Amendment which may be made prior to the Year One thousand eight hundred and eight shall in any Manner affect the first and fourth Clauses in the Ninth Section of the first Article; and that no State, without its Consent, shall be deprived of its equal Suffrage in the Senate.

Article VI.

All Debts contracted and Engagements entered into, before the Adoption of this Constitution, shall be as valid against the United States under this Constitution, as under the Confederation.

This Constitution, and the Laws of the United States which shall be made in Pursuance thereof; and all Treaties made, or which shall be made, under the Authority of the United States, shall be the supreme Law of the Land; and the Judges in every State shall be bound thereby, any Thing in the Constitution or Laws of any State to the Contrary notwithstanding.

The Senators and Representatives before mentioned, and the Members of the several State Legislatures, and all executive and judicial Officers, both of the United States and of the several States, shall be bound by Oath or Affirmation, to support this Constitution; but no religious Test shall ever be required as a Qualification to any Office or public Trust under the United States.

Article VII.

The Ratification of the Conventions of nine States, shall be sufficient for the Establishment of this Constitution between the States so ratifying the Same.

Done in Convention by the Unanimous Consent of the States present the Seventeenth Day of September in the Year of our Lord one thousand seven hundred and Eighty seven and of the Independence of the United States of America the Twelfth. In Witness whereof We have hereunto subscribed our Names.

George Washington – President and deputy from Virginia

New Hampshire – John Langdon, Nicholas Gilman

Massachusetts – Nathaniel Gorham, Rufus King

Connecticut – William Samuel Johnson, Roger Sherman

New York – Alexander Hamilton

New Jersey – William Livingston, David Brearley, William Paterson, Jonathan Dayton

Pennsylvania – Benjamin Franklin, Thomas Mifflin, Robert Morris, George Clymer, Thomas Fitzsimons, Jared Ingersoll, James Wilson, Gouvernour Morris

Delaware – George Read, Gunning Bedford Jr., John Dickinson, Richard Bassett, Jacob Broom

Maryland – James McHenry, Daniel of St Thomas Jenifer, Daniel Carroll Virginia – John Blair, James Madison Jr.

North Carolina – William Blount, Richard Dobbs Spaight, Hugh Williamson

South Carolina – John Rutledge, Charles Cotesworth Pinckney, Charles Pinckney, Pierce Butler

Georgia – William Few, Abraham Baldwin

Attest: William Jackson, Secretary

[Note: Repealed text is not noted in this version. Spelling errors have been corrected in this version. For an uncorrected, annotated version of the Constitution, visit http://www.usconstitution.net/const.html]

APPENDIX C

The Bill of Rights and other Amendments

Amendment I

Congress shall make no law respecting an establishment of religion, or prohibiting the free exercise thereof; or abridging the freedom of speech, or of the press; or the right of the people peaceably to assemble, and to petition the Government for a redress of grievances.

Amendment II

A well regulated Militia, being necessary to the security of a free State, the right of the people to keep and bear Arms, shall not be infringed.

Amendment III

No Soldier shall, in time of peace be quartered in any house, without the consent of the Owner, nor in time of war, but in a manner to be prescribed by law.

Amendment IV

The right of the people to be secure in their persons, houses, papers, and effects, against unreasonable searches and seizures, shall not be violated, and no Warrants shall issue, but upon probable cause, supported by Oath or affirmation, and particularly describing the place to be searched, and the persons or things to be seized.

Amendment V

No person shall be held to answer for a capital, or otherwise infamous crime, unless on a presentment or indictment of a Grand Jury, except in cases arising in the land or naval forces, or in the Militia, when in actual service in time of War or public danger; nor shall any person be subject for the same offense to be twice put in jeopardy of life or limb; nor shall be compelled in any criminal case to be a witness against himself, nor be deprived of life, liberty, or property, without due process of law; nor shall private property be taken for public use, without just compensation.

Amendment VI

In all criminal prosecutions, the accused shall enjoy the right to a speedy and public trial, by an impartial jury of the State and district wherein the crime shall have been committed, which district shall have been previously ascertained by law, and to be informed of the nature and cause of the accusation; to be confronted with the witnesses against him; to have compulsory process for obtaining witnesses in his favor, and to have the Assistance of Counsel for his defence.

Amendment VII

In Suits at common law, where the value in controversy shall exceed twenty dollars, the right of trial by jury shall be preserved, and no fact tried by a jury, shall be otherwise re-examined in any Court of the United States, than according to the rules of the common law.

Amendment VIII

Excessive bail shall not be required, nor excessive fines imposed, nor cruel and unusual punishments inflicted.

Amendment IX

The enumeration in the Constitution, of certain rights, shall not be construed to deny or disparage others retained by the people.

Amendment X

The powers not delegated to the United States by the Constitution, nor prohibited by it to the States, are reserved to the States respectively, or to the people.

Amendment XI

The Judicial power of the United States shall not be construed to extend to any suit in law or equity, commenced or prosecuted against one of the United States by Citizens of another State, or by Citizens or Subjects of any Foreign State.

Amendment XII

The Electors shall meet in their respective states, and vote by ballot for President and Vice-President, one of whom, at least, shall not be an inhabitant of the same state with themselves; they shall name in their ballots the person voted for as President, and in distinct ballots the person voted for as Vice-President, and they shall make distinct lists of all persons voted for as President, and of all persons voted for as Vice-President and of the number of votes for each, which lists they shall sign and certify, and transmit sealed to the seat of the government of the United States, directed to the President of the Senate;

The President of the Senate shall, in the presence of the Senate and House of Representatives, open all the certificates and the votes shall then be counted;

The person having the greatest Number of votes for President, shall be the President, if such number be a majority of the whole number of Electors appointed; and if no person have such majority, then from the persons having the highest numbers not exceeding three on the list of those voted for as President, the House of Representatives shall choose immediately, by ballot, the President. But in choosing the President, the votes shall be taken by states, the representation from each state having one vote; a quorum for this purpose shall consist of a member or members from two-thirds of the states, and a majority of all the states shall be necessary to a choice. And if the House of Representatives shall not choose a President whenever the right of choice shall devolve upon them, before the fourth day of March next following, then the Vice-President shall act as President, as in the case of the death or other constitutional disability of the President.

The person having the greatest number of votes as Vice-President, shall be the Vice-President, if such number be a majority of the whole number of Electors appointed, and if no person have a majority, then from the two highest numbers on the list, the Senate shall choose the Vice-President; a quorum for the purpose shall consist of two-thirds of the whole number of Senators, and a majority of the whole number shall be necessary to a choice. But no person constitutionally ineligible to the office of President shall be eligible to that of Vice-President of the United States.

Amendment XIII
1. Neither slavery nor involuntary servitude, except as a punishment for crime whereof the party shall have been duly convicted, shall exist within the United States, or any place subject to their jurisdiction.

2. Congress shall have power to enforce this article by appropriate legislation.

Amendment XIV

1. All persons born or naturalized in the United States, and subject to the jurisdiction thereof, are citizens of the United States and of the State wherein they reside. No State shall make or enforce any law which shall abridge the privileges or immunities of citizens of the United States; nor shall any State deprive any person of life, liberty, or property, without due process of law; nor deny to any person within its jurisdiction the equal protection of the laws.

2. Representatives shall be apportioned among the several States according to their respective numbers, counting the whole number of persons in each State, excluding Indians not taxed. But when the right to vote at any election for the choice of electors for President and Vice-President of the United States, Representatives in Congress, the Executive and Judicial officers of a State, or the members of the Legislature thereof, is denied to any of the male inhabitants of such State, being twenty-one years of age, and citizens of the United States, or in any way abridged, except for participation in rebellion, or other crime, the basis of representation therein shall be reduced in the proportion which the number of such male citizens shall bear to the whole number of male citizens twenty-one years of age in such State.

3. No person shall be a Senator or Representative in Congress, or elector of President and Vice-President, or hold any office, civil or military, under the United States, or under any State, who, having previously taken an oath, as a member of Congress, or as an officer of the United States, or as a member of any State legislature, or as an executive or judicial officer of any State, to support the Constitution of the United States, shall have engaged in insurrection or rebellion against the same, or

given aid or comfort to the enemies thereof. But Congress may by a vote of two-thirds of each House, remove such disability.

4. The validity of the public debt of the United States, authorized by law, including debts incurred for payment of pensions and bounties for services in suppressing insurrection or rebellion, shall not be questioned. But neither the United States nor any State shall assume or pay any debt or obligation incurred in aid of insurrection or rebellion against the United States, or any claim for the loss or emancipation of any slave; but all such debts, obligations and claims shall be held illegal and void.

5. The Congress shall have power to enforce, by appropriate legislation, the provisions of this article.

Amendment XV
1. The right of citizens of the United States to vote shall not be denied or abridged by the United States or by any State on account of race, color, or previous condition of servitude.

2. The Congress shall have power to enforce this article by appropriate legislation.

Amendment XVI
The Congress shall have power to lay and collect taxes on incomes, from whatever source derived, without apportionment among the several States, and without regard to any census or enumeration.

Amendment XVII
The Senate of the United States shall be composed of two Senators from each State, elected by the people thereof, for six years; and each Senator shall have one vote. The electors in each State shall have the qualifications requisite for electors of the most numerous branch of the State legislatures.

When vacancies happen in the representation of any State in the Senate, the executive authority of such State shall issue writs of election to fill such vacancies: Provided, That the legislature of any State may empower the executive thereof to make temporary appointments until the people fill the vacancies by election as the legislature may direct.

This amendment shall not be so construed as to affect the election or term of any Senator chosen before it becomes valid as part of the Constitution.

Amendment XVIII

1. After one year from the ratification of this article the manufacture, sale, or transportation of intoxicating liquors within, the importation thereof into, or the exportation thereof from the United States and all territory subject to the jurisdiction thereof for beverage purposes is hereby prohibited.

2. The Congress and the several States shall have concurrent power to enforce this article by appropriate legislation.

3. This article shall be inoperative unless it shall have been ratified as an amendment to the Constitution by the legislatures of the several States, as provided in the Constitution, within seven years from the date of the submission hereof to the States by the Congress.

Amendment XIX

The right of citizens of the United States to vote shall not be denied or abridged by the United States or by any State on account of sex.

Congress shall have power to enforce this article by appropriate legislation.

Amendment XX

1. The terms of the President and Vice President shall end at noon on the 20th day of January, and the terms of Senators and Representatives at noon on the 3d day of January, of the years in which such terms would have ended if this article had not been ratified; and the terms of their successors shall then begin.

2. The Congress shall assemble at least once in every year, and such meeting shall begin at noon on the 3d day of January, unless they shall by law appoint a different day.

3. If, at the time fixed for the beginning of the term of the President, the President elect shall have died, the Vice President elect shall become President. If a President shall not have been chosen before the time fixed for the beginning of his term, or if the President elect shall have failed to qualify, then the Vice President elect shall act as President until a President shall have qualified; and the Congress may by law provide for the case wherein neither a President elect nor a Vice President elect shall have qualified, declaring who shall then act as President, or the manner in which one who is to act shall be selected, and such person shall act accordingly until a President or Vice President shall have qualified.

4. The Congress may by law provide for the case of the death of any of the persons from whom the House of Representatives may choose a President whenever the right of choice shall have devolved upon them, and for the case of the death of any of the persons from whom the Senate may choose a Vice President whenever the right of choice shall have devolved upon them.

5. Sections 1 and 2 shall take effect on the 15th day of October following the ratification of this article.

6. This article shall be inoperative unless it shall have been ratified as an amendment to the Constitution by the legislatures of three-fourths of the several States within seven years from the date of its submission.

Amendment XXI

1. The eighteenth article of amendment to the Constitution of the United States is hereby repealed.

2. The transportation or importation into any State, Territory, or possession of the United States for delivery or use therein of intoxicating liquors, in violation of the laws thereof, is hereby prohibited.

3. The article shall be inoperative unless it shall have been ratified as an amendment to the Constitution by conventions in the several States, as provided in the Constitution, within seven years from the date of the submission hereof to the States by the Congress.

Amendment XXII

1. No person shall be elected to the office of the President more than twice, and no person who has held the office of President, or acted as President, for more than two years of a term to which some other person was elected President shall be elected to the office of the President more than once. But this Article shall not apply to any person holding the office of President, when this Article was proposed by the Congress, and shall not prevent any person who may be holding the office of President, or acting as President, during the term within which this Article becomes operative from holding the office of President or acting as President during the remainder of such term.

2. This article shall be inoperative unless it shall have been ratified as an amendment to the Constitution by the legislatures of three-fourths of the several States within seven years from the date of its submission to the States by the Congress.

Amendment XXIII

1. The District constituting the seat of Government of the United States shall appoint in such manner as the Congress may direct: A number of electors of President and Vice President equal to the whole number of Senators and Representatives in Congress to which the District would be entitled if it were a State, but in no event more than the least populous State; they shall be in addition to those appointed by the States, but they shall be considered, for the purposes of the election of President and Vice President, to be electors appointed by a State; and they shall meet in the District and perform such duties as provided by the twelfth article of amendment.

2. The Congress shall have power to enforce this article by appropriate legislation.

Amendment XXIV

1. The right of citizens of the United States to vote in any primary or other election for President or Vice President, for electors for President or Vice President, or for Senator or Representative in Congress, shall not be denied or abridged by the United States or any State by reason of failure to pay any poll tax or other tax.

2. The Congress shall have power to enforce this article by appropriate legislation.

Amendment XXV

1. In case of the removal of the President from office or of his death or resignation, the Vice President shall become President.

2. Whenever there is a vacancy in the office of the Vice President, the President shall nominate a Vice President who shall take office upon confirmation by a majority vote of both Houses of Congress.

3. Whenever the President transmits to the President pro tempore of the Senate and the Speaker of the House of Representatives his written declaration that he is unable to discharge the powers and duties of his office, and until he transmits to them a written declaration to the contrary, such powers and duties shall be discharged by the Vice President as Acting President.

4. Whenever the Vice President and a majority of either the principal officers of the executive departments or of such other body as Congress may by law provide, transmit to the President pro tempore of the Senate and the Speaker of the House of Representatives their written declaration that the President is unable to discharge the powers and duties of his office, the Vice President shall immediately assume the powers and duties of the office as Acting President.

Thereafter, when the President transmits to the President pro tempore of the Senate and the Speaker of the House of Representatives his written declaration that no inability exists, he shall resume the powers and duties of his office unless the Vice President and a majority of either the principal officers of the executive department or of such other body as Congress may by law provide, transmit within four days to the President pro tempore of the Senate and the Speaker of the House of Representatives their written declaration that the President is unable to discharge the powers and duties of his office. Thereupon Congress shall decide the issue, assembling within forty eight hours for that purpose if not in session. If the Congress, within twenty one days after receipt of the latter written declaration, or, if Congress is not in session, within twenty one days after Congress is required to assemble, determines by two thirds vote of both Houses that the President is unable to discharge the powers and duties of his office, the Vice President shall continue to discharge the same as Acting President; otherwise, the President shall resume the powers and duties of his office.

Amendment XXVI

1. The right of citizens of the United States, who are eighteen years of age or older, to vote shall not be denied or abridged by the United States or by any State on account of age.

2. The Congress shall have power to enforce this article by appropriate legislation.

Amendment XXVII

No law, varying the compensation for the services of the Senators and Representatives, shall take effect, until an election of Representatives shall have intervened.

INDEX

Made in the USA
San Bernardino, CA
02 October 2018